CONTENTS

CONTENTS

IMPROVING SCHOOL ATTENDANCE

The availability of free and compulsory education for children is generally considered a hallmark of the development of a society, and is emphasised as a basic right to which children should be entitled. Until recently, relatively little attention has been paid in literature and research to school attendance. Neither has there been much detailed or systematic dissemination of good practice. This book is a timely contribution to new thinking about improving school attendance.

Contributors to this book include professionals in teaching, social work and psychology as well as academic researchers, who provide a balance of theoretical and academic material. This not only includes material which identifies broad current concerns, such as exploring the contentious relationship between non-attendance of school and involvement in crime, but also provides a description and evaluation of work undertaken at LEA, whole school and individual level, which focuses on both preventative work and work with students for whom non-attendance has become a long-term problem.

Eric Blyth is Reader in Social Work at the University of Huddersfield. **Judith Milner** is a freelance trainer and solutions counsellor.

IMPROVING SCHOOL ATTENDANCE

Edited by Eric Blyth and Judith Milner

LEARNING RESOURCES CENTRE
Havering College
of Further and Higher Education

London and New York

First published 1999
by Routledge
11 New Fetter Lane, London EC4P 4EE

Simultaneously published in the USA and Canada
by Routledge
29 West 35th Street, New York, NY 10001

© selection and editorial matter Eric Blyth and Judith Milner;
individual chapters, the contributors

Typeset in Garamond by Routledge
Printed and bound in Great Britain by
MPG Books Ltd, Bodmin, Cornwall

British Library Cataloguing in Publication Data
A catalogue record of this book is available from the British Library

Library of Congress Cataloguing in Publication Data
Blyth, Eric
Improving school attendance / edited by Eric Blyth and Judith Milner.
p.cm.
Includes bibliographical references and indexes.
School attendance–Great Britain. I. Milner, Judith, senior lecturer.
II. Title.
LC135.G7B591999
371.2'94'0941–dc2198-38000
CIP

ISBN 0–415–17871–1 (hbk)
ISBN 0–17872–X (pbk)

ILLUSTRATIONS

Tables

Figures

LIST OF ILLUSTRATIONS

CONTRIBUTORS

Kay Bardsley has a background in teaching and youth work. She has worked with the Leeds Attendance and Behaviour Project as a seconded Education Welfare Officer since 1991.

Dr Jon Blacktop is Senior Lecturer in Statistics at the University of Huddersfield.

Eric Blyth is Reader in Social Work at the University of Huddersfield, and Director and co-founder of the university's Centre for Education Welfare Studies.

Dr Brian Boyd is Associate Director of the Centre for Research and Consultancy at Strathclyde University.

Peter Costa is an educational psychologist with the Leeds Attendance and Behaviour Project and is also involved in the Leeds LEA task group on preventing exclusions. He previously worked on the Leeds Positive Behaviour Project.

Professor Cedric Cullingford is Professor of Education at the University of Huddersfield. He has published widely in the field of education. Recent publications include *Children and Society* (1992), *Anglo-German Attitudes* (1995) and *The Effective Teacher* (1995).

Mike Haworth is Educational Psychologist, Leeds City Council.

Dorothy Jessop is administrator of the Northorpe Hall Trust and project leader of the Northorpe Hall Education of Looked After Children project.

Bob Johnson is Head Teacher of Don Valley High School, Doncaster.

Beverley Lewis has a background in secondary teaching and is Project Co-ordinator for the Improving School Attendance Project, Lancashire County Council.

CONTRIBUTORS

Douglas MacIldowie is an education trainer and consultant and an Accredited OFSTED Team Inspector. He was previously Head Teacher of Swanley School, Kent from 1983 to 1997.

Judith Milner is a freelance solutions counsellor and co-founder of the Centre for Education Welfare Studies at the University of Huddersfield, where she was previously Senior Lecturer in Social Work.

Ian Stokes is Research Officer with the Leeds Attendance and Behaviour Project.

Jo Walton worked for 10 years as a teacher in an inner city high school and since 1990 has worked with the Leeds Attendance and Behaviour Project.

INTRODUCTION

Eric Blyth and Judith Milner

The original idea for this book came as a result of contacts we made at a conference held in Leeds in 1995 with a number of educationalists involved with projects in schools and LEAs throughout the country, promoted under the 'Improving School Attendance' scheme.

There was agreement that the innovative work being carried out should be shared with a wider audience consisting not only of practitioners, managers and policy-makers but, in addition, students of vocational education and social work programmes and related academic programmes in the UK and further afield. We also recognised that the current – and continuing – concerns about pupil behaviour and exclusion from school were receiving considerable attention in a wide range of literary media (not without justification), but that, as a consequence, issues relating to school attendance were appearing to be at risk of at least relative neglect in the literature.

Although both our principal professional backgrounds are social work, we have, unusually as regards social work in the UK, been primarily concerned with issues facing children as pupils and consumers of the education system. We have at varying times worked directly with schools as social workers, one of us has been an independent adviser to a school, and the other has served as a member of school governing bodies, including acting as Deputy Chair and Chair of a school governing body.

We have been struck by the paradox offered by compulsory education in the UK. On the one hand, education via schooling offers one of the most significant avenues for individual development, 'self-improvement' and socio-economic mobility. Schools can also be a key source of emotional and social support for children and young people, especially those experiencing adversity in their lives. On the other hand, the education system is still capable of perpetuating and reinforcing existing social divisions and inequalities and socio-economic disadvantage. Further, contemporary accounts of schooling in the UK identify its capacity for promoting the oppression of children (see, for example, Carlen *et al.*, 1992; Blyth and Cooper, in press). Such tensions are evident in the small number of explicit rights that children possess within the education system and the fact of *compulsory* education and the measures available to education, social work and criminal justice personnel and agencies. These are reflected in the various contributions to this book, which draws on both original research and innovative practice being carried out in schools and local education authorities.

In chapter 1, 'Theoretical Debates and Legislative Framework', Judith Milner and Eric Blyth's overview focuses on the tensions between UK education and child care legislation and the UN Convention on the Rights of the Child. This chapter identifies the implications of the development of the education market (promoted by the Education Reform Act 1988 and the Education Act 1993) for choice, competition, social control and civic exclusion. The possibility of some of these tensions being resolved with the Crime and Disorder Act is discussed.

Brian Boyd, in 'Combating Truancy: The Scottish Approach', draws on a major Scottish project, the 'Truancy File', and other Scottish approaches to homework, discipline and bullying, to illustrate the 'Scottish approach' to attainment, attendance and behaviour based on a belief that schools and their communities – pupils, parents, teachers, school boards, external agencies and community groups – can significantly affect the outcomes by which schools are judged in the context of 'effectiveness'.

In chapter 3, 'School Attendance and the Role of Law in England and Wales', Jon Blacktop and Eric Blyth discuss policy issues and practice strategies arising from legal requirements concerning compulsory education in Britain. The chapter provides a discussion of the current legal framework and legal measures designed to promote school attendance. Up to now there has been little empirical evidence concerning the impact of such measures. The authors attempt to redress this balance by reporting on a research project conducted in four local education authorities into parental prosecution for non-attendance.

Cedric Cullingford comments on an especially controversial aspect of current debates about absenteeism in 'The Relationship between Delinquency and Non-Attendance at School'. This is based on the author's empirical research carried out with young criminals, and highlights their accounts of their experiences of school. It analyses not only how truancy and absenteeism arise but why – the sources of influence and the relationship of the individual's coping strategies (or lack of them) to external events.

Chapters 5 to 11 focus on practice issues for improving school attendance and draw on initiatives developed and implemented in a number of schools and local authorities.

Chapters 5 and 6 can be read in isolation but, written by members of the Leeds Attendance and Behaviour Project team, focus on inter-related themes and are more usefully considered together. In chapter 5, 'The Effective Collection and Analysis of Attendance Data', Ian Stokes and Jo Walton show how the collection and analysis of accurate data can be used strategically as a basis for devising schemes to improve attendance. The authors conclude with a discussion of how this method and process of school attendance policy formulation can be applied to policy formulation in related areas such as behaviour and anti-bullying policies, equal opportunities, disaffection, delivery of the curriculum, and standards of achievement. In 'The Essential Elements of an Effective Attendance Policy', Kay Bardsley, Peter Costa and Jo Walton identify the importance of both the content of an attendance policy and the process by which it is developed, implemented and maintained. The chapter usefully concludes with a sample policy based on the experience of the Leeds team.

Douglas MacIldowie in chapter 7, 'Strategies for Improving School Attendance', provides an account of the Department for Education-funded Kent Attendance Project; an initiative that involved additional support from the Education Welfare Service, improved liaison between schools and support services, and an investigation – by means of a questionnaire – of the reasons for non-attendance. The author identifies strategies contributing to improved attendance: raising the profile of attendance throughout the school; additional support from the Education Welfare Service; improved involvement with pupils' families; increased liaison between primary and secondary schools; the provision of incentives for improved attendance; identification of pupils 'at risk'; the use of 'circle time' to encourage positive attitudes towards school and attendance; 'truancy checks'; the introduction of optical mark-reader registers; and analysis of attendance data.

'Proactive Primary Approaches to Non-Attendance', by Beverley Lewis, highlights the importance of establishing patterns of punctuality and regular attendance at the point at which children have their first experiences of compulsory schooling. Drawing on work undertaken as part of the Lancashire Improving School Attendance Project, the author describes a range of initiatives and strategies aimed at building effective partnerships in the primary school involving children, their parents/carers, teachers, education welfare officers and the local community.

Bob Johnson, in 'Raising Expectations at Don Valley High School', describes the work undertaken since 1991 in one co-educational high school providing education for 11 to 18 year olds in an area of socio-economic deprivation. The chapter describes the process by which the school community became engaged in identifying both the need for change and the means by which it would be achieved. The chapter outlines the specific strategies employed in the school and evaluates their outcomes in particular on attainment and attendance.

Eric Blyth, Dorothy Jessop and Judith Milner, in 'Doing Better: Improving the Educational Experiences of Looked After Children and Young People', summarise the evidence concerning the educational disadvantages experienced by children and young people in public care and describe work in one local authority area designed to improve both their attainment and attendance.

In the final chapter, 'Student Support Groups', Mike Haworth and Kay Bardsley describe the role of groupwork in working with children and young people who have attendance problems. The authors draw on their own extensive experience of working with a number of such groups to describe the process of establishing and running groups, the content of groupwork programmes and the evaluation of their outcomes.

As work on the book progressed, we were impressed by the newly elected Labour government's determination to give further focus to non-attendance and exclusion from school, through the creation of the Social Exclusion Unit and making truancy and exclusion its first two priorities. At the same time, acknowledgement needs to be given to previous administrations that initially established the Elton Committee (DES, 1989a) to look into disruption and behaviour problems in school and that subsequently targeted funding at both behaviour and attendance through the Education Support Grant initiative, the latter now replaced by the Standards Fund.

As the manuscript was being finalised, the Social Exclusion Unit produced its report *Truancy and School Exclusion* (Social Exclusion Unit, 1998). While much that is in the report reflects what is already 'best practice' in many schools and LEAs, the report also fell prey to the more emotive assumptions associated with the British tabloid press, although even *The Times* chose the headline 'Parents Facing Jail in Campaign against Truancy' (Elliot and Pierce, 1998) in its news feature on the report. The Social Exclusion Unit itself commented, accurately enough, that: 'No one knows precisely how many children are out of school at any time because of truancy or exclusion' (1998: 1), although it also asserted that 'truancy and exclusions have reached a crisis point. The thousands of children who are not in school on most schooldays have become a significant cause of crime' (1998: 1).

Perhaps most worrying about the recommendations outlined by the Social Exclusion Unit and the government's response to these are the amendments to the Crime and Disorder Act that will extend the role of the police in relation to school attendance and provide them with powers to remove children from the streets and detain them, in the absence of the commission of any crime.

It is our hope and intention that this book penetrates the rhetoric and will be a useful source for those whose job it is to 'do something' about absenteeism from school. We hope that it also provides a commentary on perspectives about 'truancy' and absence from school at the end of the twentieth century.

1

THEORETICAL DEBATES AND LEGISLATIVE FRAMEWORK

Judith Milner and Eric Blyth

Introduction

The availability of free and compulsory education for its children, conventionally through the provision of state-funded schooling, is generally considered a hallmark of the development of a society. In the UK a system of such education has been in existence since the end of the nineteenth century, every child in Britain aged between 5 (4 in Northern Ireland) and 16 being required to receive 'efficient, full-time education suitable to his age, ability, aptitude and to any special educational needs he may have'.

Free and compulsory education is recognised as a basic entitlement under international standards, the United Nations' Universal Declaration of Human Rights and Convention on the Rights of the Child and the European Convention on Human Rights. However, since different perceptions can be – and are – held about the various purposes of education and their relative importance, so too there are a range of views about the meaning and significance of *absence from school*. Consider, for example, the 'mainstream' view propounded by the Department for Education (now the Department for Education and Employment) that:

> There is too much truancy from our schools. This undermines our educational system. It means that some schools are turning a blind eye, and some parents are not fulfilling their side of the bargain by meeting their legal obligation to see that their child attends school. Worse of all, it can lead to much unhappiness among school children themselves, as well as to greater problems for the community.
>
> (DFE, 1992a: 5)

This assumes not only that levels of school attendance and absence are unambiguous measurable matters of 'objective fact', but that education (or, more specifically, 'schooling') is invariably a 'good thing' and absence is invariably not. In reality both the concept of non-attendance (and, in particular, perceptions which are, explicitly or implicitly, value judgements, such as 'truancy' and even 'unauthorised absence') and the presumed implications of non-attendance are social constructions.

The very fact of 'compulsory' education indicates that, without compulsion, those for whom education is designed would not necessarily avail themselves of it, or might be prevented by others from availing themselves of it. Such concerns have been evident from the early days of compulsory education in the United Kingdom as nineteenth-century bylaws requiring compulsory school attendance were resisted both by employers (often well represented among the local magistracy) anxious about losing a source of cheap labour and by parents anxious about losing the earnings of their working offspring, not to mention children themselves, who were not always enthusiastic about trading the dubious pleasures of the 'dark satanic mill' for the schoolroom with its emphasis on strict discipline and moral teaching. Indeed the value of education as a mechanism of social control (rather than as a means of self-improvement or of social mobility) was never far from the surface:

> Education was desirable because it prevented juvenile delinquency and mendicancy, because it increased a labourer's skill, productivity and earning power; because it prevented the growth of criminal classes; and because it led the workman to realise his true interests lay not in Communism or Chartism but in harmony with his employers.
>
> (Finer, cited in Carlen et al., 1992: 19)

a perspective that has withstood the test of time:

> In the long run, the objective must be to ensure that education ceases to be optional. All children of school age need to be in education. No children should be left to roam the streets during school hours.
>
> (Social Exclusion Unit, 1998: 2)

Schooling, the family and the state

This perception of education, as intrinsically much more than a self-evidentially beneficent service made available, in the main, by the state rather than by private providers, is crucial for understanding the relationship between parents and their children and the state, a relationship which, in turn, is fundamental to understanding the phenomenon of non-attendance.

First, parents themselves have little real choice about whether to send their children to school. Second, by sending their children to school, parents transfer significant rights and authority over their children to individuals (teachers) acting on behalf of the state. This, together with the fact that children of school age spend a considerable proportion of their waking lives in school (15,000 hours in secondary education alone [Rutter *et al.*, 1979]), provides schools with opportunities to monitor children for signs of neglect, abuse or other forms of 'distress' and trigger formal intervention in the lives of children and their families. Finally, schools may exert both positive and negative effects on their pupils.

Compulsory education and parental choice

UK law imposes a duty on parents to ensure that their children of compulsory school age receive appropriate education, whether through attendance at a state or independent school, or by other means (such as tuition at home), in which case the parents will need to provide evidence of the suitability of the education being provided. In practice, since few parents are in a position to make alternative arrangements outside of school for their children that would meet the standards required, the concept of compulsory *education* effectively means compulsory *schooling*. As a corollary, education authorities also have legal responsibilities to make appropriate education provision for children living in their area.

If a child is not registered at a school and the education authority establishes that he or she is not being properly educated 'otherwise' it may serve a notice requiring the child's parent(s) to register the child at a school of their choosing. If the parents fail to respond to this notice within a given time, the child will be registered at a school chosen by the education authority. Parents who subsequently fail to secure the regular attendance of the child at the school at which they are registered and who fail to provide an acceptable defence are guilty of an offence.

In order to clarify the distinction between legitimate and illicit absence, the government introduced new categories of 'authorised' absence and 'unauthorised' absence in 1994 (DFE, 1994). Any absence that is not authorised by the school is, by definition, unauthorised and could place the parent(s) at risk of contravening their legal responsibilities. Despite regulations and guidance (DFE, 1994; SOED, 1995), there remains considerable discretion over which absences schools may authorise and, in English schools at least, continuing ambiguity about the categorisation of absences and the powers to authorise it (OFSTED, 1995a, 1995b). Furthermore, Hoyle (1998) claims there is an 'implicit moral bias' in the government's categorisation of absence, citing the Department for Education's (now Department for Education and Employment) selection of examples of unauthorised absence (a birthday) and authorised absence (graduation of an older sibling) (DFE, 1994: 7) – a distinction maintained by the Labour administration (DFEE, 1997a). Similarly, the classification of an educational visit as an authorised absence both assumes a narrow view of 'education' and diminishes the educational value of that activity.

In order to enforce school attendance either education authorities may prosecute parents under provisions of education legislation or they may act in respect of the child under childcare legislation. Despite some differences between the different jurisdictions, broadly similar measures exist throughout the United Kingdom. In exceptional circumstances non-attendance alone could satisfy the 'significant harm' test necessary for an application by a local authority for a care order under the provisions of the Children Act 1989 (*Re: O*, 1992). In addition to existing sanctions, the Crime and Disorder Act 1998 gives courts a new power to impose a Parenting Order where a parent is convicted of failing to comply with a School Attendance Order or of failing to secure his/her child's regular attendance at school. The government pressed ahead with the concept of parenting orders despite reservations expressed by leading independent childcare organisations such as The Children's Society and Barnados that the compulsory element of a parenting order could exacerbate existing tensions within families and be counter-productive (Scanlon, 1998). A Parenting Order may last for up to 12 months. It has two elements: a requirement on the part of the parent to attend counselling or guidance sessions where help in dealing with their children will be provided, and a requirement to exercise control over the child's behaviour, such as escorting the child to school or ensuring that he or she is home by a certain time of night and/or avoids contact with other disruptive children. Parental Orders will be piloted and evaluated in different parts of the country for an eighteen month period commencing in the autumn of 1998.

While, in practice, most parents have little choice about whether their children should attend school or not, education reforms introduced during the 1980s and 1990s made much of the concept of 'parental choice' in their children's education, an essential aspect of the new 'education market'. Parental choice found expression in two major directions. First, legislation was introduced to permit 'open' enrolment at schools, preventing artificial limits being placed on the numbers of pupils which could be registered at an individual school (and at the same time dismantling the traditional notion of a school serving the geographical area in which it is situated), providing parents with the right to 'express a preference as to where they would like their children to go to school', supplemented by information about schools (published performance data) upon which informed decisions could be made.

The development of *real* parental choice has been more limited than official rhetoric might suggest and it is important to note that parents have rights to 'express' a choice. They do not have an unequivocal legal right to exercise that choice. Proponents of the education market assume that 'all are free and equal, differentiated only by their capacity to calculate their self-interest' (Ranson, 1990: 15), so that any differences are explained and legitimated by pathologising as 'bad' parents those who do not make a choice or who make 'poor' choices. This analysis does not allow for the impact of structural (dis)advantage on the exercise of choice. Bourdieu and Passeron (1990), for example, recognise that, depending on their socio-economic status, different individuals acquire varying degrees of 'cultural capital'. Parents (the better educated and better off) with 'cultural capital', who have knowledge of schools, are able to interpret schools' promotional material and performance data, are able to 'work the system' (using such strategies as making multiple applications, applying for scholarships, using appeals procedures, even moving house to be nearer a preferred school, or being able to provide or pay for transport to enable children to attend a preferred school), are able to present a positive image of themselves when negotiating with key gatekeepers, and are in a better position to maximise their choices than those with no or little 'cultural capital'.

Moreover, the rhetoric of parental choice conceals increasing evidence that, in the deregulated education market, schools are increasingly choosing their pupils, those they consider will best contribute to the school's image through some mechanism of selection (e.g. Audit Commission, 1996; Power *et al.*, 1996). More secondary schools have reverted to some element of selection (the most efficient method of improving school performance data), while more schools are excluding 'undesirable' (i.e. high-cost/high-risk/low-achieving) pupils and indicating reluctance to accept pupils excluded from other schools – an increase at least in part fuelled by pressure on schools to demonstrate positive (popular) images. Rather than being seen as consumers of education with interests and rights to be recognised and respected, pupils are increasingly being seen as little more than the raw data of school performance statistics.

In essence, the education reforms of the 1980s and 1990s have promoted the re-emergence of a stratified state education system. Just as reforms have enhanced choice for some parents but not others, so too have they created 'schools which can afford to turn away certain clients and other schools that must take any they can get' (Ball, 1993: 8).

The second element of parental choice relates to determining via a secret ballot of parents whether the school attended by their children should remain under local authority control or 'opt out' of local authority control by securing grant-maintained status and receive its funding from central government. The Conservative government, which introduced the concept of grant-maintained schools, promoted this as a significant step for both parental choice and school autonomy:

> The Government firmly believes that self-government is best for state schools.
>
> (DFE, 1992a: 19)

Schools that have opted out have welcomed the new sense of owner-ship and independence. They can decide what they want to do and get things done without having to ask permission from the Town or County Hall. They are able to spend more in the classroom. Many schools become more popular with parents after opting out.

(DFE, 1992b: 2)

Indeed former Secretary of State for Education John Patten (1992) described grant-maintained status as the 'natural organisational model for secondary education'. In practice, few parents seemed to agree, and only 1,158 out of a total of 24,000 schools in England and Wales (approximately 5 per cent of the total) had opted out between September 1988 when opt out was intro-duced and March 1997 (Hamilton and O'Reilly, 1997). Further, the opportunity to make such a choice was restricted to certain parents only, that is, once the decision to opt out had been taken, there were no provisions for a subsequent ballot to opt back in. Government ministers also seemed lukewarm regarding the notion of parental choice. In 1995 parents' evident reluctance to more enthusiastically grasp the 'opportunity' of independence led the then Prime Minister John Major to announce proposals to dispense with parental ballots for all voluntary aided (i.e. church) schools (Charter, 1995), although this idea was abandoned in the face of combined opposition from Anglican and Roman Catholic bishops, while Kenneth Clarke, erst-while Secretary of State for Education reportedly stated: 'If I'd been Secretary of State in 1988, I would not have put in this balloting system....They [ballots] remain the biggest single obstacle in the way of moving to grant-maintained status' (cited in Hamilton and O'Reilly, 1997). Despite the rhetoric, early research into grant-maintained schools in England indicated that there was little evidence of increased parental involvement in such schools, although grant-maintained status could enhance the power of the head teacher (Power *et al.*, 1994, 1996).

Parents' and teachers' authority

The legal nature of the teacher's authority over, and responsibility for, pupils in his or her charge was established in the 1890s and outlined by Lord Esher (then Master of the Rolls) as a duty 'to take such care of his boys [*sic*] as a careful father would take care of his boys' (*Williams* v. *Eady*, 1893). The extent of teachers' responsibilities and their relationship with those of parents has been further elaborated over the years. The concept of *in loco parentis* implies that the teacher not only has authority but also a *duty* to care (*Sim* v. *Rotherham Metropolitan BC* and other actions, 1986: 405; Brazier, 1988). By the 1960s the test of the standard of care expected of teachers began to change to take account of the context of schooling, in particular the recognition that a teacher responsible for a class of 30 plus is not in the same position as a parent caring for a considerably smaller number of children at any one time and that teachers may possess knowledge not expected of the parent (*Van Oppen* v. *Clerk to the Bedford Charity Trustees*, 1989).

Delegation of parental authority to the teacher was implied, the teacher being subject only to the same legal limitations placed on parents, and where a parent disapproves of action taken by a teacher (usually over punishment), courts have determined that where a teacher has behaved 'reasonably' while acting *in loco parentis*, parents cannot over-rule their actions. In a 1938 ruling Judge Tucker stated:

> when a parent sends his [*sic*] child to school, he delegates to teachers at the school the power to inflict reasonable and moderate punishment as required...and...he delegates to the teacher the taking of such steps as are necessary to maintain discipline with regard to the child committed to the teacher's care.
>
> (cited in Harris *et al.*, 1992: 142)

While Brazier (1988) and the Elton Committee (DES, 1989a) also support the notion of the teacher's *independent* authority to discipline children, this inevitably conflicts with the concept of increasing parental rights in education. Having said this, the eventual abolition of corporal punishment in state schools in the UK in 1987 was entirely due to successful action taken by parents who contended that the administration of corporal punishment in school against their express wishes represented a breach of the European Convention on Human Rights (*Campbell and Cosans* v. *United Kingdom*, 1982). The complete abolition of corporal punishment in all maintained and independent schools and for children receiving nursery education will have to wait until late 1999, following implementation of the School Standards and Framework Act 1998. Meanwhile, the government has issued guidance designed to clarify the use of 'reasonable force' by teachers to prevent the commission of a crime by a pupil or to prevent a pupil causing damage to property, injury to themselves or others, or disruption (DFEE, 1998).

The acquisition of authority by schools acting on behalf of the state has implications for their role in the lives of children. Schools act as integral agents in the 'welfare network' and provide mechanisms for official surveillance and regulation, and as sites for the disempowerment of children.

Schools and the welfare network

Given that, in principle at least, all children over the age of 5 should be attending school, schools have unrivalled access to the child population, thus providing opportunities for early detection of children experiencing disturbance and distress, and playing an active part in their monitoring and treatment. As a corollary, since the institution of compulsory attendance itself provides a proxy indicator of parental competence, the absence from school of a child who should otherwise be attending could also be indicative of difficulties, with, in extreme circumstances, deprivation of education providing potential justification for formal intervention or compulsory measures of care (e.g. *Re: DJMS*, 1977; *Re: O*, 1992). The key place of schools in the 'welfare network' is now generally recognised (Gilligan, 1998).

The Victorian founders of the education welfare service were quick to spot the impact of poverty and material disadvantage on access to educational opportunity and the need to provide welfare assistance if children were to take advantage of the educational opportunities made available to them (Coombes and Beer, 1984), while the Plowden Committee (CACE, 1967) recognised the potential contribution of social work in combating under-achievement in schools and recommended the establishment of a school social work service to complement the work of teachers, a recommendation never implemented, although reiterated nearly three decades later on behalf of a major teaching union which claimed that 'many schools appear to have become an unfunded branch of the social services' (Webb, 1994: 71).

Research into the impact of schools on their pupils has demonstrated their value in providing support and sanctuary to children experiencing a range of adversity. Rutter, reviewing the evidence of school effectiveness research, concludes that 'Good school experiences are likely to be socially helpful to all children, *but probably they are critically important only in subgroups under stress and with a lack of other positive experiences*' (1991a, our emphasis).

It is a relatively short step from recognising the place of schools in the welfare network to a more specific appreciation of the role of schools and their staff in child protection (for a fuller discussion see, e.g., Sage, 1993; DFEE, 1995; NASUWT, 1995). However, recent consideration of the role of schools in child protection has also highlighted what may be termed the 'downside' of schooling, the part played by schools in the disempowerment of children, in extreme circumstances exposing them to abuse both by their peers and by adults. Acknowledgement of school as a potential source of disempowerment and oppression of children requires a reconsideration of conventional meanings given to absenteeism and to the motivation of absentees (Blyth and Milner, 1997; Blyth and Cooper, in press).

School as a site for the oppression of children

Dissent against mainstream perspectives on education and recognition of the role of compulsory education in promoting social control (essentially ensuring that the working class learned to know their place and stayed there) is not a new phenomenon. For example, H.G. Wells observed that: 'the Education Act of 1870 was not an act for common universal education, it was an act to educate the lower classes for employment on lower class lines and with specially trained inferior teachers who had no university qualification' (cited in Coombes and Beer, 1984: 5). That this lesson has not been forgotten in more recent times is reflected in the observations of an unidentified Department of Education and Science official: 'We are in a period of considerable social change. There may be social unrest, but we can cope with the Toxteths. But, if we have a highly educated and idle population we may possibly anticipate more serious social conflict. People must be educated once more to know their place' (cited in Ranson, 1984: 241). The tension between education as a form of social control and a means of self-advancement and socio-economic mobility remains (Bowles and Gintis, 1976). It clearly suits dominant socio-economic groups to hold out the carrot of self-improvement via education and the near-mythical figure of the self-made (wo)man as evidence that the system does reward those who are worthy and who make sufficient effort and that, conversely, failure to succeed is the result of individual rather than institutionalised shortcomings.

Devoid of such obvious ideological overtones, a survey of 8 to 15 year olds in the UK (Ghate and Daniels, 1997) showed that school provided the context for three main sources of worry for children and young people: fear of being bullied or picked on, fear of getting into trouble with teachers, and fear of failing tests and exams.

Children in the UK enjoy relatively limited educational rights. Formally children and young people of compulsory school age have an implied right to receive full-time education suitable to their age, ability and aptitude and to any special educational needs they may have, since (with certain specific exceptions, notably concerning the more limited access to education for pupils excluded from school) a legal obligation is placed on local authorities to make such education available and on parents to ensure that their children of compulsory school age receive such education.

Further safeguards are given under provisions of the European Convention on Human Rights and the United Nations' Convention on the Rights of the Child, to both of which the UK government is a signatory. Article 2 of the First Protocol to the European Convention states that:

> No person shall be denied the right to education. In the exercise of any functions which it assumes in relation to education and to teaching, the State shall respect the right of parents to ensure such education and teaching in conformity with their own religious and philosophical convictions.

As this indicates, the Convention emphasises parents' rather than children's rights. Its main impact on British education has been as the means of securing the abolition of corporal punishment in British state schools (although clearly children have been the undoubted beneficiaries) (*Campbell and Cosans* v. *United Kingdom*, 1982).

While the United Nations' Convention focuses more specifically on the rights of the child, and embraces a wide range of rights that might impinge on education, it has had limited impact on education in the UK. The standards the Convention seeks to encourage cannot be established by claims to legal entitlement. Furthermore, the initial response of the then Conservative government indicated its opinion that UK legislation and institutions *already* reflected the spirit of the Convention (HMSO, 1994), a view supported neither by critics in Britain (see, e.g., Newell, 1991; Lansdown, 1995, 1996) nor by the UN Committee on the Rights of the Child (1995) itself. While we discuss the Convention's specific references to education below, we need to recognise that education provision cannot be considered in a vacuum, in particular noting the well-documented growth of childhood poverty and the increasing 'wealth gap' between rich and poor since the 1980s (see, e.g., NCH: Action for Children, 1994; OECD, 1995) and evidence of the contribution of poverty to family difficulties which may affect children's behaviour and performance in school (Rutter, 1991a, 1991b; NUT, 1992; AMA, 1995; OFSTED, 1995a).

Specifically, education provision in the UK rests uneasily with Articles 3 (the best interests of the child), 12 (participation in decision-making) and 15 (rights to freedom of expression) of the Convention. While the government claimed: 'In some of the areas which affect children's lives very significantly, for example health and education, there is an *implicit* acceptance in the system of the best interest principle although there is no reference to it as such in the relevant legislation' (HMSO, 1994, p. 21, our emphasis), it is notable that the government deliberately chose not to make the welfare of the child an underpinning principle of the Education Act 1993 (Lansdown, 1996). In practice, this means that decisions made concerning school choice and admissions, exclusion and special educational needs procedures are not required to have regard to the welfare of the child. Moreover, while Conservative administrations made much of their efforts to encourage increased *parental* choice and participation in their children's education, there has been no recognition of the possibility of conflict between the rights of parents and of children concerning education.

Similarly, these education procedures do not allow for the participation of pupils themselves (Article 12), although government Education and Health departments considered that children and young people in public care played an insufficiently active role in decisions made about their lives, including education (DFE and DOH, 1994). Furthermore, children have no formal rights to participate in matters of school policy or administration or involvement in decisions such as school uniform, curriculum, arrangements for school meals, supervision in the playground or discipline.

Pupil's rights to freedom of expression (Article 15) are frequently severely constrained within the compulsory schooling system, usually in the guise of ensuring 'good order'. For example, school rules concerning school uniform, hair length, wearing jewellery, political and other badges will rarely take account of pupils' own views, while conflict between children and school authorities over these issues may, not infrequently, lead to their exclusion from school. Less than convincingly, the government defended its record on the grounds that 'there is no obstacle in law to prevent children themselves from making a complaint' (HMSO, 1994: 28).

However, Jeffs claims that British education legislation has always 'cast young people in the mould of powerless subjects within the system' (1995: 25), while Lansdown (1996) argues that learning about human rights and responsibilities via the formal curriculum is undermined by the failure of schools to operate as democratic communities that provide evidence that adults value the feelings and opinions of pupils, an omission that so far has not been addressed by the new administration (DFEE, 1997a).

Outcomes of failure to attend school

Despite the fact that most young people of school age in the UK attend school regularly, both politicians and the media appear caught up in a moral panic about levels of non-attendance, its presumed link with delinquency, and young people's rejection of education (e.g. DFE, 1992a; Scott-Clark and Burke, 1996; Scott-Clark and Syal, 1996; DFEE, 1997a; Social Exclusion Unit, 1998). The assumption that a child's failure to receive education is likely to be damaging for both the individual and for society more generally is buttressed by a considerable body of empirical evidence which correlates failure to attend school and failure to obtain educational qualifications with poor longer-term outcomes in education, training, employment, housing and personal relationships (see, e.g., Farrington and West, 1990; Hibbett and Fogelman, 1990; Hibbett et al., 1990; Casey and Smith, 1995; Farrington, 1996; Social Exclusion Unit, 1998) as well as ideological imperatives such as the need for social stability and cohesion and industry's needs for a well-educated, flexible workforce. Cedric Cullingford in chapter 3 of this volume examines in more detail the particularly contentious relationship between non-attendance at school and delinquency. The Crime and Disorder Act 1998 enables a court to impose a Child Safety Order in respect of a child under the age of ten years in order to protect the child from the risk of being drawn into crime. An order could prohibit specified conduct, such as truanting from school (Scanlan, 1998).

In contrast to mainstream perceptions, Holmes proposes an unfashionable assessment of the 'functional' consequences of 'truancy', which he regards as 'sometimes a sign of discovery and initiative: an opportunity for disgruntled individuals to seek solitude, space they will need in later life' (1989: 7). He suggests that:

- siblings (and parents) of 'truants' might benefit from the additional 'child-minding help';

- peers and teachers might benefit from the smaller numbers of (well-motivated) pupils in school: 'Schools can be more orderly, less crowded, and happier places if only 87% of the roll turn up each day, for whatever reason' (Holmes, 1989: 7);
- in a context of high youth unemployment, when employers can pick and choose, the 'losses' to industry as a consequence of non-attendance are less significant than officially expressed concerns would lead us to believe.

Attempts to understand the implications of 'truancy' cannot be divorced from its causes. Historically, the search for the causes of non-attendance has focused on individual and family factors, the 'pathology' model retaining an important place within official contemporary discourses of 'truancy'. For example, Graham and Bowling (1995) observe that the likelihood of truanting is increased by two to three times in families characterised by 'weak' parental supervision and 'low' family attachment, while O'Keeffe (1994) identifies a connection between high levels of absence and adverse family dynamics and socio-economic pressures.

By the early 1980s, though, research on school effectiveness having demonstrated the strong relationship between disruptive behaviour and persistent non-attendance and the organisation and ethos of particular schools, *irrespective* of the individual characteristics of their pupils and their pupils' families, the focus of attention had shifted substantially to the impact of the education system and schools. School factors found to be associated with non-attendance include curricular difficulties, the wish to avoid particular subjects and/or teachers (O'Keeffe, 1994), and bullying (Learmonth, 1995). Learmonth indicates that the development of in-school anti-bullying schemes may contribute to improved school attendance by making schools more congenial environments for children.

O'Keeffe's finding that, according to pupils' own accounts, the most important source of truancy is the school curriculum itself is reinforced by Learmonth (1995), while OFSTED (1995a) found a high correlation between rates of attendance and pupil performance in public examinations, high rates of attendance accompanying success in public examinations and low levels of attendance accompanying unsatisfactory or poor examination results. Stokes and Walton (in this volume) also cite illness, personal problems, dissatisfaction with classroom management and delivery of lessons, bullying and dissatisfaction with break times as reasons for absenteeism. These findings reinforce contentions (e.g. Grenville, 1988; Holmes, 1989) that absenteeism may, on occasions at least, represent a rational consumer response to dissatisfaction with the service on offer. Drawing on the ideology of the market, this suggests that interventions should be directed towards improving the service rather than harassing reluctant consumers.

Prevalence and patterns of non-attendance

Official concern that truancy has reached crisis point (Social Exclusion Unit, 1998) has been afforded the status of a moral panic by the media and politicians, although estimates of prevalence range widely. *The Guardian* (1990), for example, reported 'more than half a million children' absent at least once a week without 'acceptable reason' (cited in Gleeson, 1992), while in 1995 the public sector union Unison was claiming that over 800,000 children a year 'played truant' (Montgomery, 1996). A *Sunday Times* headline, 'Return of the Wagman in Crackdown on 1m Truants', derived from 1995/6 school performance statistics (O'Reilly, 1997), is qualified in the text of the report: 'About 568,000 primary school children and 410,000 secondary school pupils were estimated to have skipped class for at least *half a day* last year without permission or a note from their parents' (our emphasis). The Department for Education and Employment's own analysis of attendance data from LEAs provides information for both 'authorised' and 'unauthorised' absence in terms of '% of half days missed through absence' and 'average number of half days missed per pupil' (DFEE, 1996), neither of which of themselves provide a particularly useful account of the phenomenon and how it affects individual schools and pupils. Publication of overall absence levels reveals little useful information. A given absence rate could, for example, be indicative of a large number of pupils missing small amounts of school or a very small number of pupils permanently – or almost permanently – absent.

The basis of concerns about levels of illicit absence assumes the accuracy of school attendance records, an accuracy that cannot be assumed to exist. First, we need to acknowledge the possibility of inaccuracy resulting from 'human error' and post-registration truancy (O'Keeffe, 1994). Second, attendance registers have always been prone to more calculated misrepresentation to suit the interests of schools. In the early days of compulsory school attendance the fact that teachers' and head teachers' pay was in part based on pupil attendance led to the suspicion that attendance records might show inflated levels of attendance (Rubenstein, 1969). Today the school's position in performance tables has replaced teachers' pay as an incentive to present published attendance data in the most favourable light (i.e. redesignating ostensibly 'unauthorised' absence as 'authorised' absence), but having the similar effect of undermining the credibility of official absence data. This is clearly illustrated by the experience of some schools when details of unauthorised absences were first required to be included in published performance data in 1993. These schools, which believed they had conscientiously applied government guidance on the categorisation of absence, believed they had been penalised in 'league' table terms in comparison with schools which had adopted a less rigorous approach to absence categorisation (OFSTED, 1995a). Further doubt may be cast on the reliability and validity of official attendance records through strategies such as formally excluding truants (a manoeuvre which in England and Wales – although not Scotland – has the effect of 'authorising' erstwhile 'unauthorised' absence); enforcing parental 'withdrawal' of unwelcome pupils; informal (illegal) exclusions; illicit granting of 'study leave'; and removing absent pupils from school rolls (OFSTED, 1995a; Stirling, 1996).

The net effect of these factors is that we should remain sceptical of official data about prevalence and patterns of non-attendance. In particular it is impossible to compare current and past school attendance or absence levels.

The use of different definitions and categorisations of absence also makes for difficulties in comparing the results of different research studies. Even dedicated truancy studies (e.g. O'Keeffe, 1994), using self-reporting measures, may well underestimate true levels since they are least likely to identify the young people most likely to be absent from school.

Stoll and O'Keeffe (1989), who interviewed pupils *at school*, found two-thirds of pupils admitting to truanting at some time during their secondary schooling, although only about 30 per cent of pupils admitted to so doing in O'Keeffe's later study (O'Keeffe, 1994). 'Post-registration' truancy appears to be more prevalent than 'blanket' truancy (i.e. never getting to school in the first place), although many truants are engaged in both (Stoll and O'Keeffe, 1989; O'Keeffe, 1994). A small minority of pupils appear to be 'frequent truants', O'Keeffe identifying 2.5 per cent (Year 10) and 4.5 per cent (Year 11) pupils who admitted to truanting at least once a week, while Gray and Jesson (1990) found that 6 per cent of Year 11 pupils were absent for days or weeks at a time, and Farrington (1996) notes that by the ages of 12 to 14, 18 per cent of his (all-male) sample were identified by teachers as either 'frequent truants' (although 'frequency' is not defined) or having poor attendance attributed to truancy, while a similar percentage of 14 year olds themselves admitted 'frequent truancy'.

Truancy rates typically increase during the last two years of compulsory schooling (SCRE, 1992; O'Keeffe, 1994; Sutherland, 1995). O'Keeffe (1994) found that slightly more boys than girls admitted to truanting: 24.6 per cent of Year 10 boys; 25.5 per cent of Year 10 girls; 37.7 per cent of Year 11 boys; 30.5 per cent of Year 11 girls. However, he reports that truancy levels at single-sex boys' schools tend to be higher than at mixed schools, with single-sex girls' schools having consistently lower levels of truancy than either mixed or single-sex boys' schools. Carlen *et al.* (1992) note that girls are more likely than boys to be involved in condoned absence.

Improving school attendance

Following the recommendations of a Committee of Inquiry into behaviour in schools chaired by former education minister, Lord Elton (DES, 1989b), the government initiated a programme designed to improve school attendance throughout the UK in 1990. Funding for the programme has come from both central and local government sources. Additionally, in Northern Ireland there has been some project-based funding from the EU Peace and Reconciliation Fund.

While the precise nature of initiatives has tended to reflect local needs, many current projects involved the development of more accurate and reliable computerised methods of attendance registration, establishing co-operative inter-professional teams, employing 'whole-school' approaches, promoting school 'ownership' of attendance and emphasising measures to promote and encourage attendance rather than punish absence. Since central government has contributed the main element of funding it has been able to influence the nature of the work that will be supported; for example, in 1994/5 expressly encouraging projects that had a 'Truancy Watch' element. Although the government has maintained its financial support for this programme, the short-term nature of funding (for one year at a time only) has limited the ability of managers and workers effectively to plan ahead.

The Social Exclusion Unit (1998) considers that these initiatives provide a sufficient quantity and range of good practice to show that schools can substantially cut truancy, outlining the ingredients of an effective approach as:

- acting quickly and consistently (zero tolerance of truancy);
- making a truancy 'crack-down' an issue for the whole school and community;
- using computerised registration;
- dealing early with children's literacy and numeracy problems;
- providing an alternative curriculum for those unlikely to achieve at GCSE;
- providing extra-curricular activities to motivate those at risk of becoming disaffected.

Importantly the Social Exclusion Unit's recommendations that a genuine cross-departmental focus be brought to tackling the problem, a complex set of inter-related problems not having been well managed by government at either national or local level, have been incorporated into the Crime and Disorder Act 1998.

19

2

COMBATING TRUANCY

The Scottish approach

Brian Boyd

Introduction

In Scotland, 1977 was the 'year of the reports'. Three major committees had been established three years earlier to look at: the structure and balance of the curriculum in the last two years of compulsory schooling; assessment and certification; and the issues of truancy and indiscipline (Scottish Education Department, 1977a, 1977b, 1977c). Of the three reports that emerged (all popularly known by the surname of the chairperson – Munn, Dunning and Pack), it was, perhaps, inevitable that it would be the two, dealing with structures – of school timetables and examinations – that would make the most impact. The Pack Report dealt with what were seen as social problems, philosophy, attitudes, roles and expectation, and, furthermore, it contained a Statement of Dissent, one which radically challenged the prevailing ethos of schools. It seemed destined to be a controversial report from the outset, and Her Majesty's Deputy Senior Chief Inspector Chirnside, assessor to the Pack Committee, recalled later that he 'changed the title of the Pack Committee's report from Truancy and Discipline to Truancy and *In*discipline' (Boyd, 1993), thus departing from HMI's attempt to present issues positively and signalling the perceived link between the two headline issues.

The Committee had been set up in 1974 by the Secretary of State:

> to inquire into truancy and indiscipline among primary and secondary school pupils in Scotland; to consider what measures can be taken by the school, and by the school with the help of other services, to reduce these problems; to consider the circumstances in which suspension and exclusion of pupils from school may be justified, and what provision should be made for such pupils; and to make recommendations, having regard to the most effective use of available resources.
>
> (Scottish Education Department, 1977c: ix)

Two years previously the school leaving age had been raised, thus prompting the national review of curriculum, assessment and related matters, and in the Preface to the Report it was observed:

> The Secretary of State advised that, in interpreting the remit, we should not review the decision to raise the school leaving age. We accepted this advice *but certain consequences of the decision cannot be overlooked and have been discussed where appropriate.*
> (Scottish Education Department, 1977c: ix, my emphasis)

Thus a signal was given that the Report was going to be thorough and challenging, and remains for many Scottish educationalists the best of the three that appeared that year.

Truancy and indiscipline in schools in Scotland: an analysis of the issues

It is interesting to note now, some twenty years on, the extent to which truancy and indiscipline seemed inseparable and were perceived as social problems. The link between non-attendance and low attainment had not been made in research terms, although the analysis of the causes of truancy inevitably led the Committee to consider the curriculum. But, initially, the Report focussed on 'public concern', both about truancy and 'there was increasing concern among education authorities, the teachers' associations and the general public about the problem of unruly pupils' (Scottish Education Department, 1977c: 1).

The link between truancy and youth crime was accepted by the Committee on the basis of evidence given by the Scottish Council on Crime, which argued that the 'peak age for crimes proved was 16' and reported a 'sharp rise' (between 1950 and 1970) for each group from 8 to 14 years. Indeed the Report quoted verbatim from the Scottish Council on Crime's Memorandum on Crime and the Prevention of Crime (1975): 'We are led to understand that a substantial proportion of children who get into trouble for committing offences have, at some earlier stage in their career, been noted as truants. Truancy may be an early indication that a child is beginning to go off the rails.' (Scottish Education Department, 1977c: 1).

Thus, amid a welter of statistics and assumptions, the Committee set out to deal with truancy as an issue which could no longer be 'considered as a harmless and occasional adventure'.

As if to allay fears of the school system being in crisis, the chapter on 'Truancy' began with the sentence 'Truancy is not a new phenomenon' (Scottish Education Department, 1977c: 13). It looked historically at the issue of attendance, beginning with the 1872 Education Act, which introduced compulsory schooling. Attendance rates in the 1870s were around 75 per cent and increased to 80 per cent in the 1890s, though the figures did not relate to the population but rather to those enrolled in schools. Indeed, the figure of 89 per cent reached in 1913 was thought to be admirable and was not surpassed until 1930. But even in the mid-1970s, the Committee found that access to accurate statistics on truancy was not without its problems. The lack of centrally gathered statistics was compounded by variations in the definition of truancy itself.

Some individual schools gave written evidence to the Pack Committee. One such school in the West of Scotland submitted evidence showing that absence was 'periodic in character, with a minimum on Tuesdays and a maximum on Fridays' (Scottish Education Department, 1977c: 15). The Committee was forced to conclude that the figures available across Scotland were 'open to criticism', not sufficiently sensitive to pick up on what it called 'hidden truancy' – where pupils depart after registration – and not able to distinguish among schools, or within year groups in schools. And, most importantly, it observed that 'the absence rate tells us nothing about the causes of absence' (Scottish Education Department, 1977c: 15). The sources of statistics were varied – local authorities, social work, children's hearings – and the Committee was unhappy with the blurred nature of the picture presented to it.

The confusion over definitions of truancy was such that the Committee decided early on in its deliberations to adopt the following:

> Truancy is unauthorised absence from school, for any period, as a result of premeditated or spontaneous action on the part of pupil, parent or both.
>
> (Scottish Education Department, 1977c: 18)

Thus, what have become known in the 1990s as 'authorised' and 'unauthorised' absence could, in the view of Pack, be regarded as truancy. The Committee then commissioned a survey to be carried out by the Scottish Council for Research in Education (SCRE) in order to determine the scope of the problem. The general picture in 1976 was summarised as follows:

> That the problem of truancy is very considerable is quite clear from the fact that over 15 per cent of all children, and a quarter of all boys and girls in S4, were at some time during the 6 weeks of the survey absent from school without adequate explanation.
>
> (Scottish Education Department, 1977c: 23)

Not only were the global figures worrying to the Committee, but the survey demonstrated that 'some schools have much worse records than others' (Scottish Education Department, 1977c: 23). One school had a truancy rate four times the national average, but what alarmed the

Committee was the conclusion that: 'Even on the average figures there would be in a comprehensive school of, say, 1500 pupils a group of 30 to 50 very persistent truants' (Scottish Education Department, 1977c: 23).

The Report looked in detail at both 'Family Circumstances' and 'Factors associated with School' (Scottish Education Department, 1977c: 26–9). It considered family breakdown, family size, socio-economic disadvantage, and family history of non-attendance as being correlated with, or causes of, truancy. It considered size of school as a factor, but rejected it, and went on to consider shortages of teachers (still a problem in the expansionist 1970s), the curriculum (notwithstanding the Munn Committee's deliberations [Scottish Education Department, 1977a]), 'maladjustment' of pupils, bullying and school systems for administering attendance and absence.

The long section in the Pack Report on 'Indiscipline and Sanctions' is not immediately the subject of this book, but it did deal with the issues of 'suspensions' and 'exclusions' and recommended that 'Day Units' be established on a pilot basis in some secondary schools. The present writer was the head teacher of one such school in the 1980s and both the operation of the unit and the evolution of policy and practice from then to the present day will be picked up later in this chapter.

Perhaps the strongest section in the Pack Report was on 'Curriculum and Organisation'. The immediate backdrop was the rapid expansion of education to meet the demands of a rising pupil population and the raising of the school leaving age (ROSLA). The Report identified the increasing demands society was placing on schools and commended the efforts schools were making to fulfil these expectations. More radically, it argued that: 'Parents and pupils, it seems to us, have a right to express their own expectations of the school and to have an opportunity to do so' (Scottish Education Department, 1977c: 70). It took account of the recently published Bullock Report, *A Language for Life* (DES, 1975), and referred back to the Primary Memorandum (Scottish Education Department, 1965), which introduced 'child-centredness' into Scottish primary schools, and began to make the connections between failure to learn successfully and likeliness to truant. Anticipating the Warnock Report (there was a Scottish HMI on the Warnock Committee), it looked at 'learning difficulties' and considered the importance in the long term of pre-school provision. It had a separate section on 'Remedial Education' and, once again, anticipated the appearance of what was to become a seminal HMI report on the education of pupils with learning difficulties. In an echo of the Primary Memorandum, it still used the term 'backwardness' in relation to pupils, but looked forward also to the issues of 'learning support' which was to characterise the Scottish system in the 1980s.

The Pack Report, then, did what no other major report had done (not even its contemporaries, Munn and Dunning) and considered the impact of its arguments on how schools should be managed. It looked at 'Transition to

Secondary School', 'Curriculum Policy and Development', 'School Timetables', 'Class Organisation', 'Subject Barriers', and devoted a whole section to the issue of Guidance (the Guidance or pastoral system having been recently introduced to Scottish secondary schools). All of these issues are still topical and, indeed, contentious. What the Pack Report was doing was to challenge the educational 'policy community' to examine whether curriculum was part of the problem rather than being part of the solution. It challenged head teachers to reflect on their internal systems for meeting the needs of individual pupils, and challenged the Scottish Education Department and its curriculum advisers to ask if vulnerable pupils' needs were being met.

It went on to look at the guidance structure, the impact of social work, training of teachers and social workers, and the role of the head teacher as leader and manager. All in all, it was a radical and forward-looking report, but, its findings, all 141 of them, did not make the impact the Committee hoped they would. The Statement of Dissent contained comments such as the following that were always going to be seen as too radical:

> In general I consider that as a society we have conspired to deny the rights – the dignity and the authority – of our children....The reason that I haven't signed the final report is that in my view it offers no significant challenge to prevailing distortions in our societal attitudes towards children growing up in Scotland.
>
> (Scottish Education Department, 1977c: 130)

Yet, there have been resonances of this dissenting voice in the debate on the 1995 Children (Scotland) Act.

The 1980s: more reports and some action

The most influential document to appear in Scotland in the 1980s on matters of pupil welfare was undoubtedly *More Than Feelings of Concern* (Scottish Consultative Council on the Curriculum, 1986), a report on guidance and Scottish secondary schools. It introduced into a Scottish context the notion of the 'school as a caring community' and, as its title suggests, made the link between caring and pupil achievement. It picked up from where Pack left off, and introduced the notion of 'whole-school responsibility', echoing Bullock and Warnock and suggesting policies at a whole-school level which would impact on individual children. It quoted Pack early on in the Report:

...the organisation, curriculum and staffing structure of a school should be designed to accord with the ideas of a caring society and should meet its requirement for all pupils in so far as this is possible.
(Scottish Consultative Council on the Curriculum, 1986: para 1.24)

While there was no separate chapter of the Report on truancy, it argued that a caring community 'does not simply emerge as a by-product of good intentions'. Rather: 'It represents a goal that has to be deliberately planned and worked towards' (Scottish Consultative Council on the Curriculum, 1986: 3). Thus, *More Than Feelings of Concern* shifted the focus from society to the school. Schools could make a difference if they accepted 'a responsibility for promoting the social and personal development' of pupils. The Report introduced the concept of the 'First Level Guidance Teacher' and argued for 'Extended Guidance Teams' that might include social workers, educational psychologists, the school attendance service (where it existed), the health visitor, school nurse, and so on. More recently the idea has been developed into an extended support for learning teams, but the principle of collaborative working was to be a key part of the caring school.

Not all of the initiatives in Scotland in the 1980s were national. Strathclyde region, which represented half of Scotland and had the bulk of the country's economic and social disadvantage, was looking at a range of issues. The 'Young People in Trouble' report, a joint venture involving education, social work and the Reporter to the Children's Panel, appeared in 1988 (Strathclyde Regional Council, 1988). Its most far-reaching recommendation was the setting up in every Strathclyde school of a Joint Assessment Team (JAT), involving all the professionals and agencies involved with vulnerable young people, to consider how best their needs might be met. Thus prevention – of indiscipline, of truancy, of exclusion – would be the main aim, but the JAT would also consider cases of young people 'in trouble'. The goal of inter-departmental co-operation was paramount:

We wish to stress that inter-departmental co-operation should not be restricted to those working at what teachers call 'the chalk face', that is, to those whose duties bring them into direct contact with young people. Those responsible for the management of the various departments should establish a co-operative framework.
(Strathclyde Regional Council, 1988: para 1.3.3)

While JATs were established in most secondary schools and within many primary schools serving areas of disadvantage, the goal of inter-departmental co-operation was considerably more elusive. Nevertheless, the principle had been stated and the notion of the management of a caring community had been extended to major departments in the Council.

School effectiveness/school improvement: a changing context in the 1980s and 1990s

While the discussions continued about these vulnerable young people, the whole debate about the impact of the school was being contested. In the wake of Rutter *et al.*'s *Fifteen Thousand Hours* (1979), Scottish education had also moved towards a position where it was recognised that schools could make a difference. Management as an issue became a national and a regional imperative, and the HMI initiative on *Management Training for Head Teachers* included modules on 'The School in its Community' as well as 'Managing the Curriculum' and 'Monitoring and Evaluation' (Scottish Office Education Department, 1990). Indeed, almost every publication — reports and the increasing number of ringbound folders of indicators of various kinds — bore the legend 'For Use in School Self-Evaluation'. Against a backdrop of government initiatives to produce and publish national data on examination results, attendance, leaver destinations, cost per pupil, Her Majesty's Inspectorate were commissioning research and producing materials to enable schools to look at their own practices and manage their own improvement.

In the meantime, the issue of truancy had not gone away. In 1991, the Scottish Office Education Department (SOED) issued a consultation paper to interested bodies 'seeking their views on the nature and incidence of truancy among Scottish schoolchildren' (Scottish Office Education Department, 1991). It began by reminding readers that Section 30 of the Education Scotland Act 1988 'places a duty on parents of children of school age to provide efficient and suitable education for them, either by causing them to attend school regularly or by other means' (Scottish Office Education Department, 1991: para 2.1).

It reminded education authorities of their powers to enforce attendance at school and schools of their requirements to record absence. It asked the age-old question 'What is truancy?' and quoted Pack, but suggested, 'Views are sought on this definition'. The consultation paper asserted that 'there is a clear link between truancy and examination results; perhaps, but not overtly, drawing on successive surveys of school leavers carried out for the SOED at that time by the Centre for Educational Sociology at the University of Edinburgh. These had shown, successively, since the seminal *Tell Them From Me* (Gow and McPherson, 1980) that young people who were, in the days of 'O' Grade examinations, deemed to be 'non-certificate' or 'non-academic', or who, after the more inclusive Standard Grade examinations were introduced, were nevertheless low achievers and left school as soon as they could, had higher incidences of truancy in all categories:

- a lesson here and there
- a day here and there

- several days at a time
- weeks at a time.

The SOED paper referred also to its own 1989 School Meals Census as well as the survey for the Pack Report and reported that in the 1989 school leavers survey, 45 per cent of S4 leavers reported that they had missed a lesson here and there by truanting and 7 per cent said they had truanted for weeks at a time. The paper sought views on recording procedures, the need to distinguish between 'authorised' and 'unauthorised' absence, and how best practice could be shared. How truants and their families should be dealt with was also to be considered, and, importantly, more research was commissioned, first into a wide range of issues affecting inner city and estate schools, but more specifically on the links between non-attendance and attainment.

The 1990s – from policy to practice: national initiatives

The chapter on truancy in *Education In and Out of School* (MacBeath, 1992) confined its analysis to the Pack definition, the School Meals Census and the young leavers survey, but reinforced the link between truancy and low achievement. It suggested that in some schools there might be 'a norm of "acceptable absence"' (MacBeath, 1992: 64). It also introduced the unpalatable possibility that some teachers may not welcome attempts to improve attendance figures since for them it 'not only increases class size but of the least desirable kind' (MacBeath, 1992: 67). It went on to describe 'Lessons Learned' from the study:

- schools and teachers must set and maintain high expectations for student attendance
- it is helpful to set goals and incentives for individual students
- alternative provision and flexible approaches to the curriculum are needed, particularly at S4 stage
- parental co-operation and support is crucial
- it is important for guidance teachers to meet other workers on their territory
- home visiting is expensive but extremely helpful.

(MacBeath, 1992: 67)

The research into the relationship between truancy and attainment was commissioned in 1994 by the SOED and was carried out by the Scottish Council for Research on Education (SCRE). The resulting report, *Understanding Truancy: Links between Attendance, Truancy and Performance* (Malcolm et al., 1996), had already begun to inform policy and practice before it was published. It fed directly into the SOED project being carried out by

MacBeath to produce a 'Truancy File' for all schools (HMI Audit Unit, 1995). Malcolm *et al.* found in their study of seven pairs of schools, in each case a secondary and one associated primary, that 'pupil absences were more likely to be "explained" than "unexplained"' and that 'as the level of absence increased, the level of Standard Grade award decreased' (Malcolm *et al.*, 1996: x). More importantly, perhaps, from a policy perspective, was the finding that: 'Explained absence is comparable in its effects on attainment with unexplained absence' (Malcolm *et al.*, 1996: x).

Thus, for the government, for councils and for schools, the emphasis was to shift from truancy to non-attendance. If any kind of absence, from the traditional kinds of truancy to parents taking children away on off-season foreign holidays, could be associated with decreased attainment, then the emphasis could shift to the management of the school. The message was that schools had the ability to improve the attendance of their own pupils – and some were already doing so. Therefore, packs of materials aimed at schools, school boards and parents would enable them to improve on their practice. Thus 'The Truancy File' was born and the Scottish Initiative on Attendance, Absence and – later – Attainment was set up.

The 'Truancy File'

The 'Truancy File' followed the formula of the 'Homework File' (HMI Audit Unit, 1994a). Essentially a training pack aimed at school managers, teachers, school boards, parents and other professionals working with schools, it is an attractively presented mix of research findings, examples of good practice from across Scotland, case studies, hypothetical situations and activities to be carried out, usually in small groups. In the first section, 'Origins and Purposes', it lists four possible uses of the File:

- as a source of reference
- for training and development
- for auditing and monitoring
- for planning and prioritising

and the underlying philosophy was spelled out:

> Ultimately truancy will be only be overcome by teachers working together with parents and other bodies to improve school and class-room practice and to strengthen school–community relations.
>
> (HMI Audit Unit, 1995: 1)

This 'school effectiveness' paradigm was consistent with the approach being taken by the Audit Unit within HMI. There was an assumption that the school, working with others, could solve the problems of truancy, and that the File, if used alongside other sources of advice, such as performance indicators, school development planning, examination results, issued centrally by the Scottish Office Education and Industry Department (SOEID, as the SOED was now called), then truancy could be addressed. There was no explicit recognition of the complex debate which had gone on over decades as to the societal origins of truancy or the nature of compulsory schooling itself, but rather a belief, consistent with the growing body of school effectiveness research, that individual schools could make a difference, that truancy could be 'managed'. Thus, copies of the extensive pack were sent free of charge to every school in Scotland (some 3,500), not with any directive as to when it should be used, but, in the Scottish consensual tradition, as a helpful tool with which to address a problem facing many schools.

The breadth of the issues covered in the File is impressive, as the contents page shows:

WHY TRUANCY MATTERS

Section

1.1	Does truancy matter?
1.2	Truancy matters to the pupil
1.3	Truancy matters to the teacher
1.4	Truancy matters to the school
1.5	Truancy matters to the community
1.6	Are parents responsible?
1.7	What does truancy cost?
1.8	What the law says
1.9	What the reports say
1.10	What the research says
1.11	What the pupils say

GETTING A MEASURE OF THE ISSUE

Section

2.1	The Attendance audit
2.2	Monitoring attendance
2.3	The attendance continuum
2.4	Breaking down the figures
2.5	Tracking attendance patterns
2.6	An Attendance survey
2.7	Attendance and achievement
2.8	Using questions
2.9	Identifying pluses and minuses
2.10	Evaluating effectiveness

CAUSES AND CURES

Section
3.1   20 reasons for non-attendance
3.2   Roots and causes
3.3   Causes and cures: what schools can do
3.4   Causes and cures: who else can help?
3.5   Spotting the danger signs
3.6   Rowena is missing
3.5–3.6 Feedback notes
3.7   Three views of what really happened
3.8   Children in care
3.9   A shared responsibility
3.10   The ideal school for truants
3.11   Reviewing personal experience
3.12   A question of attitudes
3.13   So what would you do?

MAKING POLICY WORK

Section
4.1   Thinking about ways forward
4.2   Prevention or cure
4.3   Support for learning
4.4   Monitoring attendance
4.5   Using incentives
4.6   Informing parents
4.7   Home visiting
4.8   A community approach
4.9   Using joint assessment
4.10   The local attendance council
4.11   Truancy centres
4.12   The power to change

Each major issue consists of a separate A4 booklet, with a single page for each section. The format is easy to use, photocopiable for use with groups, and designed to be dipped into rather than worked through from 1.1 to 4.12.

The 'Truancy File', derived from the research carried out by SCRE, and produced by the Quality in Education (QIE) centre, is, therefore, in the mainstream of Scottish consensual policy-making. An education system 'centrally governed and locally administered' is how Scottish education has long been described, but this description fails to acknowledge the strategic role of the local authorities, who had their own policies, philosophies and structures for supporting schools. In the two decades from the mid-1970s onwards, Strathclyde as a council had been innovative (e.g. adults in schools; pre-5 centres, etc.) but had often found itself in conflict with central government and the SOEID (e.g. over National Testing). But the history of Scottish educational policy-making (Humes, 1986; McPherson and Raab, 1988; Boyd, 1993) shows a tendency to consensus. Whether the phrase 'policy community' or 'leadership class' is more accurate, ownership and implementation have been seen as key issues in Scotland. The 'Truancy File' sought to give schools 'ownership' of their own approaches to dealing with local manifestations of truancy, while the SOEID, at the same time, published school-by-school statistics, inviting comparisons and implying that schools and local authorities could 'do better' by looking at more successful examples elsewhere. There was no compulsion attached to the use of the 'Truancy File', produced, as the Acknowledgements show, with the help of senior officers of Strathclyde Regional Council.

The Scottish Initiative on Attendance, Absence and Attainment (SIAAA)

The SIAAA was a joint venture between the HMI Audit Unit and the Quality in Education centre at the University of Strathclyde. This partnership between HMI and a university signalled clearly the belief that policy should be informed by research. It underlined the idea of a partnership between the government – in this case HMI – and local authority schools and its aim was to seek out and disseminate 'good practice'. The SIAAA was grounded firmly in the SCRE research, and devised a number of 'attendance pathways' based on practice in Scottish schools, some of which addressed attendance and truancy directly and others which aimed at creating a more positive ethos in the school:

Direct Attendance Pathways

1. Attendance Policy and Procedures
2. Effective Monitoring of Attendance
3. Parental links on Attendance

Ethos Pathways which help promote Attendance

4. Support for Learning
5. Promoting Positive Behaviour and Relationships
6. Pupil Participation and Responsibilities
7. Working Together with Other Agencies

The SIAAA worked with local authorities and schools to promote and disseminate practice, mounted national and regional conferences to highlight and share insights, and, above all, set out to raise the awareness of the issues among all those with a stake in schooling. The link established by the SCRE research between attendance and attainment was by far the most powerful strand, and the SIAAA ran in parallel with the Scottish Ethos Network as part of the developmental axis of HMI strategy. The statistical publications in the 'Information for Parents' series, *Scottish Schools: Costs 1993/94 to 1995/96* (HMI Audit Unit, 1994b), *Examination Results in Scottish Schools 1994–1996* (HMI Audit Unit, 1996), *Attendance and Absence in Scottish Schools 1995/96* (HMI Audit Unit, 1997a) and *Leaver Destinations from Scottish Secondary Schools 1994/95 to 1996/97* (HMI Audit Unit, 1998), formed the other, more accountability-focused part.

The SIAAA ran for some two years and became a high-profile initiative, partly as a consequence of its charismatic director, Cameron Munro, and partly as a result of the willingness of schools and local authorities to share good practice. The final publication of the SIAAA, *Close to the Mark* (HMI Audit Unit, 1997b), had a Foreword from the new Labour Minister of State for Education, Brian Wilson, underlining the continuity in the system as well as the continuing importance of the issue. The publication contained examples of good practice from some 100 schools across Scotland – primary, secondary and special – and illustrated the extent to which schools had taken up the challenge of truancy and non-attendance. Once again, links were made to other HMI initiatives, in particular their re-launched performance indicators *How Good is Our School?* (1997). In this way, the HMI 'Quality Process' could be seen to be working in partnership with schools and local authorities, and *Close to the Mark* was a celebration of the fruits of such a partnership.

Exclusions from school

In 1997, Munn and her colleagues at Moray House Institute of Education published the findings of their research into regional authority practices, headteacher perceptions, characteristics of excluded pupils, in-school alternatives and good practice (Munn *et al.*, 1997). They found great diversity across authorities and schools in terms of practice and policy and commented on the lack of strategic overview of the issue in Scotland. They also found that in-school strategies often reflected the ethos of the school, ranging from the punitive to the positive praise-and-reward approaches. The key characteristics of excluded pupils had many similarities with those found in relation to truancy by SCRE:

- more boys than girls were excluded (9:1 in primary and 4:1 in secondary)
- the peak stages for exclusion were P5, S3 and S4

- over half the excluded secondary pupils had a previous history of indiscipline while almost all the excluded primary pupils had such a history
- the most common reasons for exclusion were fighting/assault, disruptive behaviour, failure to obey rules and abuse/insolence
- 26 pupils (19 secondary and 7 primary) had been excluded for assault on staff. Almost all were boys.

(Munn *et al.*, 1997: 5)

Among the authors' conclusions was that there should be 'a highlighting of elements of good practice' and 'the provision of examples of good practice at authority and school level' (Munn *et al.*, 1997: 8).

Tackling social exclusion and raising educational attainment: problems and opportunities

A Labour government, committed to raising achievement and tackling social exclusion, clearly saw the value of a collaborative approach, and although the SIAAA has been wound up as the new government develops its own approaches to these issues, it is worth reflecting on the lessons learned for the future. It seems clear that, in the light of the research into truancy and exclusion, the issues addressed by the Pack Report are still current. The issue of the curriculum, of 'Teaching for Effective Learning' and of the links between underachievement and non-attendance still need to be explored. At present, in Scotland, the essential dilemma facing schools is how to raise achievement for all while at the same time meeting centrally produced targets which concentrate on examination results; how to develop an inclusive school ethos, reducing exclusions and catering for pupils with emotional and behavioural difficulties while at the same time raising levels of examination results; and how to promote self-evaluation against a backdrop of national targets and published statistics.

The issue of pupil motivation remains central to the debate in many schools. Peer group pressure, underachievement among boys and lack of perceived employment prospects are often cited as contributory factors to both truancy and exclusion from school. The government has sought, through its New Deal initiative, to provide employment, and in Scotland, curricular changes, such as the 'Higher Still' programme (Scottish Office Education and Industry Department, 1995), seek to deliver 'opportunity for all'.

The outcome of such changes remains to be seen, but the essential paradox remains. While the message of the 'Truancy File' and the SIAAA is that schools can address their own problems from a local perspective, the curriculum becomes ever more centralised. Room for manoeuvre is reduced and the impact of national targets may be to narrow even further the focus of school initiatives.

But there are reasons for optimism in Scottish education. While the lack of a national strategy for ensuring that research informs practice at a school level has been pointed out (Boyd, 1995), it is true to say that the 'Truancy File' represents a belief that teachers-as-reflective-professionals can be part of self-evaluating schools. The Scottish Consultative Council on the Curriculum has contributed publications on the importance of personal and social development (pupil self-esteem, aspirations and dispositions to learning) in publications such as *The Heart of the Matter* (Scottish Consultative Council on the Curriculum, 1996a) and *Climate for Learning* (Scottish Consultative Council on the Curriculum, 1996b). National networks, on ethos, learning and teaching, and able pupils, continue to emphasise the school as a learning organisation, and HMI publications still promote school self-evaluation. The SOEID-funded 'Improving School Effectiveness Project' (ISEP) carried out across 80 schools by QIE and Mortimore's team at the Institute of Education in the University of London reported in the summer of 1998 and reinforced both the ability of individual schools to make a difference and the complexity of the processes involved in school improvement.

Most interestingly of all, perhaps, has been the acknowledgement in recent months by HMI that in order to break into the link between social disadvantage and educational underachievement, new models of schooling may need to be explored. In May 1998 the government announced the setting up of pilot 'New Community' schools in Scotland based on the American 'full-service school' concept.

Corrigan (1996: 28) has argued that education should be 'child-centred', 'family-focused', 'community-based' and 'culturally sensitive'; and he argues for an 'interprofessional village' which would unite, in training and in management, all of the agencies which impact on the lives of young people – education, social services, health, housing, justice–law and business and industry. The challenge for schools, argues Corrigan (1996: 19), is to teach relevant knowledge, connect with other agencies and collaborate with other policy-makers towards 'interprofessional partnerships' (Corrigan, 1996: 19).

The Scottish Office Crime Prevention Office has issued a document entitled *Communities that Care (UK): A New Kind of Prevention Programme*, produced by the Joseph Rowntree Foundation, which promotes a community involvement model designed to build 'safer communities where children and young people are valued' (Joseph Rowntree Foundation, 1997). Among the 'school risk factors' it identifies are:

- low achievement beginning in primary school
- lack of commitment to school, including truancy
- school disorganisation (school failure)

(Joseph Rowntree Foundation, 1997: 9–11)

Thus, some 20 years after Pack, it would appear that the elements the Report identified as being necessary to combat truancy (and indiscipline) might be coming together. It is not just 'society's fault' nor is it up to schools on their own to solve the problems. Social disadvantage and under-achievement are factors but they are not the whole picture, nor is the relationship necessarily causal.

'It takes a village to educate a child' may be a truism, but the implica-tions may now be about to be addressed in a serious way in Scotland. If they are, it will have been the result, once again, of a partnership between central government, local authorities and schools in their communities. It will only succeed if a climate of trust and collaboration can be built up and main-tained. But the price of failure in terms of the social exclusion and wastage of human potential is too high for the attempt not to be made.

3

SCHOOL ATTENDANCE AND THE ROLE OF LAW IN ENGLAND AND WALES

Jon Blacktop and Eric Blyth

Introduction

Parents who fail to secure the regular attendance of the child at the school at which they are registered are guilty of an offence. The maximum fine upon conviction is the maximum of Level 3 of the Standard Scale, currently £1,000. The law provides a number of defence grounds: that the child was absent with leave; the child was ill or prevented from attending by any unavoidable cause; the absence was due to religious observance; the school at which the child is a registered pupil is not within walking distance of the child's home and appropriate transport arrangements were not made by the LEA; and the family has a travelling lifestyle (in which case the child must attend for a minimum of 200 sessions [half days] during the preceding 12 months). In 1997, magistrates considering a case brought by Lincolnshire County Council against the mother of 15-year-old Kelly Turner extended the existing definition of 'avoidable cause' in accepting a defence argument that Kelly was prevented from attending school by virtue of 'unavoidable cause', the need to care for her own baby (Golden and Hopkins, 1997).

In 1994 the government introduced two new categories of absence, 'authorised' and 'unauthorised' (DFE, 1991), in an attempt to clarify the situation with regard to absence 'with leave'. Accordingly, parents may not 'authorise' absence, only schools may do so, although, despite regulations and guidance, there remains considerable discretion – and ambiguity – about the categorisation of absences and the powers to authorise it (OFSTED, 1995a, 1995b).

Such problems were highlighted when details of unauthorised absences were first required to be included in published school performance data. Some schools, considering they had conscientiously applied government guidance on the categorisation of absence, complained that other schools that had adopted a less rigorous approach to absence categorisation had received a better placing in the 'league' tables (OFSTED, 1995b), casting doubt on the credibility of published absence data.

Currently the law in England and Wales may be used in one of two major, but inter-related, ways. The parents of children whose school attendance is unsatisfactory may be prosecuted under provisions of the Education Act 1996 or the child may be deemed to be in need of supervision under the provisions of the Children Act 1989. (Broadly similar measures exist in other UK jurisdictions, despite different legal frameworks.) The principal option available under the Children Act is for an LEA to apply for an Education Supervision Order (ESO); however, in exceptional circumstances non-attendance alone has been considered sufficient to satisfy the 'significant harm' test necessary for a successful application by a local authority for a Care Order (see, e.g., *Re: O*, 1992 – a ruling which could open up the possibility of social services, in consultation with the LEA, making use of other provisions, for example orders under Section 8 of the Act, a Child Assessment Order [Section 43], or even using non-attendance as the basis for an application for an Emergency Protection Order [Section 44] [Robertson, 1996]). At the time of writing, however, there are no recorded instances of the use of measures available under the Children Act in relation to school attendance other than Education Supervision or Care Orders.

This is a vastly different state of affairs to the common image of Section 1(2)(e) of the Children and Young Persons Act 1969, where this legislation was exploited by the juvenile court in Leeds, particularly where adjournments and the ultimate threat of removal from home were used to compel children to go to school (Berg *et al.*, 1977, 1978). By the early 1980s nearly four times as many children were in local authority care under Section 1(2)(e) in Leeds compared to the country as a whole (Bowen, 1985). What became known as the 'Leeds scheme' was adopted by many juvenile courts despite considerable criticism (e.g. House of Commons, 1984; Bowen, 1985; Blyth and Milner, 1987). This 'artificial use' of care proceedings was partially instrumental in creating the pressure for legislative reform that saw the replacement of the Children and Young Persons Act with the Children Act 1989.

The scope for local authority and court intervention in family life where children were not attending school was given greater force following a High Court judgment (*Re: DJMS*, 1977) in which Lord Denning ruled that the fact that a child was not attending school was sufficient to satisfy the 'care and control test' for care proceedings. This ruling had wider repercussions than simply facilitating state intrusion into the families of children who were not going to school. Because the care and control test in respect of Section 1(2)(e) proceedings was considered easier to prove than any of the other grounds for care, it was widely believed that many children found their way into local authority care through this route when the real concerns about their welfare more appropriately focused on grounds whose existence would be more difficult to prove to a court, such as 'neglect' or 'moral danger'.

Re: O (1992) effectively reapplies the ruling of *Re: DJMS* in relation to the imposition of a Care Order under the provisions of the Children Act 1989. In considering an appeal against the making of a Care Order, the court ruled that extensive non-attendance at school itself demonstrated that a child had suffered 'such an impairment of educational, social and intellectual development' that it warranted the imposition of a Care Order, and that 'where a child is suffering harm in not going to school and is living at home it will follow that either the child is beyond her parents' control or that they are not giving the child the care that it would be reasonable for the child to receive'.

Education Supervision Orders

Provision for LEAs to apply to a court for an Education Supervision Order (ESO) was introduced in the Children Act 1989 to replace the discredited (ab)use of Care Orders under the 1969 Act, and to provide a more focused, and less intrusive, form of intervention where a young person of compulsory school age was not receiving appropriate education.

LEAs are required to consider the appropriateness of applying for an ESO before initiating parental prosecution. It is also open to a magistrates' court considering a parental prosecution to direct the LEA to consider applying for an ESO, although the court cannot oblige the LEA to do so. If the LEA decides not to apply for an ESO, it must report its reasons to the court.

The principal aim of an ESO is 'to establish and strengthen parental responsibility and to enable the parents to discharge their responsibility towards the child'. Before applying for an ESO, 'all reasonable efforts should have been made to resolve a problem of poor school attendance without the use of legal sanctions' (DOH, 1991a: 25). The court may only make the order if the child is of compulsory school age and is not being properly educated, although an order cannot be made if the child is already in the care of the local authority. In addition, in keeping with the principles of the Children Act, the court must take account of the welfare of the child (Section 1[1]), including the factors identified in the welfare checklist requiring the court to take account of the child's ascertainable wishes and feelings, his or her educational needs, any harm that has been suffered, the capability of the parents in meeting the child's needs and the range of powers available to the court under the Act. Finally the court needs to be satisfied that making the order will be more beneficial to the child than making no order at all, although Judge Brown in the case of *Essex CC* v. *B* (1993) stated that, provided an LEA can put together a credible plan to ensure the child is educated, such an attempt must always be better for the child than allowing the situation to 'drift'. Even in the face of parental indifference and limited hope of success, it might still be appropriate for the LEA to try all means at its disposal rather than do nothing.

Schedule 3 to Part III of the Children Act provides further details of the role of the supervisor under an ESO and the sanctions available for non-compliance. The supervisor's role is to 'advise, assist and befriend' the child. He or she may give directions to the child/young person and/or his or her parents that address the objective of ensuring the child's proper education. The supervisor is required to consult with the child and the child's parents and to give appropriate consideration to their wishes and feelings. The supervisor has limited powers in case of either the child or the parent failing to co-operate. If the parent 'persistently fails to comply with a direction' given under the order, he or she is guilty of an offence that is punishable by a fine on Level 3 of the Standard Scale. If the child 'persistently fails to comply with a direction given under the order', the LEA is required to notify the appropriate local authority (i.e. social services department), who must then investigate the child's circumstances, with a view to considering the appropriateness of proceedings under other provisions of the 1989 Children Act.

An ESO may last for one year and may be extended for a period up to three years, but ceases once the child reaches school leaving age and may be discharged by the court on the application of the LEA, the parent(s) or the child. While an ESO is in force it supersedes the statutory duties and rights of parents under education legislation and terminates any existing School Attendance Order.

According to data produced by the government (DFE, 1995) and the National Association of Social Workers in Education (NASWE) (1996), relatively few applications for ESOs have been made since the introduction of the Children Act in 1991, although the number of applications appears to be rising. Between 1991 and 1994 the annual number of ESOs granted by courts increased from 81 to 314 (DFE, 1995).

NASWE (1996) data show that the success rate of applications made by LEAs for ESOs increased from 67.2 per cent in 1991–2 to 80.2 per cent in 1993–4. Over the same period the rate of courts' directions to LEAs to initiate an application for an Education Supervision Order decreased from 8.3 per cent of all prosecutions in 1991/2 to 5.4 per cent in 1993/4, while LEAs' 'compliance rates' increased from 23.9 per cent in 1991/2 to 34.6 per cent in 1993/4, suggesting a gradual convergence of magistrates' and LEAs' positions, possibly as a result of increased familiarity and confidence with the new procedures. The relatively small number of ESOs that have been sought means that little attempt has been made to evaluate their effectiveness in improving school attendance.

Doubts about cost effectiveness appear to provide the main explanations for the low rate of ESO applications. The Department of Health expectation that LEAs should have 'tried everything' before applying for an ESO suggests that there may be little to be gained from an order. Nothing that could be provided with an ESO could not also be provided without one and an order may do little more than put an official stamp on what is already being provided. Indeed the judge in *Re: O* (1992), in which a 15-year-old girl who had effectively failed to attend school for the previous three years was eventually made subject to a Care Order, agreed with the submission by both the local authority and the guardian *ad litem*, that there was no point in applying for an ESO since 'everything which an education supervisor would do under [an ESO] has already been done and tried by the local authority over the last 2 or 3 years' (*Re: O*, 1992: 9). ESOs are likely to be of use only in situations where parents are not 'actively hostile to intervention through an ESO', where they:

> find it difficult to exercise a proper influence over their child and the child's school attendance is irregular. It gives a court's backing to the supervising officer's work and can help bring home to parents the need to meet their legal responsibilities for their child's education.
>
> (DFEE, 1997a: Annex F 'Guidance on ESOs')

Pressures on LEA resources – the financial and administrative costs associated with applying for an order, demonstrating the attempts which have been tried already and the existence of the necessary criteria for making an order, and outlining a detailed action plan – may act as a further disincentive. Whitney (1994) notes that Education Welfare Officers seem to have little enthusiasm for ESOs, a view he regards as mistaken, while OFSTED report that 'the most commonly held view appeared to be that [ESOs] are unnecessary, burdensome and costly' (1995a: 8). In comparison, parental prosecution may be seen as administratively less complex and time-consuming and more likely to produce a 'result'.

Parental prosecution

In contrast to the low rate of applications for ESOs, prosecution of parents remains the dominant legal measure taken in respect of unauthorised absence. In so far as guidance on preferred courses of intervention has been prescribed by government, parental prosecution appears to have been dominant:

> Some authorities have found early prosecution of parents to be particularly effective, not only in relation to the individual child, but also as a signal to other parents that such conduct will not be accepted.
>
> (DES, 1991)

Although the Department failed to provide supporting evidence for this assertion, figures it produced in 1995 relating to the number of parental prosecutions initiated throughout the country suggest a complex relationship between LEAs' prosecution and unauthorised absence rates (DFE, 1995; DFEE, 1995a), albeit they provide evidence of increased use of parental prosecution, which rose by nearly a third between 1991–2 (2,803 prosecutions) and 1993–4 (3,688 prosecutions). Some LEAs appear to be able to produce low overall rates of unauthorised absence without recourse to legal action at all. For example, no parent in Wigan LEA had been prosecuted in the previous two years, yet the LEA's unauthorised absence rate of 0.8 was lower than average. In contrast, Derbyshire had an unauthorised absence rate of 1.2 and prosecuted 40 parents during the academic year 1993/4, whilst its neighbour Nottinghamshire had a slightly worse unauthorised absence rate of 1.6, yet prosecuted over five times as many parents (229).

Even if the accuracy of these data can be accepted at face value, rigorous analysis of more sophisticated statistics would be required to establish whether parental prosecutions exerted any effect.

The new Labour government appears to have picked up where the previous administration left off (see Chapter 1). At the launch of the Social Exclusion Unit, Schools Minister Estelle Morris identified both exclusions from school and truancy as 'top priorities' for the unit and stated that 'EWOs [Education Welfare Officers] should not be afraid to prosecute [parents] whenever…appropriate' (Cooper and Brown, 1997)

Further, the DFEE's draft guidance on School Attendance articulates the Secretary of State for Education's view

> that LEAs should adopt a vigorous stance in prosecuting parents of non-attenders. Where, for example, a school has a significant level of unauthorised absence, there may be a case for the EWS [Education Welfare Services] mounting, in consultation with the school, a block of prosecutions in order to demonstrate to parents how seriously the LEA regards truancy and condoned unjustified absence.
>
> (DFEE, 1997a: para. 73)

Perhaps not surprisingly, the measures recommended by the Social Exclusion Unit (1998) itself also include a robust use of law enforcement:

- the encouragement by the DFEE of LEAs to inform magistrates of 'local truancy problems so [the magistrates] will have them in mind when considering cases';
- use of the Crime and Disorder Act 1998 to give courts the power, following a parent's conviction for failing to secure their child's attendance, to impose a Parenting Order for up to 12 months; and

- use of Crime and Disorder Act 1998 to give the police explicit powers to pick up children out of school and to remove them to 'designated premises in a police area'.

(Social Exclusion Unit, 1998)

However, evidence of either direct or indirect effects of parental prosecution appears sparse. While an OFSTED study of education welfare services found some evidence among LEAs in support of the deterrent effect of prosecution, it also concluded that prosecution 'was still most often seen as a last resort rather than as part of a plan to return children to school' (OFSTED, 1995a: p. 7).

Sue Withers (former president of the NASWE) describes what appears a somewhat futile process:

> What usually happens in this type of case is that we take the parent to court, they are given a fine, it makes no difference to the children's attendance, they go back to court again and get another fine, they don't pay the fine, so they go back to court yet again with the possibility of a prison sentence.

(cited in White, 1996: 17)

Attempts to evaluate the effectiveness of parental prosecution in individual local authorities have produced little evidence in support of the practice. For example, Solihull Metropolitan Borough Council (1992) concluded that, 'as far as fourth and fifth year pupils are concerned and irrespective of the adjudication of the Court, the institution of legal proceedings is an ineffective way of actually improving a pupil's school attendance', and decided to cease prosecuting parents, although the practice was subsequently resumed.

It may be that – despite its apparent failure to improve the attendance of those children whose parents are actually prosecuted – parental prosecution may exercise some general deterrent effect or possess symbolic value in setting the boundaries of acceptable behaviour (e.g. Whitney, 1994; OFSTED, 1995a; DFEE, 1997a, Hoyle, 1998). However, whether or not the reality – or possibility – of court action exerts any deterrent effect on other pupils and their parents or has any symbolic value in setting the boundaries of acceptable behaviour remains unproven; the Solihull study, for example, concluded that parental prosecution had no discernible 'knock-on' effect on the attendance pattern of any other children in the family.

The Magistrates' Association, the professional association representing magistrates, has itself openly expressed concern that prosecutions appear to target poor parents, in particular lone mothers dependent on state benefits (e.g. Petre, 1994). Furthermore, in direct contrast to the views expressed by the government, magistrates have voiced scepticism about the efficacy of prosecution:

> The Association is far from convinced that the Adult Court is the proper forum with which to deal with this matter and believes that measures designed to prevent truancy would be preferable and probably more effective than any of the disposals realistically available to a criminal court.
>
> (Magistrates' Association, 1994)

As an apparent response to the lack of success in parental prosecution influencing school attendance, media reports indicate the application of novel 'solutions' by some magistrates. Montgomery (1996), for example, refers to a mother in the West Midlands who was prosecuted and placed on probation after ESOs imposed in respect of her two school-age sons were considered to have failed. Scott-Clark and Burke (1996) cite the example of a Solihull mother placed on probation for three years for failing to ensure her three children's attendance at school. Whitehead (1996) refers to two cases where Lewisham magistrates postponed sentencing two mothers and placed them on bail with a condition that they take their children to school and hand them over to the teacher. Whitehead cites the chair of Lewisham Education Committee, Gavin Moore, as asserting that magistrates were having to resort to a 'legal sleight of hand' and that magistrates should have powers to impose 'escort orders backed up by the threat of a substantial fine' (a request subsequently endorsed by the Social Exclusion Unit (1998), and provisions contained in the Crime and Disorder Act 1998).

While making Probation Orders in these instances is itself lawful, the development has been viewed with some concern by the National Association of Probation Officers (personal communication, 1996) and appears to make a parent's failure to secure his or her child's proper education a more serious offence than that envisaged in education legislation. The use of bail following conviction in such circumstances appears more ambiguous legally; Rodgers (personal communication) suggests that deferring sentence for a period might be more appropriate. The use of both post-sentence bail and sentence deferral would, of course, bear striking similarities to the adjournment procedures implemented by juvenile magistrates in Leeds in the 1970s and would make magistrates the enforcers of school attendance. Whether this is either appropriate or something magistrates would want to take on is, of course, open to question.

The outcome of parental prosecutions in four local authority areas

It is against this background that a small study involving four LEAs was undertaken, based on all cases taken to court in each of the four authorities during the 1995/6 academic year, a total of 150 cases. Data were collected in respect of each pupil whose parent was prosecuted over this period concerning socio-economic details (to ascertain whether the concerns expressed by magistrates were reflected in practice). In addition to pre-court attendance, attendance data were also collected for up to 24 weeks following the court appearance.

Socio-economic data

The sample consisted of 75 boys and 67 girls (the gender of the pupil was not recorded on eight returned questionnaires). This statistic requires explanation in the light of previous literature and research that highlights the preponderance of boys among those most likely to absent themselves from school. In three of the four LEAs boys did, indeed, outnumber girls by a ratio of approximately 2:1. However, in the fourth and largest LEA (both in respect of total school population and in the number of prosecutions), 46 per cent of prosecutions related to boys and 54 per cent to girls, thus skewing the entire sample. Pupils ranged in age from school years 1 through to 11. Only 13 pupils (8 per cent) were from Years 1 to 6, while 51 (34 per cent) pupils were from Year 10, the largest number from any year, outstripping the 29 (19 per cent) from Year 9 and the 27 (18 per cent) from Year 11. Over 90 per cent of the pupils for whom ethnic origin was recorded were of White UK origin (120). Of the remaining pupils, nine were Black Pakistani, two were categorised as 'other', and ethnic origin was not recorded for 19 pupils. The family type was recorded for 142 children and shows that six (4 per cent) were from lone-father families, 89 (63 per cent) from lone-mother families and 47 (33 per cent) from two-parent families. LEAs were asked to include information about the occupation of the head of household, although this was provided for only 46 cases (33 per cent of the total). Of these, 32 (70 per cent) were not engaged in paid work. A more accurate measure of socio-economic status was provided by information concerning family entitlement to benefits. Three measures were used, namely entitlement to: state benefits; free school meals; and local authority clothing grant. Eighty (71 per cent) of the 113 families for whom information was provided were in receipt of state benefits; 79 (63 per cent) of the 126 families for whom information was provided were in receipt of free school meals; 78 (65 per cent) of the 120 families for whom information was provided received a clothing grant. Information on all three types of benefit was provided for 106 cases. Of these 55 (52 per cent) received all three benefits, compared with 21 (20 per cent) who received none of the benefits. Lone-mother and dual-parent households were more likely than households headed by a lone father to be in receipt of benefits, free school meals or a clothing grant.

As the local authorities were unable to provide data about the level of socio-economic disadvantage either among their general populations or, more specifically, among the EWS clientele, it is therefore not possible to indicate whether those families existing at the lower margins of socio-economic viability are disproportionately represented among those who are prosecuted for their children's non-attendance. Other studies (e.g. Sutherland, 1995), however, have shown that persistent absentees are more likely to be socially disadvantaged than the general school population. Nevertheless, the study provides general support for the Magistrates' Association views about the type of parents who are likely to be prosecuted.

Court sanctions

Data provided by the local authorities included the type of plea entered by the parent, whether or not he or she was legally represented, and the sanction imposed by the court. Analysis and interpretation of this data proved difficult, however, because of the fact that if a parent did not attend the court hearing, a not-infrequent eventuality, the court would invariably enter a 'not guilty' plea and proceed with the case in the parent's absence. A formally recorded 'not guilty' plea cannot, therefore, be assumed to represent an overt challenge on the part of a parent to the LEA case against them.

There are 93 cases where all three variables are recorded. Of these, 34 (37 per cent) were legally represented, 71 (76 per cent), were fined while the remaining 22 received lesser sentences. Sixty-one (66 per cent) pleaded guilty, with the other 32 pleading not guilty.

Of the 59 who were not legally represented, 28 (47 per cent) pleaded guilty. This compares with all except one of those 34 who were legally represented (97 per cent). This suggests that legal advice is generally to plead guilty.

The wisdom of the legal advice is seen in the outcome. All of those who pleaded not guilty received fines (32 out of 32), compared with only 39 out of the 61 who pleaded guilty (64 per cent).

Because all who pleaded not guilty were fined and all except one of those who were legally represented pleaded guilty, there is insufficient data to separate the specific effects of being legally represented and entering either a guilty or a not guilty plea. Being legally represented influences the plea and the plea influences the outcome. Being legally represented may also alter the outcome, but this connection is hidden.

Fines were imposed in 110 cases. Of these, five were father-only families,

65 were mother-only, 33 two-parent and the remaining seven from unknown family types. Figure 3.1 shows the pattern of fines by household type.

Superficially, it would appear that single fathers are more likely to be fined than other family types. However, four out of the six single fathers pleaded not guilty (66 per cent) and were consequently fined. This compares with 19 out 63 single mothers who pleaded not guilty (30 per cent) and 8 out of 36 two-parent families (22 per cent).

Of the parents pleading guilty, two were single fathers, of whom one was fined, 44 were single mothers, of whom 26 were fined (59 per cent), and 28 were two-parent, of whom 19 were fined (68 per cent). This might suggest that a fine is equally likely for all family types who plead guilty.

The rate of legal representation in those families not receiving state benefits is 41 per cent, which is slightly higher than the 34 per cent representation among those in receipt of benefits. Despite this the proportion of those not receiving benefits who were fined is only 24 out of 33 (73 per cent), compared with 59 out of 75 (72 per cent) for those receiving benefits. This discrepancy appears related to the greater willingness of those receiving benefit to plead guilty (77 per cent) compared with the 68 per cent of those not on benefits.

Because taking legal advice seems nearly always to lead to a guilty plea, it

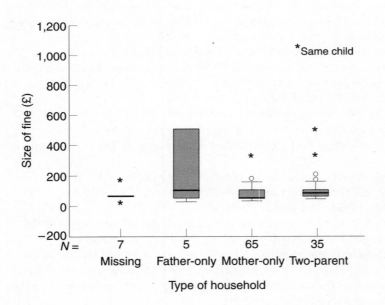

Figure 3.1 Boxplot of fine by household type (outliers labelled with previous convictions, if any)

seems reasonable to assume that of the parents who are not legally represented, those receiving benefits will be more likely to plead guilty. Of the 15 parents neither in receipt of benefits nor legally represented, only six (40 per cent) pleaded guilty, compared with 18 out of the 31 (58 per cent) who were in receipt of benefits.

Details of the plea were recorded for 26 of the 40 parents with previous convictions for one or more similar offences. Of these, 20 (77 per cent) pleaded guilty. Of the 20 for whom legal representation is recorded, nine (45 per cent) were represented, and of the 38 for whom the outcome is recorded, 28 (74 per cent) were fined. This suggests that parents with previous convictions were slightly more likely to be legally represented, more likely to plead guilty and as likely as other parents to be fined.

The minimum fine in each family type is £25, except for the two-parent families, whose minimum was £40. The maximum ranged from £150 for the missing families through £300 for the mother-only families and £500 for the father-only families to the maximum permissible fine of £1,000 for a two-parent family. As can be seen from Figure 3.1, this case followed a previous conviction for the same child. The other outliers are not labelled and this indicates that no previous convictions were recorded for these cases. The heavy positive skew on the fines must presumably result from some other cause.

The mean fine for those who pleaded guilty and were fined (48 cases) was £73 (median = £50) compared with £133 (median = £100) for those (33 cases) who pleaded not guilty. Legal representation also seemed to reduce the mean size of the fine from £107 (median = £70) for those not represented (53 cases) to £80 (median = £50) for those represented. Costs seemed not to be influenced by the same factors and mean cost was slightly higher for those who were represented (£47) than for those who were not (£39).

Because of the skew, it did not seem sensible to use the mean fine as a measure of average fine. The median fine for the missing and mother-only families is £50, while it is £80 for the two-parent families and £100 for father-only families.

There seemed little difference in the proportion of those on benefits who received a fine. Out of 33 cases recorded as coming from families not on benefit, 24 received a fine (73 per cent) compared with 59 cases (75 per cent) of the 79 cases from families receiving benefit. The size of the fine did seem to be somewhat different for cases from families on benefit. Figure 3.2 shows the distribution of fines for cases from families both receiving and not receiving benefit. The cases where receipt of benefit is not known or missing are also shown.

For the 59 cases from families recorded as receiving benefit, the fines range from a minimum of £25 to a maximum of £500 with a median of £60. For those not receiving benefit, the range is similar, but with the one case of a £1,000 fine. The median fine is somewhat higher for those not

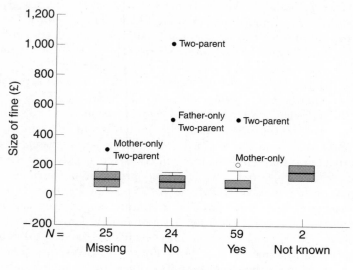

Figure 3.2 Boxplot of fine by entitlement to state benefits

receiving benefit at £85. This compares with medians of £150 for the two cases where benefit receipt is not known and £100 for the 25 cases where it is not recorded.

The data also allowed us to analyse the fines imposed by courts in each of the four LEAs (Figure 3.3). The pattern of penalty varied across the four LEA areas. Of the nine cases in local authority A with penalty recorded, all were fined. In local authority B, only six out of 12 were fined, five receiving a 12-month conditional discharge and the other an absolute discharge. In local authority C 72 out of 96 (75 per cent) and in local authority D 23 out of 31 (74 per cent) were fined. Figure 3.3 shows the pattern of fines across the four areas. The fining policy of courts in local authority areas A and B seems very subdued. The median fine in local authority A is £50 (mean = £60) and in local authority B the median fine is £60 (mean = £66). The upward struggle seen in local authorities C and D tends to suggest that fines are larger in these districts. However, the median fine in local authority C is only £55, but the mean is £102. In local authority D, the median fine is much larger at £100 and the mean fine has reached as high as £157.

Given the reservations expressed above about interpreting these particular data, the only safe conclusion that can be reached is that parents finding themselves before the court because of their child's non-attendance at school would be advised to plead guilty. Those not eligible for legal aid might wonder about the benefit of legal representation since, unless the parent is

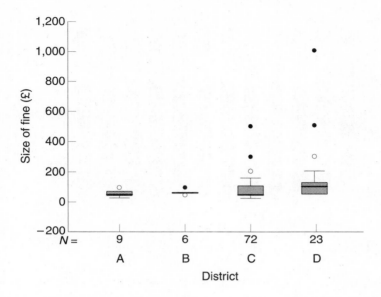

Figure 3.3 Boxplot of fine by local authority area

legally aided, it is unlikely that the lower fine the court is likely to impose on a legally represented defendant compared to one who is not legally represented would compensate for the solicitor's bill! Of the 28 cases where the parent pleaded guilty but was not legally represented, 18 (64 per cent) resulted in a fine; where the parents (all of whom pleaded guilty) were legally represented 21 out of 33 (64 per cent) were fined.

Attendance records

School attendance was recorded for 12 weeks prior to the court hearing and up to 24 weeks after. Figure 3.4 shows the numbers of pupils attending on zero, one, two, and so on, days in each of the 12 weeks before the hearing.

It is obvious that the most common outcome for any week is that a pupil will not attend school at all. Out of a total of 1,691 pupil-weeks, zero attendance was recorded in 956 (51 per cent). All other attendance levels seem about equally popular. Averaged over all 12 weeks, one, two, three, four or five days attendance each account for between 7 and 10 per cent of all attendances. The hypothesis that pupils are equally likely to attend for one, two, three, four or five days could be accepted on the basis of these figures. It almost appears that pupils have a clear idea of how many times they are going to attend each week. Possibly they have some idea of how many

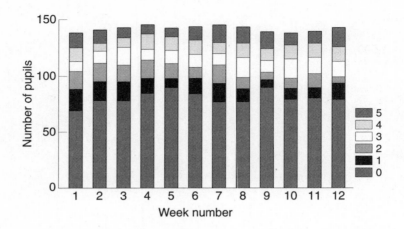

Figure 3.4 Number of days attended in the 12 weeks prior to court hearing

attendances they can 'get away with' in the next week, or maybe they have other activities to undertake on certain days.

Figure 3.5 shows the numbers of pupils attending on zero, one, two, and so on, days in each of the 24 weeks following the hearing. This figure illustrates the steady decline in the number of pupils, due primarily to the elimination from the sample of pupils reaching school leaving age. The number of pupils not attending at all each week remains approximately constant, as does the number attending on all five days. There seems to be a squeeze on those attending for part of the week. This might suggest that prosecution has polarised pupils into those who are going to attend in future and those who are not. In these 24 weeks, there is a total of 3,050 pupil weeks, of which 1,562 (51 per cent) contained no attendance. This is apparently lower than the 57 per cent in the 12 weeks prior to the court hearing, but it is important to notice that many of those who disappeared from the records because they reached school leaving age are the pupils who had persistently low attendance records. In total 414, or 13 per cent, of the pupil-weeks showed attendance on five days. This is an increase on that shown in the pre-court data.

The mean numbers of attendances per week in the 12 weeks before and the 24 weeks following prosecution were calculated (Figure 3.6). This shows a strong indication of regression towards the mean; those who had good attendance before prosecution had poorer attendance after and vice versa. This is as expected. The effect is very highly significant (p <0.01), but only accounts for about 30 per cent of the variance in attendance after prosecution.

The gain in mean weekly attendance following prosecution was calculated

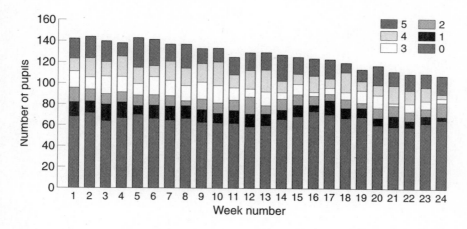

Figure 3.5 Number of days attended in the 24 weeks following court hearing

after allowing for the tendency for regression. Pupils were then divided into those whose attendance had improved and those whose attendance had deteriorated. Overall, 42 per cent (60) of the pupils for whom an attendance record was available (N = 143) showed better attendance after prosecution than before, but 58 per cent (83) showed a poorer attendance record. Factors that appear to be correlated with outcomes appear to be age; ethnic origin; plea entered by the parent; sanction imposed by the court; and family entitlement to benefits.

Pupils in higher school years were less likely to show an improvement. Out of the 13 prosecutions in school Years 1 to 6 (the primary school years), nine (69 per cent) showed improved attendance compared with only 41 out of 119 (34 per cent) of those in Years 7 to 11. This difference is statistically significant (p < .05). As might be expected, the deterioration in post-court attendance amongst older pupils is reflected within the secondary school population. However, since the absolute number of cases is small, these data should be interpreted with some caution. Of the six Year 7 pupils in the sample, four showed a post-court improvement in attendance, while two did not. However, by Year 11 only four (17 per cent) of the 24 pupils in the sample showed a post-court improvement in attendance, while the attendance of the remaining 83 per cent deteriorated further.

A most noticeable feature of the results is that while only 41 out of 114 white pupils improved their attendance (36 per cent), the proportion of black pupils showing an improvement was seven out of nine (78 per cent). This difference is statistically significant (p < .05) and cannot be explained by differences in age distribution. However, the number of black pupils is small compared with the number of pupils with no ethnic origin recorded and the findings must be interpreted with caution.

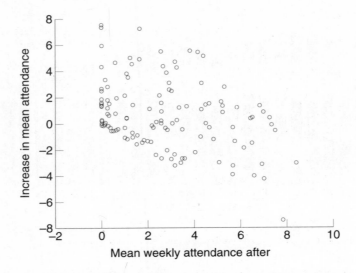

Figure 3.6 Increase in mean weekly attendance after court appearance

Attendance where parents had pleaded guilty was more likely to show improvement (37 out of 77 – 48 per cent) than where parents had pleaded not guilty (11 out of 32 – 34 per cent). There were differences between families receiving benefit, where attendance improved in only 29 out of 77 cases (38 per cent), and those not receiving benefit, where attendance improved in 16 out of 31 cases (52 per cent). Although possibly indicative, these differences are not statistically significant.

Improved attendance is about as likely whether parents were fined (43 out of 106 – 41 per cent), or not fined (17 out of 37 – 46 per cent). Plea and legal representation also had little apparent influence on improved attendance rates.

Finally, there were also major differences between the four LEAs. The percentage of cases showing improved attendance following prosecution in each of the LEAs was 19 per cent, 33 per cent, 46 per cent and 67 per cent. This difference in improvement rates is highly significant, despite the small numbers of prosecutions initiated by the smaller authorities. Given the small numbers of younger pupils and black pupils, it is difficult to be sure that the differences between LEAs are not confounded with the effects of age and ethnic origin.

A better flavour of the range of outcomes is provided by the vignettes below, illustrating three pupils whose post-court attendance improved and three whose post-court attendance deteriorated.

Pupil A is a white boy in Year 10 living with his mother only, who is in receipt of state benefits, free school meals and clothing grant. Before prosecution, he attended on an average of only two half-day sessions a week. His mother pleaded guilty, was not legally represented and was granted an absolute discharge. Pupil A's attendance rose to an average of nine half-day sessions a week after the prosecution.

Pupil B is a pupil in Year 3, of Black Pakistani origin and living with his mother only. No information is available about entitlement to benefits. Before prosecution, Pupil B hardly attended school at all. His mother was legally represented, pleaded guilty and received a conditional discharge, although an order for £50 costs was made against her. After the prosecution Pupil B was attending for an average of eight half-day sessions a week.

Pupil C is a girl in Year 9 and of 'Other' ethnic origin. She is living with her mother, who is described as unemployed, and the family is in receipt of free school meals and clothing grant. Prior to prosecution, Pupil C was hardly attending school at all. We do not know whether her mother was legally represented, or how she pleaded, but she was fined £50 with £50 costs. After prosecution, Pupil C's attendance rose to seven half-day sessions per week on average.

Pupil D is a girl in Year 7, of undisclosed ethnic origin, and lives with her mother only. The family is in receipt of state benefits and a clothing grant. Before prosecution, Pupil D was attending an average of six half-day sessions per week. We do not know if her mother was legally represented. She pleaded guilty and was fined £40. No costs were awarded against her. Pupil D's attendance after the court hearing fell to two half-day sessions per week.

Pupil E is a girl in Year 10, is white and lives with her mother only. There is no information about the family's financial status. Before prosecution, Pupil E was averaging three half-day sessions per week. In court her mother was not legally represented, pleaded not guilty and was fined £25 with £50 costs. Pupil E stopped attending school altogether following her mother's prosecution.

Pupil F is a girl in Year 8, is white and lives with both parents. Before prosecution she averaged eight half-day sessions per week. The family is in receipt of state benefits, but not free meals, or clothing grant. Her parents were not legally represented and pleaded not guilty. However, the case against them was proven and they were fined £160 with £50 costs. Pupil F stopped attending school altogether following her parents' prosecution.

Prosecution: does it work?

Critics of parental prosecution for non-attendance at school have suggested that it may be little more than 'symbolic and procedural retribution' (Hoyle, 1998: 109). The evidence from the study reported in this chapter would tend to endorse such sentiments in the majority of cases. There is a clearly recognisable group of older pupils (predominantly in Year 11) whose attendance is not going to be influenced by the prosecution of their parents and who simply disappear from the statistics as they reach school leaving age. Overall, 58 per cent of the cases studied showed worse levels of attendance following prosecution. Arguably, in these cases, the use of legal sanctions could be seen as worse than ineffective, since it runs the risk of undermining the credibility of legal enforcement. Furthermore, where post-court attendance is worse than it was before prosecution *and* the pupil still has a considerable period of schooling before him or her, future intervention strategies would appear to be problematic.

Given also the high proportion of low-income parents who are prosecuted, and the fact that size of fine appears unrelated to subsequent attendance, the imposition of heavier fines appears to offer little hope of improving school attendance. It is evident that, whatever else was going on in the lives of those youngsters who were particularly resistant to attending school, the prosecution of their parents was ineffective in affecting their school attendance.

On the other hand, 42 per cent of the young people whose parents were prosecuted subsequently showed improved attendance. Obviously the data do not permit a causal relationship to be inferred in any of these cases, since the study did not take account of any events or processes other than prosecution that might have influenced attendance. Given the prevailing political agenda that regards – indeed encourages – the prosecution of parents as a legitimate form of intervention to improve school attendance, the variation in outcomes behoves practitioners and policy-makers to identify the factors that might be associated with improved post-prosecution attendance. While this study indicates the probability of scope for more effective targeting, further research is needed to identify such factors. We need to know more about the sort of pupils who are most likely to respond to the prosecution of their parents with improved attendance. At the same time, unless we are prepared to 'write off' those absentees who are impervious to legal sanctions, we need to develop more effective strategies to ensure the engagement of this group with the process of schooling.

4

THE RELATIONSHIP BETWEEN DELINQUENCY AND NON-ATTENDANCE AT SCHOOL

Cedric Cullingford

It's just like school, this place.

(Young offender)

Introduction

The growing concern with unauthorised absences from school is fuelled by a number of different motivations. One example is the assumption that a skilled workforce is needed, and that the National Curriculum, delivered to those to receive it, is there to provide it. This curriculum might be named in the Act as an 'entitlement' to the pupil but it is also seen as an expectation, or a duty for that pupil to achieve set levels that include the duty to attend. Another reason for concern is the supposed links between non-attendance and delinquency (DFE, 1992a). That truancy and exclusion are part of the pattern that characterises the lives of criminals is well supported (Farrington and West, 1990; West and Farrington, 1997; Social Exclusion Unit, 1998). Both these motivations for concern lead to the third: non-attendance is seen as one of the symptoms of a failing school.

In a time of educational bench-marking, targets and league tables, the use of unauthorised absences as a particular measure has tended to divert research away from the causes to the definitions and amounts of different kinds of non-attendance. Certainly the almost punitive tone presented by government statements (e.g. DFE, 1992a) means that many schools and local authorities are rather defensive about the figures they reveal (OFSTED, 1995a). But this is understandable given both the correlation between socio-economic status and truancy – the role of parents, in particular, will be explored later – and the complexity of the subject. What exactly is 'absence'? Officially, it is being away during registration, and yet many pupils walk out of school soon afterwards. Or it is the absence of 'authorisation' from the parents, and yet there are many instances of false or forged sickness notes.

'Absence' or 'non-attendance' are not cut and dried issues. Pupils often choose not to go to particular lessons, for all kinds of reasons. They can choose to miss a part of the day because they feel it is irrelevant or because they do not feel well enough to undertake physical exercise. There is also a close relationship between truancy and exclusion and it is often difficult to make a sharp distinction, certainly in the mind of the pupils. As we will see, many feel excluded from particular lessons, or disliked by particular teachers. Those who are at last officially excluded from school will not only have been familiar with regular truanting but will have acknowledged the effects of playing truant – nefarious activities with their peer group – as part of the reason for exclusion. But even if physically present at school and attending every lesson, there are many pupils who feel themselves to be psychologically excluded from school (Cullingford and Morrison, 1995). Disaffection from school is a common experience that does not have to be demonstrated solely by non-attendance (Pye, 1992).

This chapter explores the actual experience of school by those who have been habitual non-attenders, both regular truants and, almost inevitably in the end, excluded. It shows how disaffection from school builds up and delineates the different sources of influence. It wants to answer the question of *why* particular individuals feel 'alienated' from school (Williamson and Cullingford, 1997), and what could be done about it. It is not about the figures of non-attendance but the complex experience. The title might suggest a simple causal link between exclusion and crime, but this is because the sample is of young offenders who have all had great difficulties with school. That this disaffection is an important part of their formative experience is clear, but in place of a simple correlation we wish to explore all the different factors that have a part to play.

There is always going to be a tension between parents' and teachers' authority and the extent to which a school is *in loco parentis* (see Milner and Blyth in this volume). Most of the current debate seems to hinge on the question of who is most responsible, say, for discipline and morality (Broadfoot and Osborn, 1986; DES, 1989). But from the pupils' point of view, the school is an extremely important experience as it is the first real insight into organised society. It is the symbol of the community at large, with rules and regulations, hierarchies and tensions between different sources of power. It comes to represent the official public world. 'Dropping out' of school has, therefore, great social implications. One particular world, public, rule-bound and organised, is rejected for an alternative.

The research

The data from which this chapter is derived were not confined to the experience of school, let alone the experience of non-attendance. The interviewees had no idea of any design the researcher might have on them – or on the hoped-for evidence. They talked at length and freely about a whole range of their experiences, from early childhood and their early memories to their recent styles of living. But they all talked about their experiences of school, especially those that they remembered most vividly and those that related most closely to their personal lives. This openness of approach gives validity as well as richness to the findings and what emerges is a clear picture of the relationship of the disenfranchised with school. With some exceptions (White with Brockington, 1983; Cullingford, 1991, 1993) there have been few attempts to try to understand the attitudes towards school *and* society, including the influence of schools, from the individual's point of view. Most studies have concentrated on correlation or observations of behaviour, testing hypotheses rather than exploring the inner workings of the mind.

In this research, qualitative methods were employed as they offer the required degree of sensitivity and flexibility essential to the investigation of social processes and the generation of attitudes. Qualitative data from systematic open-ended questions can help discover underlying social processes of stability and change. Lengthy semi-structured interviews were conducted with 25 young offenders between the ages of 16 and 21 in order to gain the empirical data. The 'structure' consisted of the discipline of making sure that all the interviews covered the same ground. These were usually about an hour in length. The research was undertaken at one male and one female young offender institution and the number of males to females interviewed reflects the disproportionate number of males to females in the prison population as a whole (19:6). Contact was made in the form of a letter, sent to each of the young people, requesting their permission and reassuring them of total confidentiality and anonymity. Each respondent was interviewed individually in a private room within the institution, away from wardens and other members of staff.

The results were then analysed in order to establish how the interviewees view, categorise and experience the world and to identify sources of knowledge. The interviews were semi-structured and certain set themes were explored in every interview. In order to avoid contamination of the data, however, it was crucial that questions were open-ended and not directed by the interviewer. 'Open-ended' implies several things. Whilst there was a structure to the interview, to make sure that the points covered in each interview were the same, the definitions and the exploration of the sources of information came from the interviewee. There were no 'closed' questions of the type designed to elicit specific information. The early questions were there as a placebo, and an introduction, designed to enable the interviewees to relax and feel confident in the confidentiality of the proceedings. They were encouraged to present a narrative of their lives, with the possibility of the interviewer returning to an earlier point and checking on it. In order to avoid any assumptions, hints or guessing of the 'right' responses, the participants were not aware of exactly what it was the interviewer was seeking. They were being asked for general reflections on their experiences of school, unaware of the specific focus of the research, lest they thought they were being typecast into a particular role.

This technique allowed the young people to develop their ideas and define attitudes, concepts and experiences that were important to them. Throughout the conversations the interviewer explored childhood memories and retrospective accounts of young offenders' whole experience of school that included their feelings and attitudes towards the curriculum, bullying, truancy, friendships, relationships with teachers, and life outside school, including family relationships.

No pre-formulated definitions were imposed. A central premise of the research was that concepts could only be defined through actual experience. For definitions to be accurate, the perceptions of those involved were given prominence. Concepts were allowed to emerge from the empirical data after careful and complex analysis. For example, terms such as 'truancy' and 'exclusion' were invoked by the respondents themselves, rather than by the interviewer. If the interviewee can guess what the interviewer would like to hear there is a marked tendency to give the desired information. Even mentioning words like 'truancy', 'peers' and 'bullying' might provoke the idea of the closed question as if there were a desire to explore all that is negative in schools. The atmosphere was such that the subjects were relieved to be listened to in a spirit of anonymity and there was no possibility of the contamination of the data. Nevertheless, the 'structure' of the interview was more a matter of making sure that every period of experience was covered than a superimposition of set terminology.

This approach provided rich data that sought to uncover the thought patterns of young offenders. The findings are very consistent, not in the particular or ephemeral terms of factual and personal details, but in terms of underlying tone, attitude and circumstances.

A crucial point in such rich data is its analysis, to make sure that any comment is not seen as a generalisation from the particular but is validated. Analysis can discover clusters of differences and/or consistencies. In this case the consistencies prevailed and were double-checked. There were three levels of analysis: the facts that the interviewees gave in terms of life experiences; the description of their feelings and reactions to these experiences; and the style and tone of their responses. The use of quotation is important as a demonstration of two factors: the consistency of the ideas; and the way in which one idea is embedded in another. Whilst quotations are used to demonstrate the idea as in the argument, there will be ample opportunity to see the consistency of the ideas even when attention is not being drawn to them.

Results

There are a number of studies which suggest that it is the pathology of the parents that is essentially to blame for instances of truancy (e.g. O'Keeffe, 1994), and a great deal of evidence about the significance of the early years (e.g. Pugh, 1997) well before pupils enter formal schooling. That different kinds of parenting have profound effects on children are clear. The attitudes and expectations that young children have of school are very important, and this importance continues into the secondary school. So are the attitudes of parents to the schools. Schools are symbolic of a certain kind of society and can be seen as distant, official and off-putting by parents as well as by pupils.

Some of the young offenders indicated that their parents were concerned when they (the young offenders) were excluded or played truant. But none of the parents were seen to be comfortable with school. There is a tendency for some parents to feel excluded, either because the school seems dominated by a particular clique (often the more advantaged and articulate), or because of the recent demands on schools to have more and more *formal* meetings with parents (Cullingford, 1995). Many parents would *like* to feel a part of the school, supporting teachers through informal links. But the moment that the school is seen as an opposing or formal institution there are difficulties. Clearly for some pupils the movement from one background to another, in terms of style, language and conversation, is as easy as it is difficult for others (Heath, 1983). It tends to be certain kinds of parents, often the disadvantaged, who do not have the cultural 'capital' or the self-confidence, who have a sense of being outsiders.

Parents may wish to support the school but still feel that those in authority do not like them. Every 'difficult' pupil tends to be explained by the background from which he or she comes, which gives an automatically uncomfortable edge to the relationship. The majority of parents in this study were perceived as indifferent to what their children did, including whether they attended school or not, but there were some who were angry about the first signs of truancy. In either case they were confused and did not know how to co-operate with the authorities, and whatever stance they took therefore seemed to make little difference. There were those parents who themselves felt completely indifferent to, even cynical, about the school system:

My Dad. He's just mad. He didn't even want me to go to school in the first place. Said it was a waste of time, he'd teach me anything I needed to know. Taught me how to fight, that's about it.

(Male, 20)

That, coupled with the mother's indifference, suggests that the schools never had a chance, but the interviewee suggests that his peers were a far greater influence. Some parents, however, attempted to approach the schools, to intervene on their children's behalf. In every case that is described the parents feel humiliated by the school and neglected by the system:

Me mum went to see the headmaster, but me mum didn't know, sort of, what to do, do you know what I mean? She was sort of confused.

(Female, 21)

Me mum explained it to him and said, 'well, as long as they tell me the truth I'll go up to school,' and like when she did go up, teacher slammed his hand on the table and treated her like a kid, so she stood up and give him a mouthful, started accusing him of this, that and the other and I never went back to school then.

(Female, 20)

The problem for schools is that when a pupil is excluded there is a clear reason for them to be unwelcome, and the same attitudes are applied to the parents. Whilst many schools make a point of close parental co-operation, this is more difficult if there are seen to be two 'sides', if there is a perceived psychological confrontation.

Whether the barriers are of the schools' making or the parents' or both, they reinforce the pupils' sense of being excluded. But perhaps the most worrying finding to emerge is not so much the confrontations as the indifference, as if the two worlds, public and private, were happy to ignore each other. Parents may be indifferent if their children are excluded:

So they were debating about what to do with me, so I was like suspended again, and I got a warning, they rung me up and said I could go back and I just says to me mum, 'I don't wanna go back. I'll look for a job.' So, I didn't go...messed me life up really.

(Male 19)

The lack of parental pressure is reflected in the system. Disruptive pupils are never welcome in school so the pressure to bring them back is never as emotionally strong as it could be. With the connivance or ignorance of a parent it is easy for an individual to leave the 'system':

Like they rung me up to speak to me mum, say I could go back to school, and I answered the phone. He says, 'Michael is that you?' and I said 'Yeah'. He goes, 'well I'm just ringing to let you know you can go back to school'. And I told me mum, I says, 'oh, they don't want me to go back to school'....She was just waiting for a letter through the post...me and me mum thought that she'd get done 'cos I didn't go to school. But none of that came through or anything, so....

(Male, 20)

Once excluded, there seems little chance of going back. While the process of moving out of the education system is usually a slow and complex one, at the heart there is a consistent and deep dividing line between 'us' and 'them', the officials, including Education Welfare Officers – seen by the young offenders as moral policemen – and the undemanding ease of being at home in bed, or with friends. The crucial distinction, from the first sign of trouble at school to the final exclusion, is between what is seen as an alien official 'system', symbolised by roles, and the warm, lubricious series of relationships, close – if stormy – contacts with other people. The distinction, between the public and the private, between role and personality, is the more important because it leads to tensions and violent clashes. The two overlap and cause difficulties, as demonstrated in the quarrels and the bullying. The violence within the peer group cannot altogether be extricated from the violence expressed against the system, but once personal violence takes over from the rules, once personal feelings and expressions rather than public decorum dominate, the consequences are fatal. Teachers are, of course, human and react humanly. Even when they try to disguise the fact, their feelings will inevitably be detected.

State schools open their doors to all, the more so since there is so little real parental choice (Cullingford, 1995), and because it is only those in favourable positions who can afford to turn pupils away. This suggests that a significant number of schools are dealing with the impoverished and also the difficult. They are part of the state's response in coping with the needs of those who have nowhere else to turn, as if schools were not so much 'deliverers' of the curriculum but attempting to meet with the requirements of the socially deprived (Webb, 1994). That schools often find themselves in the position of offering support to vulnerable and unhappy children (Gilligan, 1998) is not in doubt, given the sensitivity and responsiveness of teachers and what they hear from, and about, their pupils. But, from the point of view of those who have absented themselves from the school system, or who have been excluded, schools are no such safe havens.

To many of those who, perhaps, most need support, schools are anything but sanctuaries. On the contrary, they appear as threatening or indifferent, anonymous and difficult. From such an experience exclusion is a happy relief. Schools are disliked. They contain, for a minority of pupils at least, all the ingredients of threat. There is competition and institutionalised failure; bullying in its public and private forms. One young offender tried to get away from school specifically because of the bullying from others; but the exclusion arose from the way in which she dealt with it:

> It got to the point in the end where when she kept on hitting me and things like that and pulling me hair out, I took a knife out the kitchen drawer and I took it to school and she started bullying me first thing in the morning, and I just pulled a knife out on her...she told the teacher.
>
> (Female, 21)

As we will see, schools are social centres, institutions and meeting places, a combination of personal relationships and formal ones. The mixture can be dramatic.

The young offenders uniformly share the dislike of school, but it must be pointed out that it arises from particular experiences and certain moments. It is, at first, a dislike not of the whole system but of particular manifestations of it. All the subjects recall good moments as well as bad, good teachers and subjects they like and fruitful relationships. But schools have the potential for bringing out all that is worst in people. Those who have drawn an analogy between school and prison are provided with a lot of subconscious echoes given by these young people who have experienced both:

> Just like the atmosphere and that around. The teachers were horrible, just don't like getting told what to do. But since I've been in here I've got used to it now.
>
> (Male, 20)

It is natural that those who have been excluded should blame the system that excluded them. But they all realise that they brought trouble on themselves. And they all regret it.

Given the ways in which schools are forced to operate, by their constitutions and the law, it is not surprising that there are many factors with which some pupils find it hard to cope. Many of the experiences that the young offenders share overlap, and they certainly form a coherent whole – a telling coherence given the unguarded and unaffected narration of the facts. But there are several distinct factors which either by themselves, or more significantly in their combination, serve to force the individual into non-attendance, first by choice and then by institutional will.

The first of these factors is a dislike of taking orders. It is not so much a dislike of rules as a resentment of being told what to do, as if the command were not so much a relaying of social norms as a *personal* order:

> ...just sucking up...but they're the ones who get all the jobs now isn't it?...Just didn't like getting told what to do and that, just didn't like it.
>
> (Male, 20)

> Just being told what to do, it's always been my problem.
>
> (Male, 17)

Those who do not conform to the rules are always a problem. Schools, as institutions, with a large number of people in a confined space, some of whom become reluctant to be there, need rules. But the rules are conveyed, necessarily, through individuals, and it is taking 'orders' like that which is found difficult.

The difficulty lies in the fact that the 'orders' are conveyed not so much as the outcome of shared social circumstances as the result of one person's superiority over another. The individual feels patronised:

> If yours didn't turn out right she used to patronise you, you didn't try hard enough.
>
> (Female, 20)

> They should like talk to you as if you're a normal person, instead of treating you like a big kid.
>
> (Male, 20)

These are the reactions of vulnerable young people, vulnerable in the sense that they lack self-confidence and try to compensate for this with self-assertive aggression. It is their sense that they are 'picked' on and therefore humiliated in a personal way. The reason for this is that they feel 'stupid', that they are exposed as being 'shown up' as failures. Not all these young people were bad at school, and they all cite particular subjects at which they did well and which they enjoyed. But it is part of the culture of school, reinforced by legislation, to have assessment targets, competition and rank orders. All pupils, at some time or another, will feel embarrassed, or worse, at doing less well than their peers. In the culture of the classroom, pupils are aware of their own performance in relation to each other. One central reason for avoiding school, then, is the avoidance of a sense of failure, of being found wanting:

> Some of the work at school I found really hard and I couldn't do it...and that used to put me off as well. It used to make me angry

inside 'cos I couldn't do it, and all the others used to be there writing and I couldn't, teacher had to help me all the time. I used to feel stupid.

(Female, 21)

Even with help and support, the sense of anger and humiliation continues. In the many incidents of bullying and teasing, academic failure is always one of the potential taunts:

You can't really forget about that when they say it....It was either that or am not good at, erm, maths, English and things, if they called me about my work, or I used to, or me writing, 'you can't spell, you're thick' and things like that.

(Male, 18)

The problem is that there always seems to be an audience that relishes their failure. Sometimes they perceive this as including the teachers:

You had to have spellings...and like I couldn't remember one of them....Some teachers used to make me go into other classrooms and spell words on the board that I couldn't, that they knew I couldn't spell, to show me up and I didn't like that either.

(Male, 17)

There are two characteristics of schools that affect all pupils, although the majority manage to cope with them. The first is the growing realisation, from around the age of 8, that hard work does not in itself lead to success, that some are more naturally gifted than others are. This might seem an inevitability when young people are put into groups, but it is compounded by the narrow way in which the curriculum is defined, with stress on the memory of facts rather than the different types of intelligence (Quinn, 1997). The second is the sense of competition. The school system demands conformity to tests, to closed questions and the ordering of memory. The sense of comparison and competition is therefore reinforced by the system. Personal psychological comparisons gradually become enshrined in the way the 'system' is seen to operate. For those who find this most difficult, it seems natural to try to avoid it. From their point of view they question why they should submit to a sense of humiliation when they can absent themselves from it. The sense of waiting to be excluded from normal conforming society can have roots in small beginnings. The sense of alienation from school does not, however, always mean an inability to cope with work. For many young people school does not seem to have any particular relevance. It does not relate to them a sense of purpose that they find coherent. It then becomes 'boring':

I could do all the work and that, even the teachers said like I was bright at school, but I just didn't like bother with it, dunno, just used to find it boring.

(Male, 20)

One of the main reasons for finding work 'boring', however, is not because of the curriculum itself but because of styles of teaching and learning, typical of large classes and standard assessment tests. All children express a dislike of copying texts, writing rather than thinking and doing (Cullingford, 1991). The young offenders cite the ways in which classes are run as particularly off-putting:

...most of the time you're only copying from books, and you learn nothing, you don't learn nothing. Or, they give you a text book, three add three, and you write it down, on your book, it's simple 'cos you just copying it out of there...they should have like teachers to so many pupils....

(Male, 21)

Well, 'cos how they put the work across as well, was boring. Like, I just used to read the books instead of listening to what they'd do....

(Male 20)

It should be noted that what is being complained about is not so much the individual teachers but the system in which there are such large classes that they feel there is bound to be neglect.

The sense of not 'belonging' in the school, the sense of exclusion, begins far earlier than actual truancy or the incident that triggers exclusion. The sense of being an outsider, of not following normal rules is not just a physical statement, which ends up with being arrested and charged, but a state of mind. Whilst this is not the place to explore the very equivocal attitudes of young offenders to the law, their victims and themselves, they all recognise how long they have felt a sense of tension between social demands and the alternative peer pressures. They not only find schooling inimical to their preferred, less challenging, way of life, but they feel psychologically excluded from the processes of school even whilst there. The most powerful form of this was the sense that even the teachers didn't care about them:

I used to think they had their favourites. D'you know what I mean? And I used to sit there and they just sort of blanked me out and talked to the others all the time....I'd sit there most of the time on me own, nobody to talk to, and then I used to think, oh god, I'm not coming tomorrow....

(Female, 21)

The teachers just seemed to be different like. If you didn't turn up for school they weren't really bothered.

(Male, 17)

...used to walk in classroom and there'd be people sat with faces long and like all in their own little worlds. Then some of 'em would be doing stupid things and you'd think oh god, please get me out.

(Female, 20)

The picture that is being presented is of a sense of loneliness in the school and thoughts of escape. But it is a loneliness that derives from a feeling that the system of the school is essentially indifferent to them. A personal sense of exclusion is then made palpable, even within a school, by having 'exclusion rooms'. The experience of being 'sent out' of the class draws attention to the distinction between those who fit in and those who do not:

And if you don't do it you get like detention after school....I used to just go to the exclusion room every time we had a language lesson, 'cos I knew for a fact that if I went to the class he'd end up sending me there anyway.

(Male, 16)

The sense of anticipating that there will be trouble pervades all the interviews. They suggest that it is to the benefit of the school if they are excluded, and to the pleasure of the teachers if they are not there. Non-attendance is not so much a positive choice – to be with their peers and indulge in criminal activities – as a negative one, a result of a series of experiences:

Because they embarrass you, 'cos they know, probably, you ain't very good at reading and that, they'll just pick you out of the whole class and say 'stand up and read that paragraph to the class', and all that and you say, 'no I'm not doing it' and they'll say 'right, if you're not doing it you're going to the exclusion room'. So I just grabbed my bag and just walked out and everyone was taking the piss and that....

(Male, 16)

This combines many of the features of the school experience that lead to exclusion, the sense of embarrassment both from teachers and other pupils and a feeling that if exclusion takes place within the class, and within the school, then it might as well become formalised. And this is from a young man who, like nearly all the others, says that schooling is important. The comments on teaching styles are usually followed by remarks on the size of classes. They seem to recognise the difficulties that teachers face, which is why there is so much emphasis on the 'system'. There are many critical remarks about teachers, and clashes with individual teachers. The final exclusion often comes about because of confrontations with teachers. But it must be emphasised that all the young offenders recall their liking for individual teachers. They remember acts of kindness and signs of concern from particular ones. There is no sense of blanket blame against all teachers. Instead they cite clashes with particular teachers acting within the frameworks of the discipline of a school. Long before they absent themselves from school, they avoid particular lessons (O'Keeffe, 1994). The defining moments of exclusion centre on confrontations with particular teachers:

> It was in music, I just stood up and said, 'oh fuck off. I've had enough of you' and just walked out and everyone burst into hysterics....Everyone used to take the piss out of him....he was really horrible. He just, he used to grumble and all that about everything you done, even if you made an effort....He just done my head in.
>
> (Female, 18)

Each defining moment is the culmination of a series of experiences and a sudden refusal to accept authority, both personalised and, by extrapolation, symbolic of society:

> Teacher'll come in, you probably have your coat on, he'd say 'take it off' and me mate, he didn't take his coat off, and he says, 'take it off', and he says 'I'll take it off in a minute'. He says 'you won't, you'll take it off now', and he tried to rip it off his back, so me mate started fighting with him and that....
>
> (Male, 16)

Fighting with teachers is, of course, the most extreme form of disobedience, and the one most dreaded by a school. The same young offender asked to be readmitted, but no school would accept him, so that he, like the others, ended up 'just dossed round the streets all day, nothing else you could do'. The reasons for exclusion were nearly all for disobedience and fighting teachers, not for bullying and never for academic failure.

In all the accounts of school experiences there was one moment when the young offenders recall finding it all too much. They suggest they finally 'snapped', but this incident is neither sudden, nor out of context:

> I had a Walkman. It was in class and the teacher told me to pull it off and that and I was young at the time and I wasn't listening to her so I answered her back and she just like dragged it off me and it

like broke. It fell on the floor and broke, so I just like went mad
and told her to fuck off....

(Male, 19)

And he was just naggin' me like, and just naggin', naggin' and
that, and I couldn't take it so, so I just slammed the work down
and just walked off...walked over to him ...so's I says 'will you?'
and just ran up there and just jumped up and headbutted him,
glasses flew off, stamped on them....

(Male, 16)

These reactions are at the extreme end of pathologically bad behaviour,
the culmination of a great deal of anger. In several cases there are stories of
fighting with a whole group of teachers, of extremes of violence. But despite
this, and despite the fact that they have ended up in prison for such acts,
there is no sense of inevitability about them, except in the sense of being
unable to show any self-control. The problem is that they see all teachers as
individuals, with their own personal styles and approaches, rather than as
individuals fulfilling a role. Being made to obey rules, and pass tests,
becomes personalised. For young people who are not good at making relationships there is an irony in this:

Some teachers are alright, but most of them it's, like when they
have problems and that at home, the most of 'em bring it to school,
take it out on people.

(Male, 16)

They find it difficult to make a distinction between the private and the
public as they find it difficult to adapt to different modes of discourse.

It must be remembered that the context of their peer group relationships
is that of quarrelling and bullying (Cullingford and Morrison, 1995).
Fighting abounds. It is no surprise that fighting, against teachers or particularly violent examples against each other, is a common reason for exclusion.
Bullying contributes to truancy, but fighting against authority leads to
exclusion. Sometimes, as in the case of using a knife, exclusion is the result
of a particularly violent act:

Just smacked him, punching him in the face and dragged his hair
across the floor. 'Cos he tripped me up and I went flying and that.
'Cos it's not right though is it, tripping a girl up, so I went off me
head and I got done for it.

(Female, 16)

Sometimes exclusion results from acts of violence against the teachers. And sometimes it is the result of both:

> Just hitting teachers and everything, fighting with all me mates, best mates as well.
>
> (Male, 21)

The crucial point about the reasons for fighting is that it is a sign of lack of control, as if the violence of the feelings were uncontrolled and unsuppressed. These young offenders all recognise their lack of self-control. They know that it is a primary cause both for non-attendance at school and for criminality. Whilst the causes of the inability to relate rationally with others can be traced to the relationships at home (Cullingford and Morrison, 1997), the outcomes manifest themselves in school, especially as it is not only a demanding system but the social centre of their lives. The problem with the loss of self-control is that it becomes a focus for teasing. Others find it difficult to resist 'winding them up' until they 'snap':

> I used to get really mad when they used to say it and they just used to wind me up and wind me up all the time...you know 'til they'd really get you mad and you'd do something....It sort of like builds the temper up inside.
>
> (Female, 21)

Again and again we hear of teasing that leads to retaliation, of 'aggression problems', of phrases like 'I can get worked up really easily', 'I just lose my temper all the time', and 'that gets me going'. In this way the distinction between the private and the public is again broken down; the pressure from teasing and from academic demands becoming so strong that they find no way out except in violence. Fighting is the most central breaking of the rules, but it also seems a central part of their lives. Just as it is difficult to make a clear distinction between truancy and exclusion, so it is difficult to separate bullies and victims. All are teased and all retaliate; all inflict bullying on others and are bullied in their turn.

School has been described as young people's chief social centre. For those who are in school, it remains so. For those who are cast adrift, the social milieu is far vaguer and wider, and has no such tight social organisation. But the school contains two societies in one. It is the official face of the state, of work and preparation for future responsibilities. But it is also the meeting place for all who are engaged in other activities. Not only is it a place with the potential for acts of indiscipline, the pushing and tripping, teasing and name-calling of young people in close proximity to each other, but the natural centre of attention for people of that age. It is the place where friends and 'twockers' (car-thieves) meet:

I used to enjoy being in school 'cos I had loads of friends there.

(Female, 19)

We used to like get to school, that's where we used to all meet, then we'd just decide to get off.

(Male, 20)

Sometimes I'd like I wouldn't go to school. I'd wait 'til school finished and then wait outside for everyone, walk home with them, like.

(Male, 20)

Much of what they learned of social behaviour they have learned at school, but the significant part of this is informal. The curriculum seems a separate entity and teachers doing jobs which are perceived as necessary but inexplicable.

Schools, as centres of social activity, can both be the meeting ground of 'gangs' and places of distraction, where the sheer number of people causes difficulties. Schools are not just about lessons but about breaks:

It was better than just sittin' there quiet, if there's a lot of messin' about the time'd just go faster....it got you out of class, and you could go out, have a smoke. Somethin' like that, messing about, so it was OK.

(Male, 20)

In all the gaps between lessons, including lunchtime, there are opportunities for interactions and for escape. Not all these unofficial periods were relished:

I used to hate playtimes....'Cos that's when I used to get bullied mostly. Like I used to have stuff, like if I was playin' marbles and stuff, even I'd nicked them....

(Female, 21)

One has to remind oneself that schools are complex places. The messages that are received about them depend not just on the 'authorised' version of the National Curriculum but on the points of view of peer groups, and not just on those aiming for their futures in a competitive society but those who find its structures and demands distinctly unattractive.

All these factors, illuminated by the examples we have taken from the evidence, form a coherent whole. For young offenders, schools became places from which non-attendance was the way out, as if there were no alternative. Threatening tests, a sense of failure, quarrels with teachers, a sense of alienation from the system, compounded with bullying and peer-group pressure, all were part of the experience that led to criminality. The question is the extent to which we should look at schools as reasons for non-attendance, and what could be done to prevent what, with hindsight, looks like an almost inexorable outcome in crime.

Conclusions

I have briefly described and summarised the individual experiences of young criminals and the part that schooling played. They form a coherent and consistent pattern. The question remains whether schools in themselves were definite if unwitting causes of criminality, or whether non-attendance at school is all to do with other factors but school.

What is clear is that non-attendance and crime *are* linked, even if not in a simple balance of cause and effect. For some young people coming from an extremely difficult background, school is a particularly traumatic experience. For all pupils it can be difficult, for the same reasons that this chapter elucidates. But most have learned how to cope, how to adapt and how to meet the particular demands of school. They know when to remain invisible, when to ignore what goes on. Above all, they have learned the academic discourse of school.

It is very easy to be critical of schools. Each of these young offenders is left with a sense of failure, with a feeling of rejection and alienation. Other, alternative, unstructured aspects of society become the more attractive. But we must remind ourselves that they also, too late, see the purpose and relevance of school. They all, with one exception, wish their experience had been different. We should also remind ourselves that the young offenders, whilst quarrelling violently with some, even most, teachers, also rated some, who cared for them or who interested them, very highly. This might sound, at first, as if I am being critical of certain teachers. But this is not so. What the witnesses to failure all stress is that the teachers, however personal and individual as human beings, are also a part of a system. Large classes, tests and a narrow timetable make conditions impossible for the more intractable of pupils. Who has the time to deal with all manifestations of bullying and teasing? Who has the time to give that individual tuition to those who would gain self-confidence? It is tempting to say that until attention is paid in a supportive rather than punitive way to parenting, particularly in the early years, schools will, by their very circumstances, continue to nurture young criminals.

What, then, if we accept the present system, could be done? The first thing is to be sensitive to the issues. This involves understanding the experiences and backgrounds of individual pupils. Their lives are far more traumatic than seems apparent until the results are manifested in anger. This means also being far more sensitive to the difficulties of teachers, beleaguered both with enormous demands and layer on layer of blame. The

71

combination of 'difficult' pupils and large classes is too volatile. The second response to the dilemma is to rethink the nature of the curriculum. For all pupils it remains meaningless, since no one explains its purpose. There is a consistent finding here and elsewhere (White with Brockington, 1983; Cullingford, 1996) that those who feel failures wish that there had been far more explanation. They all have regrets. The third response to the issues is, in the absence of any national guidelines about the purpose of the curriculum (beyond facts suitable for testing), for the school itself to attempt to foster a sense of responsibility and critical thinking. For those who adapt to and survive the system it does not need explaining. But for those who find themselves alienated, it is the responsibility of the school to create some credible communication: why they are in school and how social education is as important as knowledge.

5

THE EFFECTIVE COLLECTION AND ANALYSIS OF ATTENDANCE DATA

Ian Stokes and Jo Walton

Introduction

Schools' attendance data need 'interpreting to produce a greater understanding of trends and patterns of attendance. Such analysis is rare' (DES, 1989b: 13).

Although the raw material for producing attendance analysis has been available in the form of class registers since the advent of compulsory school attendance, the demand for attendance analysis, and the ability to produce it, has only developed in the 1990s.

The increased use of information technology in school management now means that nearly all schools at secondary level, and many at primary level, collect attendance data through some form of computerised registration, but schools and LEAs differ widely in the format and extent of the analysis they produce from this information. Some education professionals have even cast doubt on the benefits of producing school attendance figures, and the publication of performance tables has lent weight to this argument as they have been seen by many as inaccurate, divisive and misleading when taken out of context.

This chapter demonstrates how valuable and informative attendance data can be collected and suggests some pertinent lines of inquiry which schools and LEAs can follow when investigating attendance trends. The ultimate purpose of data analysis should be to inform action; in this case, to inform the development and implementation of school and LEA attendance policies.

Using attendance data at LEA level

While the benefits and justifications of performance tables can be debated, it should be recognised that the data which LEAs must now collect for both primary and secondary sectors can be used to investigate a number of areas of strategic importance. LEAs should now be able to answer the following questions:

- How do our attendance rates compare with other similar LEAs?
- Are there any areas within the LEA which display differing patterns of attendance?
- Are there any factors that may contribute to different levels of attendance at different schools?
- Where should we target our resources to solve specific problems?

The DFEE has been publishing aggregated LEA data in relation to absence from school since the early 1990s, and this now includes both 'authorised' and 'unauthorised' attendance data. LEAs can now use these data to compare their attendance rates with other similar authorities.

Table 5.1 shows the 1994/5 published absence rates for five LEAs in South and West Yorkshire. All have similar numbers of pupils drawn from similar demographic areas; they also share similar rates of authorised absence. LEA 1, however, has a significantly higher rate of unauthorised absence and may want to investigate the reasons for this. LEAs facing similar challenges may also gain valuable experience from sharing information and co-operating with each other on joint initiatives.

An aggregated LEA attendance figure will only give the most basic insight into the overall picture of attendance within the area as a whole. Investigation of spatial patterns of attendance within the LEA can reveal important issues which are hidden by the bigger picture but which are also influencing it. By plotting the location of schools on maps of the areas concerned, LEAs can build a picture of levels of attendance in different sectors of their authority. When this was done in Leeds some striking, if not entirely surprising, results were obtained. The Leeds demographic profile is characterised by a dense urban core situated in the centre of the authority, surrounded by a suburban ring. The northern and eastern outskirts of the authority are characterised by large areas of sparsely populated rural land while the south and west areas merge into the conurbations of Bradford and

Table 5.1 Absence rates 1994–5: Selected LEAS, South and West Yorkshire

	No. pupils	% Auth. absence	% Unauth. absence
LEA 1	30,743	5.9	1.6
LEA 2	22,033	6.1	0.4
LEA 3	31,921	5.6	0.9
LEA 4	21,968	6.2	0.6
LEA 5	24,861	5.6	0.8

Wakefield. Figure 5.1 shows a map of the Leeds area onto which the locations of all secondary schools have been plotted.

Schools have also been tagged as being either above or below the aggregated LEA attendance rate for secondary schools (91.71 per cent), for the academic year 1996/7. The map immediately demonstrates a clear demarcation between attendance rates in the centre of Leeds compared with those in the outer areas, with all the schools with below average attendance located in the urban core. While the results of such analysis could be fairly easily predicted in the case of a metropolitan authority like Leeds, this exercise still has its uses; schools could, for example, be grouped into more homogeneous families for the purpose of comparisons and LEA services can be directed to those specific areas where the need is greatest.

Figure 5.2 shows the aggregated 1996/7 attendance levels for primary schools grouped into four 'bands' for each postal sector of Leeds. This representation allows very detailed questions to be asked, for example: 'Why are the schools in one postal sector achieving higher levels of attendance than all of their neighbouring sectors?' or even 'Why is the attendance level of a particular school significantly higher or lower than the other schools in its locality?'

Such anomalies uncovered by the mapping of attendance data may be at least partially explained by investigating other factors that might be exerting an influence on attendance rates in school. Studies in Leeds have looked at a number of these factors.

Observation of lower attendance rates in the urban core of Leeds

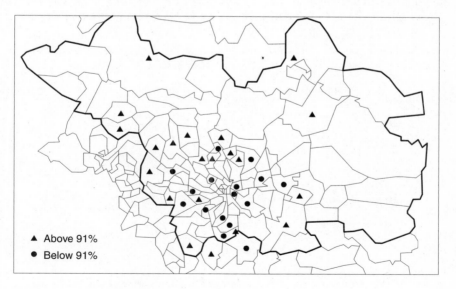

Figure 5.1 Attendance at Leeds secondary schools 1996–7

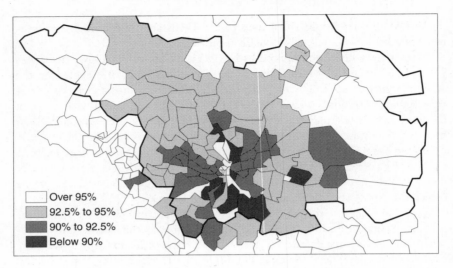

Figure 5.2 Attendance at Leeds primary schools 1996–7

immediately suggests a possible link between social deprivation and poverty and higher rates of absence. In order to confirm this the proportion of pupils in each school who are entitled to free school meals (FSM) was used as a measure of social deprivation and then compared to absence rates. Figure 5.3 demonstrates the strong relationship between the two factors: schools with low levels of FSM entitlement generally have low levels of absence; schools with high levels of FSM entitlement generally have high levels of absence.

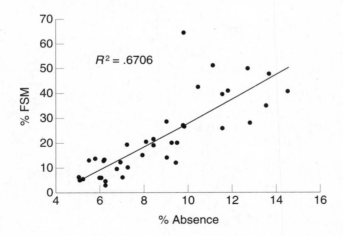

Figure 5.3 Percentage absence and percentage free school meals (FSM) for Leeds secondary schools, 1996–7

We have also investigated the relationship between attendance rates and levels of achievement. Figure 5.4 plots percentage attendance rates for Leeds secondary schools against the proportion of Year 11 pupils achieving five or more GCSE grades A–C. Again, a clear link is displayed: schools with low attendance levels generally have lower achievement rates than schools with high attendance rates.

Of course, establishing a link between two factors does not identify which, if any, is the causal factor; this can only be achieved through long-term studies of change, and even then the scientific validity of such experiments could be called into question when they are conducted in environments where a multitude of different factors are at work at any one time. However, the usefulness of producing such analysis should not be overlooked, if only for the benefits of being able to identify individual schools which are not conforming to the expected pattern and demonstrating that while 'rates of attendance depend to some extent on factors outside the school's control...attendance is also substantially affected by what schools themselves do' (DES, 1989b: 2). For example, it may be discovered that one school with large numbers of pupils who are entitled to FSM is managing to minimise absence while another school with high attendance rates is not producing the expected level of achievement at GCSE.

Investigations into the links between attendance and other factors such as ethnicity and behaviour/exclusions have also been carried out in Leeds, and while the results of these studies have not been conclusive, they do demonstrate the need to be aware of the existence of a multitude of factors which may be affecting schools' attendance levels.

With the information obtained from these analyses, LEAs can

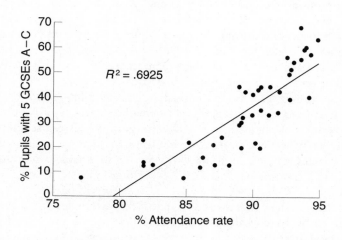

Figure 5.4 Percentage attendance rates and percentage GCSE A–Cs for Leeds secondary schools, 1996–7

strategically target their resources at the specific areas and specific schools whose need is greatest. In Leeds, information of this nature has been used to assist in the formulation of Service Level Entitlements for Education Welfare and Educational Psychology and for the allocation of funding for special project activities.

Using attendance data at the whole-school level

Every school has its own particular socio-economic and ethnic intake that may vary from year to year, and each will have its own peculiar mixture of staff gender, ethnicity, age and experience. This means that different strategies will be effective in different combinations at any one time in improving and maintaining good attendance rates. In order for a school to be able to build upon its successes through the policy formulation and review procedure, and to address its problems through the same process, it must first identify each aspect through examination of its attendance data.

Collection of the required data can be an exceedingly time-consuming procedure unless systems have already been formulated to enable the process. The most efficient way of collecting and collating such information is by the use of a computerised system. It is possible very quickly to compile weekly, termly and annual attendance figures by the registration group, year and whole school, which can be easily imported into spreadsheets from which graphical representations of the data may be produced. If, however, a computerised system is not being used in school, registration procedures which require each member of staff to produce his or her own information on a weekly basis over the course of the year will reduce the amount of time spent collating figures at the end of the year and allow the school to keep track of attendance patterns throughout the year. Schools within this authority are given forms like the one shown in Figure 5.5 to record possible and actual attendance for each registration group within the school. This can be entered onto a spreadsheet that calculates percentages on a weekly basis and aggregates data on a termly and annual basis.

Schools can use weekly, termly and annual figures in different ways as indicators of their attendance trends and identifiers of a variety of problems. Subsequent breakdown of these figures into year groups and registration groups can provide other more detailed information about trends and provide school managers with information which will enable them to provide support and training to members of pastoral staff or direct the efforts of the Education Welfare Service to particular groups of pupils.

Figures 5.6 and 5.7 show the weekly attendance pattern for the same school but separated by seven years. It can be clearly seen from the comparison that the school has achieved an improvement in overall attendance rates and that the variations in attendance rate over the year has been considerably reduced.

Statistics data collection sheet

(Complete **EITHER** present **OR** absent column)

School ....   School ....

Yr group .... Form ....   Yr group .... Form ....

Wk beginning	possible	present	absent	Wk beginning	possible	present	absent
02/09/96				02/09/96			
09/09/96				09/09/96			
16/09/96				16/09/96			
23/09/96				23/09/96			
30/09/96				30/09/96			
07/10/96				07/10/96			
14/10/96				14/10/96			
21/10/96				21/10/96			

Figure 5.5 Statistics data collection sheet

It is noticeable that such charts often show similarities across schools. For example, there is normally a drop in attendance prior to the Christmas and summer holidays, regardless of the overall level of attendance. Those schools with the highest overall attendance, however, will experience the lowest fall in attendance. Year 11 mock exams, study leave for GCSEs and SAT (Standard Attainment Test) testing are usually causes of increased

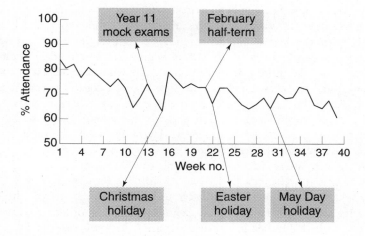

Figure 5.6 High school weekly attendance, 1989–90

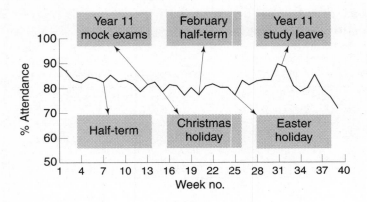

Figure 5.7 High school weekly attendance, 1996–7

attendance. Work experience time can also cause a rise in attendance. Events such as these, however, timed too close to major holidays, can cause corresponding drops in attendance during the course of the last week before that holiday.

Schools experiencing such falls in attendance have reorganised mock exams and work experience to occur right up to the end of the term time period, that is, finishing on the day that the school breaks up or at the beginning of the school term or half-term, giving pupils time to debrief after such events.

The positioning of teacher training days can be equally crucial. Monitoring over a number of years indicates that training days held on a Friday or Monday have least effect on pupil attendance. Training days in the middle of the week, however, can have a drastic effect on attendance over the course of the whole week, with the greatest disruption being experienced by those schools with the lowest overall attendance figures. It would appear that parents and pupils feel that if the school is going to be closed for a day mid-week, then they are quite justified in taking the whole or the rest of the week off. Individual teachers, especially in high schools, complain that it is unfair that training days always happen on the same school day, effectively reducing any given subject's time with a particular group. Some schools have got round this problem by keeping the day of the week the same but altering timetable days for the rest of the week.

Some events can affect the whole school adversely, for example bad weather conditions or religious holidays. It is difficult to see any way of avoiding these completely, but it is valuable to be able to explain how these factors may affect the attendance of some schools and not of others. Absence as a result of the bad weather has actually caused, in some cases, a fall in attendance over the whole year of almost 2 per cent. Those schools that closed during the bad weather, however, have experienced no such fall in attendance. There appear to be a variety of reasons why pupils stay away from school as a result of inclement weather. Some are to do with the difficulty of transport over disrupted bus routes, but some are also caused by the lack of appropriate clothing to deal with the weather conditions, so parents keep at home even primary school children who live within walking distance of the school. As schools are important community resources as well as education establishments, it would seem appropriate to take all steps to ensure that they stay open even in the most inclement weather so that young people have somewhere safe, dry and warm to come. However, those schools that do struggle to maintain some sort of normality for their community are penalised in league tables for their efforts while those that don't are rewarded.

The celebration of religious holidays also causes problems in terms of attendance rates for some schools. The two Eid festivals, Eid ul Fittr and Eid ul Addhah, occur during the Spring Term and the Summer Term respectively. It is occasionally possible with judicious planning of the school calendar by LEAs to have the festivals occur during half-term or Easter holidays. These events are similar in significance to the Christian festivals of Christmas and Easter that, fortunately for those celebrating them, occur during long holidays. All these festivals have a family as well as a religious aspect to them and often families travel across the country to celebrate together. This will effectively mean that absence for some pupils for such festivals may exceed any agreement that has been negotiated between the school and the local community as being necessary for religious requirements. Research has shown that in some schools the attendance rate for the year would have been up to 3 percentage points higher if the absences for religious reasons during the relevant Eid weeks were discounted, and these schools are therefore disadvantaged in terms of league tables compared to other schools of similar size with different ethnic intakes. Some schools try to reduce the effect of these absences by planning training days for the expected dates of the festival. This is, however, further complicated by the fact that sometimes mosques in the same area will declare the festivals on different days because of varying interpretations of the lunar cycle.

The general trend of all schools' weekly attendance rates across the year is to show a gradual reduction in attendance from September to July. This can be seen more clearly in the termly attendance block graphs as those shown in Figure 5.8. The lower the overall attendance rate of the school and the greater the problem with attendance, the greater the fall-off rate between the terms tends to be.

Comparison between year groups can indicate to schools where they need to focus their resources in order to achieve improvements. Within the normal school environment the trend in high school is for attendance rates to fall as pupils get older. As with the variation between the terms the greatest

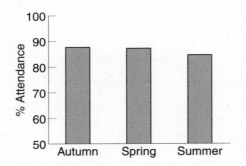

Figure 5.8 High school termly attendance, 1993–4

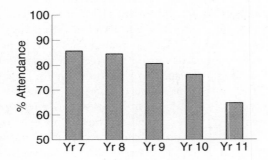

Figure 5.9 High school with average attendance of 78 per cent

differences in attendance between Year 7 and Year 11 (up to 15 or 20 per cent in some cases) are seen in those schools that have the greatest problems with attendance overall, whereas those schools with good overall attendance rates show only a small variation, usually 1 or 2 per cent (Figures 5.9 and 5.10).

Primary schools tend to show slightly different patterns, with attendance peaking in the middle years, 2, 3 and 4, with Year 6 and reception being the lowest attenders. It has also been observed that schools with nursery units often show lower attendance in the reception year than those without, as seen in Figures 5.11 and 5.12. Some parents seem to find it difficult to make the adjustment from non-compulsory to compulsory education, and schools therefore need to make strenuous efforts to reinforce parental responsibilities with regard to attendance at the time of transfer from nursery to reception (see Lewis in this volume).

Monitoring of the effectiveness of attendance policy and interventions can be undertaken during the course of the year and over the years by comparing previous years on the same graph. Schools should be looking for an overall improvement in the annual figure followed by more consistency over the

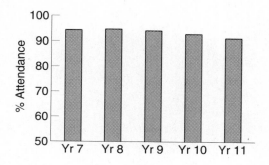

Figure 5.10 High school with average attendance of 93 per cent

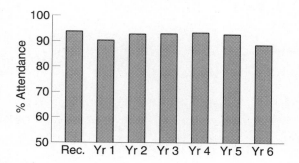

Figure 5.11 Primary school annual attendance (without nursery)

termly figures and the year group figures. The weekly attendance graphs should also demonstrate consistent levels of attendance and a maintenance of the rates of the first week of the Autumn Term throughout the course of the year.

Individual class groups often display a far more erratic weekly attendance pattern since the absence of individuals has a far greater effect with the smaller overall group number. It is possible, however, to use the absence and unauthorised absence figures plotted against each other to research the effectiveness of class or form tutors in gathering information about pupil absence. Figures 5.13–5.15 show three form groups within the same year group of an inner city high school.

Figure 5.13 shows a form group with little unauthorised absence, and although the total absence line varies over the course of the year, the overall trend is steady at around the tenth percentile. Figure 5.14 shows a form group with two long-term non-attenders. Despite this, the overall absence of the group remains fairly constant around the twentieth percentile over the

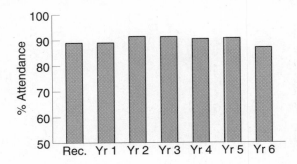

Figure 5.12 Primary school annual attendance (with nursery)

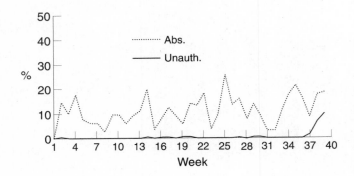

Figure 5.13 Absence v. unauthorised absence Form 1

rest of the year. Figure 5.15 shows a form group that are demonstrating a pattern of increasing absence and increasing unauthorised absence over the course of the year, starting at about 10 to 15 per cent and increasing to around 30 per cent.

The first two form groups had tutors who practised regular first day contact for their absent pupils and followed up the pupils' return to school with requests for notes from parents. In the last form group, follow-up was erratic and inconsistent and absences were rarely followed up on the first day. Using these data it is possible to distinguish those tutor groups where follow-up of absence was undertaken from those groups where it was not, thus enabling management at the school to target resources to those form tutors who needed support.

An effective policy addresses issues which have been identified by accurate information. There is little point in attempting to address the issue of parental holidays, for example, if the major problem within school is absence

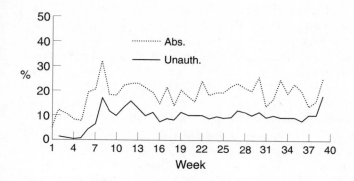

Figure 5.14 Absence v. unauthorised absence Form 2

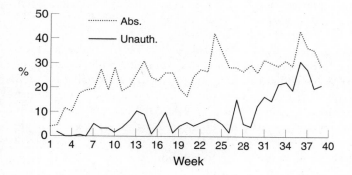

Figure 5.15 Absence v. unauthorised absence Form 3

caused through illegal employment; or tackling the issues surrounding truancy with parents and pupils if the major cause of absence is excessive parental holiday. In order to allow policies to develop, there is a need to continue to collect and analyse data in order to establish the effectiveness of the policy strategies and to identify changing factors, which require new or modified strategies.

Analysing individual pupils' attendance: the Combined Absence Index and the Combined Absence Rating

> The persistent non-attender is not hard to spot on any register, but closer analysis can identify the intermittent non-attender, whether casual or regular.
>
> (DES, 1989b: 13)

Identifying individual pupils whose attendance is showing cause for concern from form or year groups can often be a difficult, time-consuming and sometimes ineffective process if percentage attendance rates are being calculated and analysed from class registers. However, this is a task which vigilant form tutors and Education Welfare Officers (EWOs) need to do on a regular basis. The Combined Absence Index (CAI), which was developed by Gill Gant, formerly of the Derbyshire Education Welfare Service, is a tool which gives the process of identifying pupils for EWS involvement a greater degree of regularity and consistency and can provide a framework for 'thresholds' of attendance levels to be set as criteria for referral to the service. The Leeds Attendance and Behaviour Project piloted the use of CAIs in Leeds between 1990 and 1993 and has continued its use, both for purposes of referrals for work with individual pupils and in the development of whole-school attendance policies.

The CAI is a two-fold measure of a pupil's attendance, taking account of percentage absence and spread of absence within a specified period. The following examples illustrate how it can be used.

Over a five-week period, pupil A may have a 20 per cent absence rate. This consists of one full week's absence due to a throat infection; a pattern of absence that is acceptable and after which the pupil is generally able to catch up quickly. Over the same five-week period pupil B may also have a 20 per cent absence rate. However, this consists of odd-day absences affecting all five weeks. This is obviously a situation of concern and much more difficult to remedy.

The CAI for each pupil is reached by combining the percentage absence and the number of broken weeks within the period under examination, hence pupil A receives a CAI of 20/1, pupil B receives a CAI of 20/5.

Individual schools or welfare services can set their own thresholds for a child to be deemed as having attendance which shows 'cause for concern' in relation to whatever are considered to be 'normal' or 'acceptable' levels of attendance, but Derbyshire Education Welfare Service recommended that the criterion should be set at 20/3 over a five-week period.

Returning to the examples: with the criteria set by Derbyshire, pupil A would be seen as not having attendance problems, while pupil B would be identified as showing cause for concern.

CAIs can therefore be used as a regular record of individual pupils' acceptable/ unacceptable attendance. *Ad hoc* referrals from schools can never ensure that all pupils with attendance problems are identified and given the support they require. This system, however, provides comprehensive referral criteria, which makes it much more difficult for a child to 'slip through the net'.

While the CAI is very valuable in analysing a pupil's attendance in relation to a specific threshold, it is, however, limited in its usefulness in comparing the spread of absence of individual pupils with their peers. The presence of two variables, broken weeks and percentage absence, means that it is not always possible to list a group of pupils in rank order of attendance as expressed by a CAI.

The concept of the Combined Absence Rating (CAR) is fairly simple: the calculation of a single figure that enables pupils to be ranked in relation to both their percentage absence and the number of weeks broken with absence over a specified period.

The difficulty with CARs is in their calculation. The project originally used the following equation:

$$\left(\frac{\dfrac{\text{total weeks}}{\text{broken weeks}}}{\% \text{ absence}} \right) \times 100$$

Using this formula, the worst possible CAR, namely that representing 100 per cent absence, is 1. The best possible CAR, namely that representing 100 per cent attendance, is infinity.

Following helpful suggestions from HMI, a second equation was produced:

$$(\% \text{ absence}) \times \left(\frac{\text{no. broken weeks}}{\text{total weeks}} \right)$$

Using this formula, the worst possible CAR, namely that representing 100 per cent absence, is 100. The best possible CAR, namely that representing full attendance, is 0.

Whichever formula is used, however, the fairly lengthy calculations involved could prove to be prohibitive if calculated manually for whole form/class or year groups on a regular basis. It is for this reason that the project has used spreadsheet software to calculate CARs, speeding up the process immeasurably.

A teacher or EWO who has decided that they have the resources to do some attendance-related work with five pupils can use the CAR to identify either the five whose attendance is the worst in relation to both absence and broken weeks, or five from the middle of the group who may benefit from input at the early stages of a worsening attendance pattern.

As with CAIs, thresholds of acceptable attendance can be set using the CAR, with the added advantage that they can remain constant regardless of changes in the length of time (total weeks) under investigation. Using CAIs to compare periods of varying length would be difficult as the number of broken weeks stated in the expression would relate to different total weeks.

Threshold CARs can also be used to identify any discrepancy between resources available to work with poor attenders and the actual number of pupils who need to be given attention. It may be found, for example, that there are more pupils exceeding the threshold CAR than available resources for extra work can accommodate.

Another benefit of producing regular lists of CARs for groups of pupils is that changes in an individual's attendance can be compared with his or her peers. The attendance of groups of students quite often falls over the course of the year. It is therefore quite difficult to quantify the significance of a pupil's attendance change if it is considered in isolation. If, however, a pupil has a CAR that puts him or her near the top of an attendance list for his/her form or year group in one half-term, but whose CAR in following half-terms shows him/her slipping progressively down the list, s/he can be swiftly identified as developing an attendance problem, even if s/he has not yet reached the threshold set for pupils who are a 'cause for concern'.

CARs are a useful complement to CAIs if more detailed analysis of attendance trends are required, but they should not be seen as a replacement of CAIs. The CAI is the easiest and most effective method of producing a representation of the spread of absence.

Post-registration truancy

Stoll and O'Keeffe's (1989) findings suggest that post-registration truancy is an activity common to a majority of students and that existing structures for the monitoring of attendance only serve to hide its prevalence. The main reasons for post-registration truancy were found to be a dislike of particular lessons, that is, primarily a curricular issue, rather than a general dislike of school.

Leeds Attendance and Behaviour Project has conducted a number of studies to ascertain the extent of and reasons for post-registration truancy in Leeds schools. These have included questionnaire surveys, interviews and post-registration truancy audits. The Education Support Grant-funded Improving Attendance Project of 1990–3 ran a number of questionnaires with pupils from Years 9–11 in five Leeds schools. Out of 1,379 pupils questioned, 20 per cent admitted to leaving school or missing a lesson without permission on at least one occasion during the first term of the academic year. In a questionnaire administered to a smaller sample of 258 Year 10 and 11 students, 37 per cent said they had never absconded, 51 per cent admitted to up to five separate incidences, 6 per cent said they had 'bunked off' between five and 20 times, and 5 per cent said they had left lessons on over 20 separate occasions. These figures point to post-registration truancy on a similar scale to that identified by Stoll and

O'Keeffe, but also suggest that there are a minority of students in the senior year groups who abscond on a very regular basis. Additional comments solicited from students included criticisms of the curriculum, such as: 'School was boring and I didn't get the subjects I wanted.' However, many alternative reasons for missing lessons were given, including personal problems, criticism of classroom management and delivery of lessons, bullying and dissatisfaction with the length of break times. From these comments it seems that a rejection of the curriculum is only one possible reason for post-registration truancy.

All schools involved with the 1993/4 project ran questionnaires with their staff and students. Twenty per cent of students admitted to post-registration truancy at least once in the three weeks preceding the administration of the questionnaire and 8 per cent said that they had absconded from lessons on three or more occasions in that period. If the trend of 20 per cent of pupils missing lessons at least once in the first three weeks of the academic year were maintained, the total proportion of students who would have truanted after registration by the end of the year would be very high, quite possibly equivalent to the numbers estimated by Stoll and O'Keeffe.

Students were also asked where they went when they left lessons. Of the students who answered, the largest group (45 per cent) succeeded in keeping their destinations undisclosed, choosing the 'Other' category from the options. Twenty-five per cent said they went to their own or a friend's house, 12 per cent said they went to local shops or town, while only 15 per cent said they stayed in or around the school building (6 per cent went to the toilets).

A range of options was offered to students in giving reasons for truanting from lessons. The most frequent answer, with twice as many respondents choosing this as the second most popular reason, was that they were ill (31 per cent). This seemed a surprising result, although it highlights an important point that large numbers of students may be going home ill without notifying staff. While these pupils are not 'truanting' in the normal sense of the word, they are leaving school without permission and are causing the same problems for school and themselves that any other truant causes. It would also be useful to investigate why these students feel that they cannot tell staff that they are ill. Are they using illness as an excuse? Do they think that staff will not believe that they are ill? Is it too much trouble for them to find someone who can take a message? Are they embarrassed by their illness?

The second most popular reason for students absconding was that they had 'something else better to do' (12 per cent). Dissatisfaction with the lesson (the main reason for absence in Stoll and O'Keeffe's study) came out only third favourite among Leeds students, with 10 per cent of respondents identifying this as the reason for their last unauthorised absence from a lesson.

As part of a separate activity, project staff working with an identified group of poor attenders in five project schools interviewed these pupils about a number of attendance-related issues, including post-registration truancy. Most of the high school students admitted to 'bunking off' on a regular basis, and many of them said that they had started this practice at middle school. The information from these interviews points to the possibility that pupils with poor overall attendance may often begin their slide to block absence with periods where they truant from individual lessons.

Further questioning about these students' attitudes towards school also highlights the fact that even among these poor attenders there is rarely a general dissatisfaction or disillusionment with school as a whole, and that their absences are often due to severe problems with one particular subject, with one particular teacher, or with a specific non-curricular problem.

The least favourite subjects amongst the students were English and Maths. PE also received significant mentions in this respect. These choices are very similar to the opinions of the students in Stoll and O'Keeffe's study.

Nine project schools conducted an audit to identify pupil absence following registration. A third of the schools did not identify anyone without an authorised reason for their absence from lessons. The others generally only identified a handful. With one or two exceptions, the small number of truants identified seems quite surprising at first. However, in a school of about 700 students, it only takes two or three different pupils absconding every day to satisfy Stoll and O'Keeffe's estimate of two-thirds of students undertaking at least one act of post-registration truancy. Of course, all schools will have a minority of pupils who consistently 'bunk off' lessons, but it seems quite probable from these figures that a sizeable proportion of the schools involved with the project will have an internal truancy problem of similar proportions to that which is estimated by the North London team. What this exercise does demonstrate is that numbers of post-registration truants, even on the scale identified by Stoll and O'Keeffe, can easily remain invisible and untraced unless active checking is introduced.

More boys than girls truanted from lessons, although the difference is not greatly significant. What does stand out is the predominance of missing senior pupils. Post-registration truancy does seem to be most common among Year 9, 10 and 11 students, the same age group whose overall attendance is generally the poorest.

The most commonly missed subjects from these audits were English, Maths, PE and French, but a number of other subjects were also affected, and it seems that truanting from individual lessons could well be widespread across the curriculum.

One of the schools started running internal truancy audits on a daily basis the week before the official project audit took place. Its first audit identified seven truants, but after three days of checking, there were no truants found in the project audit at all. It seems clear that in the case of this school, regular checks on lesson attendance succeeded in temporarily eradicating post-registration truancy. Running daily lesson checks on a long-term basis, however, may prove to be counter-productive. While daily audits may be an effective deterrent against 'opportunistic' truants who want to miss the odd lesson, pupils who are absconding regularly from lessons in which they are having problems and getting into trouble for it as a result of daily lesson checks may be tempted to stay away from school altogether if their problems are not treated sympathetically by staff. As we are already aware from our pupil interviews, post-registration truancy can easily develop into block truancy if it is not identified and dealt with in an appropriate manner.

In view of the level of post-registration truancy being admitted by pupils via surveys, it was considered important within this authority to consider systems to deal with the problem. Schools require effective strategies that take as little time and effort as possible and preferably with low cost implications. Pupils need to know that any system is highly likely to identify lesson truants. In this way opportunists are far less likely to try to truant since there is a distinct possibility that they will be caught and have to face the consequences.

Most high schools operate some form of lesson registration. This has become even more important with annual report systems that indicate lesson attendance over the course of the year. It is therefore relatively easy on a manual or computerised registration system to institute mechanisms that make these easy to check. Several different methods are being used effectively within the Leeds LEA.

Some schools using manual registers require staff members to produce a list of absentees for each session that are collated at the office. Sometimes these are circulated to staff for checking against lesson registers. In other schools members of teaching staff are themselves expected to check their lesson registers at some point during the school day. Schools using computerised registration will produce an absence list after registration which is either placed in staff areas around the school to facilitate checking or is combined onto a sheet of A4 paper and reproduced so that every member of staff has his or her own copy. One school began this process the same morning as computerised registration began within the school. The number of identified absentees reduced from eight on the first morning to none by the end of the week. Students became convinced that the computer could 'see' them leaving school.

Other schools have developed a system of random checks. At any point during the week members of staff are required to identify the pupils who are not present at their lesson and this list will be checked centrally against the session absentees.

Schools operating the SIMS[1] attendance module have the facility to operate a similar check to that above using optically mark-read forms and with the report produced by the computer. Other computerised systems enable schools to check at every lesson for absentees, but these often require a considerable investment by the school that may well be disproportionate to the problem that the school is facing.

Any of the above systems make it possible for schools to identify those pupils who are truanting and give staff an opportunity to address the situation. Opportunist lesson truants will be easily dealt with by such a system, but for those pupils who have a problem, either in or out of school, the way that the truancy is handled may mean the difference between encouraging the pupil back into the education system or forcing him or her into full-time truancy instead.

Conclusion

Having established the usefulness of data in the development of effective attendance policies, it is not an unexpected conclusion that data can also be used to feed the development of other policies within the school. Such data input within this authority is already common in many related areas such as behaviour, anti-bullying, delivery of the curriculum and raising standards of achievement.

The need for adequate accurate data has led to the development of a variety of information technology tools. Several years ago the Leeds Attendance and Behaviour Project was approached by two schools within the authority who were concerned that valuable strategic information with regard to improving behaviour was being left unused in pupils' files. Both schools operated a system affectionately referred to as 'pink slip systems'. Incidents of poor behaviour in or out of the classroom were recorded on pink slips and passed on to pastoral staff (form tutors, heads of year, key stage co-ordinators) for information, where the incident had been dealt with, or for further action if the incident was sufficiently serious. Invariably, once finished with, the slips went into pupils' files and were never seen again unless the young person was unfortunate enough to end up in the position of being excluded. What both schools wanted was some way of analysing the information on these slips so that they were able to identify individuals' problems earlier and address trends across the school with more targeted and informed behaviour and anti-bullying policies. The result of this request has been the development of the Behaviour Database© that performs the exact functions which the schools required plus many more. Positive as well as negative behaviour reports can now be recorded and analysed, giving school managers accurate information on which to base their strategies for improvement. The development of such a powerful tool has met a demand in schools and the LEA for ways to maximise the efficiency of limited resources.

The production of behaviour questionnaires for parents, pupils and staff has enabled schools to produce policies which address common concerns expressed by the respondents and to develop ways to advertise and reinforce schools' work in the area of improving behaviour within the communities which they serve.

Exclusions analysis on an authority-wide basis using specifically constructed databases enables schools to look at their own exclusion rate in comparison to other similar schools and promotes the sharing of good practice by searching for creative solutions to behaviour problems. It also gives authorities information necessary to target resources into specific schools or areas or into categories of exclusion, whether specific types of behaviour or problems with imbalance in gender, ethnicity of age of these pupils being excluded. Such targeted activity has been responsible for an estimated reduction of over 30 per cent in permanent exclusions within this authority over the last two years.

Schools for many years have gathered information about their exam performance as a measure of how they are performing. The expanded national programme of assessment has made it possible for authorities to feed back to schools information based upon their own performance at different ages, in a range of areas, and in comparison to other schools across the authority. Such information allows schools to highlight areas of weakness and focus activity on overcoming problems and raising standards specifically, thus maximising the efficiency of their efforts.

If data are to be used effectively, they must be seen as part of a process and not an end in themselves. Whilst nationally data are distributed as a means for parents and the public to grade success on an individual, school or authority level, their most powerful use is in enabling managers to focus on areas for improvement and to monitor the methods being used to further such aims. The flow of information also facilitates the review process with changing situations within LEAs and schools highlighted, enabling changes in strategies to meet these changing needs.

Note

1 The SIMS Attendance Module is a management information system for schools. It consists of basic administration information such as pupil data and staff data, provides a financial system for schools, and also provides timetabling, achievement and reporting systems for schools and their pupils. The Attendance Module is an integrated part of that system drawing relevant information from other modules. The system was first designed to be used with optically mark-read forms but can also be used with swipe cards and with BROMCOM, a system which uses keypads to collect the information in class and radio to send that information immediately to the office. The optically mark-read system gives good accurate information which will enable most schools to effectively manage their attendance without having massive implications on school budgets. Once the attendance information is read from the forms, schools can immediately obtain absence lists with home information to enable the pursuance of first-day absence contact systems, to provide information for teaching staff for the monitoring and prevention of post-registration truancy,

and to enable primary schools to provide information to dining rooms about pupil numbers. Statistical information about individual pupils and groups of pupils for any time periods can be easily produced to assist in the support of schools' attendance policies, and indeed to focus the strategies of the developing policy taking account of emerging problems identified through the use of the system.

6

THE ESSENTIAL ELEMENTS
OF AN EFFECTIVE
ATTENDANCE POLICY

Kay Bardsley, Peter Costa and Jo Walton

Why have an attendance policy?

The advent of school inspections led by the Office for Standards in Education (OFSTED) has produced a plethora of policies in schools. It is not unusual for individuals – or exceptionally small groups – of teachers to work late into the night to produce policies to quench the inspectorial thirst for documentation, thereafter to become consigned to dust-gathering shelves. Such policies are destined to fail for the simple reason that the extent of their ownership is limited to one person, or at best a few people. Policies in schools have three main functions:

- to reconcile external requirements and legislation with the ethos and character of the school;
- to reinforce the consensus and values of the school; and
- to improve consistency between staff.

Attendance policies need to fulfil *all* of these functions if they are to be effective. In the case of external requirements, there is a substantial body of legislation and local practice that schools need to incorporate. Policies are also excellent vehicles for stressing the values of the school in order to persuade pupils that school is an important place to be. Finally one of the most important factors in improving attendance is a high level of staff consistency in registration procedures and the follow-up of absence. A good, well-thought-out and well-negotiated policy can be a potent way of encouraging staff consistency.

The policy formation process

Any locally determined policy will need to take account of legislation and other requirements which are to be found in the Education Acts, departmental circulars (DFE, 1991; DFE, 1994) and in statutory instruments (Education [Pupils' Attendance Records] Regulations 1991; Pupils' Registration [Amendment] Regulations 1994; Education [Pupil Registration] Regulations 1995). (See also Milner and Blyth and Blacktop and Blyth in this volume for a general discussion of the legislative framework concerning school attendance.)

While there are principles that can be applied to any attendance policy, no two attendance policies will be exactly the same. Policies of any type need to reflect the nature of the school, its intake and its existing procedures and set-up. In order to ensure the most appropriate strategies are being employed, schools need, in advance of policy formulation, to gather relevant information and analyse it with due regard to their own position. There are three major areas of information to be explored, and these include good practice, the hard data of attendance figures and the soft data of attitude and opinions of pupils, parents/carers, staff and governors.

Teachers, administrators and Education Welfare Officers (EWOs) have over the years developed many solid and ingenious techniques for improving attendance with individuals and groups and for maintaining good attendance rates once achieved. Discussion between schools, especially in the immediate area, with the EWO for the school and with teachers within the school, will elicit much good practice. Across the country, authorities and GEST (Grants for Education Support and Training) funded projects have produced documentation on the accumulated areas of good practice and these provide a relevant source of information for schools. HMI (DES, 1991), the DFEE (Learmonth, 1995) and OFSTED (1995a) have produced information, providing schools with an idea of what they expect to find in place at school.

Attendance data are a mainstay of the policy because they will indicate to the school the problems that the policy needs to address. There is, for example, little point in the policy addressing the issue of excessive lateness in great detail if this is not a substantial problem and instead the major cause of absence over the course of the school year is parental holidays in school time. Whole-school, year group, individual class and individual pupil figures can tell schools a great deal about their own trends and the effectiveness of strategies being used to improve attendance. What is important is that schools address within their policies constructive and effective registration procedures to ensure the ease of gathering data for analysis and to serve the policy implementation.

In order for policies to be living documents, it is important that all those persons involved in the policy feel ownership. The easiest way to consult with staff, governors, parents/carers and pupils is to survey them. This gives them the opportunity to give their opinion on the problems and solutions and can provide valuable insights for staff into the perceptions of other groups. Having consulted the various groups about their opinions, they are more likely to feel part of the process and accept the resulting demands of the policy on their time. Most parents/carers, for example, who say that they would welcome some system of first-day absence contact, will not be opposed towards its introduction. Surveys also provide a different perception on the causes of absence. It is significant that absences that are regarded by many staff as a result of lack of parental support are seen by pupils and parents/carers to be a result of domestic difficulty, and a lack of motivation is seen by pupils as being insufficient interesting work to do.

Registration procedures

Essential to all policies are effective registration procedures. The way in which registers are taken not only affects the accuracy of the data held by the school but also gives a clear message to pupils about the school's attitude to attendance and punctuality. Our research indicates that a clear time framework for what happens when is essential so that all staff treat all pupils in a consistent way. Consider, for example, a situation where one member of staff marks his register at 9.00 a.m. and another marks hers at 9.10 a.m. Two children walking to schools together and arriving at their different classrooms at 9.05 a.m. will have different marks: one being marked present and the other present late. Any late follow-up will be totally unfair and the pupils' records at the end of the school year will portray the same information in a completely different way. A year head writing a reference for each child for a job or a college placement may well be in the position of consciously choosing between them based on inaccurate information.

The time the registers are to be returned to the office will influence the school's routines for dealing with late-comers. It is important for health and safety reasons that all pupils who arrive on site irrespective of arrival time are recorded in some way. This also facilitates follow-up of excessive lateness, especially where this results in the pupil 'losing his or her mark'. Where the school has adopted other areas of good practice, other information may need to be produced from the registers on a regular basis. Where the school is following a system of first-day absence contact, for example, it may be necessary to produce an absence list after registration. Such lists can also be circulated for staff, especially in secondary schools, to check against subject registers in strategies to prevent post-registration truancy.

Letters of follow-up for children who have been absent without explanation should be designed in advance and be available for use by relevant members of staff. Systems need to be designed to ensure that those letters are used at the right times and are sent out consistently.

On a weekly, monthly or termly basis, attendance statistics may be required to promote good attendance through reward systems. Class rewards may require staff to maintain totals and calculate percentages for individuals or their own class on a daily, weekly or termly basis, and these requirements should be written into procedures to ensure their consistent application.

Computerised registration considerably reduces the amount of time spent by staff in the production of any necessary lists or figures and releases staff to perform those tasks for which they are trained, that is, delivering the curriculum effectively.

Consideration also needs to be given to the production of reports required at various times of the year. A 'who?, what?, where?' analysis has been found valuable in this respect. Accurate information is essential to the smooth running of any attendance policy and its development depends upon feedback of its effectiveness. Rigorous registration procedures will promote the production of such information and will also ensure fair and consistent application of the policy to all staff, pupils and parents/carers, for the benefit of all.

Immediate response to absence

Official guidelines on improving school attendance point to the follow-up of short-term absence as being a crucial factor in the establishment and maintenance of good attendance rates in school (DES, 1989; DFEE, 1994). A system which effectively follows up short-term absence will help to ensure that the number of unauthorised absences are kept to a minimum; it will also alert schools to emerging patterns of authorised absence as noted by the DFEE (1994).

At the Leeds Attendance and Behaviour Project it has been found that an immediate response to short-term absence is the single most effective strategy a school can use to improve its attendance rates. The essence of good practice is prompt action by vigilant form or class teachers.

We advocate a system of first-day absence contact. This places responsibility for notifying the school about a child's absence on the parents/carers. Leaflets inform carers that the school expects them to tell the school about a child's absence on the first day. Some parents/carers will find it difficult to send in written notification, others find it difficult to contact the school by phone during school hours because of time constraints, or because school telephone lines are heavily used at the beginning of the day. In response to this, some schools have found it very useful to install a dedicated telephone line, with an answer machine for times when the phone cannot be staffed, solely for taking absence messages.

If parents/carers have not contacted the school by a predetermined time, a member of the school staff will contact them. Telephone contact is preferred but letters are used where this is not possible. Parents/carers are asked to provide a telephone number where they can be contacted during the day. If they are not on the phone a relative or friend may be prepared to take and pass on messages. In Leeds schools operating the system, inner city schools estimate that they can contact 80 per cent of parents/carers in this way; in outer area schools the figure rises to 90 per cent.

In school, a list is produced each day of the pupils who are absent from morning registration. Those pupils whose absences have been explained and late arrivals are eliminated from the list, as are those pupils who are chronic non-attenders and have an EWO working with them. The list is passed to the member of staff who is assigned to make telephone contact with the carers. This person should preferably be someone in authority in the school.

Where schools are operating computerised registration systems, an absence list can be produced easily with the relevant information to enable home contact. Where manual systems are used, it may be necessary for those staff registering pupils to produce an absence list at the time of registration which can be collated for those members of staff performing the function of parent/carer contact. Reasons for absence can then be recorded and any problems that come to light can be resolved or a strategy determined in order to tackle them. Consistency is the key to the effective use of the system. To benefit from the system a school must pursue the contact with all first-day absentees in the school every day. The system seems to have three main benefits to the schools. It enables staff to identify problems as they emerge; enables schools to work in partnership with parents/carers, thereby improving home–school links; and helps to maintain and improve attendance rates in the school.

Our research suggests that a strength of the system is in identifying problems as they emerge. It may be, for example, that a child is being bullied or is having difficulties with a lesson or a teacher. Difficulties can be dealt with at an early stage, preventing them becoming entrenched and resulting in a long-term attendance problem.

Our evidence suggests that a majority of parents/carers appreciate the system and see it as a sign that the school cares about its pupils. In a survey of 425 primary school carers by the Leeds Attendance and Behaviour Project, 70 per cent answered 'yes' to the question: 'Do you think it is a good idea for schools to contact home on your child's first day of absence?' A similar question answered by 680 high school carers in a postal questionnaire elicited 65 per cent support. Notably, in the latter sample, only 5 per cent of respondents did not think it was a good idea. Anecdotal evidence from the schools supports this.

Improved attendance rates

In a survey of 1,379 pupils in five inner city high schools in Leeds, all of which had developed a system to follow up short-term absence, pupils were asked: 'Have school ever phoned home when you were absent and what effect did this have?' Nineteen per cent of the pupils who had been contacted at home said that the contact had made them return from the absence sooner than they would otherwise have done. A further 9 per cent of the sample said the contact had prompted them not to take any further days off.

A postal survey of 17 high schools found that eight undertook first-day absence contact; of these, six said they thought their attendance had improved as a result of the system.

Awards, incentives and raising the profile of good attendance

The emphasis of much of the attendance policy will be on reactive work, that is, follow-up procedures and monitoring strategies. However, policy-makers must also consider the positive and the proactive; to promote regular attendance at school amongst the whole school community (DFEE, 1994). The work of the Leeds Attendance and Behaviour Project has identified two interconnected areas that help do this: raising the profile of attendance issues amongst the whole-school community; and the recognition of good attendance through a system of incentives and awards. These should form an integral part of the school's attendance policy:

> The positive recognition of good school attendance forms an essential part of a whole school approach to promoting good attendance within the school. It gives cohesion to a positive school ethos which routinely recognises good behaviour and good work and provides incentives for pupils to aim at and maintain a high level of attendance.
>
> (Leeds City Council, 1993, DI)

OFSTED inspectors expect schools to have active monitoring systems and strategies for monitoring good attendance. Any system of awards must operate consistently across the school. If the head of Year 7 promotes the system but the head of Year 8 does not, then the system will falter and fail. Each member of staff within a school must be committed to the scheme if it is to succeed. Senior management support is essential and within the senior management team there should be a member of staff responsible for monitoring its effectiveness and ensuring that the scheme is practised consistently.

Rewarding attendance must be looked at creatively. While the achievement of 100 per cent attendance may deserve special accolade, it is unrealistic to set that target for all pupils. Some may have had illnesses or other unavoidable problems that have prevented them attending every day. Many schools have set up a graduated system of awards whereby bronze certificates are available for those with 90 per cent attendance, silver for those with 95 per cent and gold for 100 per cent. A structured system like this will encourage good attendance by giving recognition to attainable targets. Consideration should also be given to the time periods over which good attendance is recognised. The guiding principle should be to strike a balance between maintaining the value of the awards while making them realistic and accessible to all pupils.

The majority of children attend school most of the time; some of them in difficult circumstances, and this achievement deserves recognition. There is also a group of children who attend most of the time but may be poor time-keepers or have a tendency to take a few more days off than are really necessary. This group could be persuaded to attend more often and more punctually through form and year tutors' efforts in informing pupils at regular intervals of the importance of good attendance. There is scope for covering attendance-related topics as part of the curriculum: for example, the history of compulsory school attendance and truancy in History; the life of a truant in English or Drama; analysis of attendance data in Maths; how pupils get to school/where they live in Geography. Many schools encourage pupils to monitor their own attendance by completing a card each week in tutor time.

Graphs charting class attendance rates are displayed in some schools. Several have used this as a basis for group awards. The danger with this is that the same group will be recognised each week and a group with a chronic non-attender may never be rewarded. To overcome this difficulty, the basis on which the award is given can be changed on a week-by-week basis. The best-attended class may get the award one week, followed by the group with the best punctuality or the least unauthorised absence. Primary schools in particular have commented on the usefulness of this. In a recent survey of 28 schools that had worked on the project, 96 per cent had some method of recognising good attendance. Having a system which awards good attendance will raise the profile of attendance around the school. In surveys of pupils about attendance at school, individual awards are generally rated highly as incentives for good attendance. Most popular are those things that can be taken home to parents/carers.

Home–school contact

Research within Leeds (Leeds City Council, 1993b) has found that attempts to improve home–school links through recognising parents/carers as partners in their child's education have had positive influences on attendance rates and are further reinforced by raising the profile of attendance matters. Contact with parents/carers can be achieved through a variety of means both relating to attendance matters and by promoting general information with parents/carers on areas of school life.

If the partnership is to work to its full potential, parents/carers need to feel that their input is important and their opinions matter. Where communications are good and schools keep parents/carers informed and vice versa, pupils are enabled to concentrate their efforts on getting the best out of their education. Some children take advantage of poor lines of communication to 'play off' home against school to the detriment of their own school career. Where parents/carers feel at ease with the system they are willing to make use of it.

It is clear that the route through which most parents/carers get their first information about the school is the prospectus. This should contain clear statements about all the school's expectations, including attendance and punctuality. The school's requirements and system for receiving information in the event of absence should also be clearly explained, together with advice on the nature of authorised and unauthorised absence. This needs to be clearly communicated to parents/carers, however. Many schools produce leaflets aimed specifically at attendance and punctuality matters that are regularly issued to parents/carers throughout the school year. These

- need to be direct and easy to read;
- should be as short as possible; and
- should make use of graphics instead of reams of text wherever possible.

Efforts should also be made to provide letters in appropriate community languages as well as English. Pupils from minority ethnic groups should always be given communications in both languages so that those parents/carers who are unable to read English can be saved the embarrassment of requesting a translation of the English document.

Newsletters may also be used as a way to get information home to parents/carers about attendance. Regular feedback on the overall attendance rate at school – for example, the difficulties being experienced in terms of parental holidays or bad weather – keeps parents/carers in the picture about the effect that their child's absence is having on overall school attendance. Highlighting the achievement of pupils with 100 per cent attendance or punctuality will also serve to raise the profile of attendance and give talking points for parents/carers with their children at home about school. Feedback to parents/carers about their own child's attendance on a regular basis, once a term instead of once a year, will serve to remind parents/carers of their responsibilities and encourage children. Informing parents/carers quickly when their child's attendance is causing concern gives them the opportunity to intervene with their own child or opens the lines of communication which enable parents/carers to ask school for help when they are having difficulties.

One high school identified a lesson every week for each form tutor when he or she would be kept off the substitution list if an appointment had been arranged with a parent/carer. Within the first two terms, form tutors had met most of their pupils' parents/carers and dialogue had begun. Having identified a person in school, parents/carers were far more likely to phone into school to give prompt information about problems and make possible early interventions.

Parents/carers' rooms are a valuable resource. Such a room signifies to parents/carers that staff welcome their visits and that they want them to share in helping their child make the best of his or her education. Many parents'/carers' own experience of school was not good and provision of a room where they do not feel under scrutiny by staff and pupils helps to put them at their ease and make school a more welcoming and friendly establishment.

Attention needs to be paid to clear signposting in schools. In the first instance, is the school's position obvious from the main roads? Many parents/carers are put off by the difficulty of getting to the school and then into the school building.

When parents/carers need to come into school to meet with specific members of staff it is always worth considering the offer of transport. It may be possible for the school's EWO or someone with responsibility for home–school liaison to perform such a task. Often once the first visit is completed parents/carers find school less intimidating and are prepared to make the trip themselves in the future.

It may be appropriate to involve other members of the community, perhaps community leaders or interpreters, to faciliate good communication when meeting with parents/carers from minority ethnic groups.

When teachers visit parents/carers at home it clearly indicates that school staff care since such activities fall outside their normal activities. Schools have often found joint home visits between teachers and EWOs effective where pupils are causing concern. Many schools are finding that visiting the new intake is a valuable exercise in promoting co-operation between school and home. This has become common practice on intake to nursery, and where it is practised at reception or transfer between primary and high school it has also proved useful.

One of the easiest ways of involving parents is asking for their opinions. Parents/carers like to feel included in their child's education and asking for their views promotes good relations, whether it is on the best ways to improve attendance rates, school uniform or their homework expectations.

Schools can also be useful in involving parents/carers in their own continuing education; whether this is the provision of parenting classes or the opportunity to pursue qualifications, education breaks down barriers. Becoming a community resource raises the profile of school and education in general with parents/carers and thus enhances pupil experiences of their own education.

Education Welfare Officers

EWOs are pivotal to the success of an attendance policy. As such they should be involved in the formulation of the policy. Their expertise in improving school attendance and knowledge about strategies used in other schools are invaluable resources. Indeed, the EWO's time must be employed strategically to ensure the best attendance for the school as a whole. Time should be spent analysing where the attendance problems within school are at their most acute. For example, it may be that there is a particular problem in a year group with a group of pupils who are at risk of exclusion. The EWO could work together with them in a groupwork context. In a primary school situation, a group of carers might be identified who are experiencing difficulty organising their children to get to school in the morning. The EWO may decide to form a support group for these parents/carers. He or she may also be involved in campaign work – addressing assemblies to give information about these issues, or raising the profile of his or her own role around the school and in the community. The EWO will have a wide variety of contacts with other agencies and can thus be a valuable source of information about initiatives and help. Within the policy there should be clear guidelines about the stages that school staff should go through before the EWO becomes actively involved in tackling the attendance problem.

Child employment

Young people can gain useful experience and income from having jobs while they are at school, with positive effects on their attendance and educational performance (Lavalette *et al.*, 1995). However, a large-scale study of 1,827 secondary school children in Birmingham found that of the 43 per cent of children employed, three-quarters were employed illegally (Pond and Searle, 1991). A similar study in Leeds found over a third of secondary school children in employment (Leeds City Council, 1993c), with a large proportion working illegally. In most LEAs the enforcement of child employment legislation falls to the Education Welfare Service. However, EWOs, already doing school attendance work, are often over-stretched, and this additional duty may tend to take a lower priority.

The employment of children can affect attendance and the issue should therefore form part of the policy on attendance. How, then, can schools ensure that the work their pupils are engaging in falls within the law and will not be to the detriment of their attendance or performance at school? Part of the attendance policy can be proactive in informing children and parents/carers about the law on child employment regarding permitted working hours and types of employment and practical issues such as obtaining a work permit.

These can be addressed in a variety of forums, including assemblies, Personal and Social Education (PSE) lessons and tutor time. Again, these can be integrated into the curriculum and made a learning experience by, for example, conducting surveys about pupil employment.

The school EWO may be invited to address groups of pupils about the legislation governing child employment and his or her role in enforcing it. He or she may also be able to run drop-in sessions giving pupils advice about obtaining work permits and so on. The Education Welfare Service may run forums for local businesses that inform and educate the business community in ensuring that their employment of youngsters is legal. Members of the governing body may be instrumental in setting up these forums.

Transfers

> Where a school manages the induction of new pupils skilfully, and explains the process to new parents/carers with care, the conditions for the highest rates of attendance can be set from the beginning.
>
> (DES, 1989b: 27)

Transfers of pupils fall into two broad categories: those that occur when a child moves into the education system or between phases; and those when a child moves between schools within the same phase. The principles behind induction remain the same in both cases, but the handling in terms of schools policy is likely to be different.

Much good practice in the area of ordinary transfer is already seen in the primary phase. Many nursery pupils are visited prior to intake so that parents/carers are given an idea of what to expect, pupils are able to meet the staff with whom they will be working in school, and staff have the opportunity of assessing the pupils' ability and background and preparing a smooth entry for them. Some high schools have also found this a useful exercise. Parents/carers invariably see home visits as a sign of the school's concern for the child in their care. Where visits to all the new intake are impracticable because of numbers, then some high schools have operated a system of identifying pupils who may be at risk of developing attendance or behaviour problems and making home visits with the EWO.

Information is made available to parents/carers of potential pupils through a variety of outlets. Local community resources such as health centres, libraries, religious buildings and even supermarkets are often willing to mount display materials or to have leaflet information available. Parents/carers and pupils are invited to visit schools on specific open days or by appointment and parents/carers receive information directly by post once allocations have taken place.

'Buddying' schemes, where pupils from the high school make friends with pupils from feeder primary schools before transfer and continue to meet with them after transfer, have also proved very effective in promoting smooth transfer.

Once pupils are due to start at a new school, staggered entry may be considered as appropriate, with each group of pupils being allowed to settle in before the next group arrives. In the case of nursery and reception, this process may be completed over several weeks, although in high schools it usually involves the new intake being with their own form tutors for a morning or a day while other pupils come in later.

Extraordinary transfers cause most problems for schools, who often complain that the pupils with the worst attendance or behaviour records came to them 'late' or they were directed to take them because the school was not full. The handling of such transfers can, however, make an impact on pupils' attendance and attitudes in their new school. Extraordinary transfers happen for a number of reasons and each needs to be looked at separately, with a course of action decided upon and executed depending on the circumstances to ensure positive results. An individual assessment needs to be made about the pupil's own development to ensure correct placing within the school's own curriculum and pastoral structure. This will involve, wherever possible, negotiating with the school from which the pupil is transferring. Where the pupil has been excluded from one school or has been transferred because of a 'care' move, it is important to negotiate with the previous school to establish an appropriate reintegration programme which may be similar to those produced for reintegrating long-term absentees. Liaison with the EWO is also advisable, especially if there is an ongoing problem or involvement with the family. Parents/carers should be involved in the negotiation process and encouraged as far as possible to resolve differences with the previous school.

Pupils should begin at the start of a week when all relevant information has been gathered and all staff are aware of the new pupil's arrival.

Reintegration of long-term absentees

Long-term absentees can be divided into two broad categories: those who will not go to school; and those who cannot go to school because of some physical or psychological difficulty. Experience tends to suggest that the longer an absence continues, the more an individual pupil's problems become entrenched, moving the pupil into the second of these categories. Long-term absentees present huge problems to schools staff when they do eventually return to school. The reintegration of a long-term absentee, therefore, involves a co-ordinated effort between school, parents/carers, the pupil and the Education Welfare Service and any other agency that has been involved with the young person.

It may be valuable for schools to devote a section of their attendance policy to the reintegration of long-term absentees. This can range from simple strategies that all staff and pupils are encouraged to adopt, to outlining the pastoral structure through which all long-term absentees will be fed.

Cheerful greetings, sensitivity towards the absentee who has turned up but wants to hide his or her embarrassment, alertness to the pupil who comes in looking fraught or under the weather, all convey positive hidden messages about the school's interest in pupils.

Agreement needs to be met by all parties involved in the return of a long-term absentee as to the individual plan to be followed, taking into account the individual's unique circumstances. It may be appropriate for the young person to return in a phased re-entry, only attending for a set number of hours in the first week and gradually building up the time spent in school until he or she is attending full-time at the end of the third or fourth week. Some pupils may require support away from specific subject classrooms to enable them to get to a stage where they can understand the work being done in those classrooms. Alternatively, it may be appropriate to have extra support available for them in the classroom. Other pupils with the same timetable may be enlisted to help the returning pupil to get to grips with the school timetable again and prevent him or her from getting lost. It may also be appropriate to prepare social groups in advance to accept pupils into their circle and thus make 'fitting in' easier. Teachers also need to make sure that their attitude to pupils is a positive one. Long-term absentees are pupils with special needs and should be seen as such within the school. Success will not occur overnight and there may be difficulties and setbacks to overcome on the way. Patience is the key.

Steering the policy development process

The attendance policy as developed by the Leeds Attendance and Behaviour Project (Leeds City Council, 1994) has a definite structure:

- *Introduction to the policy and its links with the values of the school.* This would include a statement of rights and responsibilities which links to the mission statement of the school. This part of the policy embodies the values of the school and links the policy to all the other policies of the school. The mission statement may therefore be the mission statement for the whole school. The general statement of rights and responsibilities needs to be made more specific through a series of statements of expectations: what the school expects from pupils; what the school expects from parents/carers; and what parents/carers and pupils can expect from the school.
- *How good attendance will be encouraged.* A description of the ways in which the school intends to encourage good attendance. This will include rewards that are to be used as well as other aspects of the way in which attendance is to be encouraged: recording and charting, Records of Achievement, Compact[1], and so on, but also through the curriculum and parental involvement.

- *How the school will respond to poor attendance.* A description of the way in which the school will respond when faced with poor attendance or punctuality. This will include sanctions, such as late detentions, as well as other, more supportive aspects such as: letters home, first day of absence contact and follow-up. Other things a school will need to consider will be: links with outside agencies (e.g. EWS); meetings with parents/carers; support and reintegration procedures.
- *Clarification of roles and responsibilities.* This section of the policy describes the way in which the school intends to put the rest of the policy into practice on a day-to-day basis. This will include the roles and responsibilities of staff, especially the pastoral staff of the school, but will also include details of what subject teachers are required to do, especially with respect to the keeping of lesson registers, internal truancy controls and follow-up of non-attendance.

A policy is not just a document, rather, to be effective, it has to represent and reinforce a real consensus in the school. The process by which a policy is developed, introduced and implemented and owned by all members of the school community is absolutely essential to its success (see also Samson and Hart, 1995). A good action plan details the way in which the various parts of the policy will be brought into operation and outlines the strategy that the school may engage in to raise the profile of attendance issues and publicise the policy to the student body as well as parents/carers. The action plan could also detail the way in which the work on attendance and attendance issues can be integrated into the curriculum. At the centre of the action plan is the target for attendance. Except in very rare situations, this will involve some improvement in attendance. In many cases it is possible for schools quickly and easily to achieve large increases in attendance in a short time as a result of a campaign. However, such increases are almost always short-lived because the necessary organisational changes have not been made, and attendance levels fall back. It is more realistic for schools to set smaller targets such as sustained year-on-year growth in attendance of 2–3 per cent and aim to achieve this through underlying structural changes and improvements in practice.

Conclusion

This chapter has concerned itself with the development of a good attendance policy. It has been written with the intention of showing the degree of preparation and development work that would go into such a good attendance policy. It is clear that a vibrant living policy cannot be produced in a short time but requires much work. This is work that is worthwhile because it will not be limited to attendance issues alone, for the improved staff consistency resulting from the detailed planning for good attendance will yield results in almost every other area of school life.

Appendix: A sample attendance policy

1. Aims

Bramley Grange School is committed to providing a full and efficient education for all pupils. We believe that all pupils benefit from education and from regular school attendance. To this end we will organise and do all we can to ensure that all pupils attend school to their fullest and that any problems that impede full attendance are identified and acted upon as soon as possible.

2. Expectations

We expect the following from all pupils:

- that they will attend school regularly;
- that they will arrive on time and be appropriately prepared for the day;
- that they will inform a member of staff of any problem that may hinder them from attending school.

We expect the following from parents/carers:

- to encourage their children to attend school;
- to ensure that they contact the school whenever their child is unable to attend school;
- to ensure that their children arrive in school well prepared for the school day and to check that they have done their homework;
- to contact the school in confidence whenever any problem occurs that may keep them away from school.

Parents/carers and pupils can expect the following from the school:

- regular, efficient and accurate recording of attendance;
- early contact with parents/carers when a pupil fails to attend school without providing good reason;
- immediate and confidential action on any problem notified to us (confidential means that the member of staff notified will not disclose that information to anybody without the consent of the pupil or their parent/carer);
- we will take steps to encourage good attendance;
- a quality education.

3. Encouraging attendance

We will encourage attendance in the following ways:

- accurate completion of the registers at the beginning of each session and within 30 minutes of the start of the session;
- attendance checks at appropriate time;
- recording of good attendance on individual Records of Attainment and in relation to Compact schemes;
- a certificate for 95 per cent and 100 per cent attendance for any one half-term; and a 'Gold' Award for 100 per cent attendance through the year (attendance is 100 per cent if there has been no unauthorised absence);
- an improved attendance certificate for any pupil achieving a greater than 10 per cent improvement in attendance in any one half-term;
- a class trophy to be awarded to the tutor set with the most improved attendance each month and awards for any group with 100 per cent attendance in any month;
- all awards to be presented by the Head of Year;
- targeting and visiting pupils who have attendance problems in the feeder primary;
- holding a special parents'/carers' Consultation Evening for those parents/carers who are concerned that their children may be experiencing difficulty in school;
- sending parents/carers termly attendance figures.

Attendance for each tutor set will be charted and displayed in the entrance foyer.

4. Responding to non-attendance

When a pupil does not attend school, we will respond in the following manner:

- If no note or telephone call is received from parents/carers, the parents/carers will be contacted on the first day of absence by telephone, or, if not on the telephone, then by letter.
- Where there is no response, a second letter will be sent after three days of unexplained non-attendance, or there may be a visit from a member of the school staff (usually the Form Tutor or Head of Year).
- In the event of continued non-attendance, the case will be discussed with the Education Welfare Officer (EWO) for the school and further action planned. This may, in appropriate cases, result in a referral to the Education Welfare Service (EWS).

- After ten days, unless other action is planned, the parents/carers will be invited to attend a meeting in school by the Head of Year. This meeting will include the Form Tutor, EWO, parent/carer and pupil and will aim to identify and solve the problems that are preventing the pupil from attending school.
- If there is no improvement, then the case will be discussed again with the Educational Welfare Service focal worker with a view to a referral being made to the Education Welfare Service. If a referral has already been made, then the case will be reviewed and the meeting used to plan further action.
- The return to school and reintegration for a pupil after long-term absence requires special planning. The Head of Year will be responsible for deciding on the programme for return and the management of that programme. All staff need to be aware that this is a difficult process that will require careful handling and that any problems should be notified to the Head of Year as soon as possible. Programmes will be tailored to individual needs and may involve phased, part-time re-entry with support in lessons as appropriate. Support will be arranged between the Head of Year and the Special Educational Needs Co-ordinator.

The success of the programme will also require liaison between the Head of Year, parents/carers and the EWO.

Staff will be notified of the return of long-term absentees via the staff notices.

5. Organisation

In order for this policy to be successful, every member of staff must make attendance a high priority and convey to the pupils the importance of the education being provided. This means ensuring that all staff arrive on time to lessons and are well prepared.

In addition to this there are the following specific responsibilities:

Head Teacher

- to oversee the whole policy;
- to report to governors.

Pastoral Deputy Head Teacher

- to liaise with Heads of Year;
- to oversee the operation of the SIMS (see Stokes and Walton in this volume, pp. 93–4) system and the collation of attendance data;
- to oversee the work of administrative staff;

- to produce an attendance profile for the whole school;
- to report to the school Senior Management Team on attendance matters.

Heads of Year

- to collate attendance data for the year group;
- to oversee the registration process and ensure that registers are completed accurately and on time;
- to reinforce good practice at year meetings;
- to organise attendance assemblies;
- to initiate contact with parents/carers in cases of prolonged unexplained absence;
- to liaise with EWOs as appropriate;
- to organise returns of long-term absentees in conjunction with the Special Educational Needs department.

Form Tutor

- to complete registers accurately and on time;
- to follow up immediately any unexplained non-attendance by contacting parents/carers;
- to display information on attendance;
- to record all reasons for absence in the register;
- to inform the Head of Year of concerns.

Source: Composite of policies produced as a part of the Leeds Attendance and Behaviour Project (1993–4).

Note

1 Compact schemes are agreements between education and commerce whereby young people, usually at risk of failure at school, are set targets to achieve, for which they receive an award. Rewards can range from a certificate, to work experience, to placement with the company on a youth employment scheme. In the case of attendance, the target to achieve will usually be full attendance at school.

7

STRATEGIES FOR IMPROVING SCHOOL ATTENDANCE

Douglas MacIldowie

Introduction to the Kent Attendance Project[1]

In July 1991 the Department for Education (DFE, 1991) announced that 30 local education authorities had been given Education Support Grant (ESG) funding for initiatives aimed at promoting new strategies for the positive management of attendance issues. From April 1990 to March 1993, Swanley School, a mixed 11–18 comprehensive in north-west Kent, joined forces with the Education Welfare Service (EWS) and four other Kent secondary schools in an ESG-funded project to investigate the reasons for truancy and to develop strategies for improving attendance. Each school appointed an attendance officer from the pastoral staff (where such a role did not already exist), but the greater part of the ESG funding was spent on significantly enhancing each school's allocation of dedicated Education Welfare Officer (EWO) time. The head teachers, attendance officers and EWOs met together regularly to share information, to develop initiatives and to evaluate progress. The LEA gave further support by equipping each school with the SIMS Attendance Module for recording and processing data related to levels and categories of attendance.

Every school likes to report success. In telling a round, unvarnished tale about the progress we made during the attendance project at my former school, I hope to avoid the natural pitfalls of overstating the positive achievements and glossing over the disappointments. Truancy is a subject on which schools have felt sensitive, even vulnerable, especially since DFE Circular 11/91 (DFE, 1991) required the inclusion of unauthorised attendance levels in school prospectuses and governors' annual reports from autumn 1992, and in published school performance tables from autumn 1993. Working on a collaborative venture with neighbouring schools called for a high level of professional trust and mutual respect. Throughout the project, I found my colleagues in the other schools prepared to exchange information and to give frank accounts of their successes and failures.

Consequently each school became a critical friend of the others, providing valuable lessons about strategies for improving attendance.

Any collaborative venture also requires time: time for opposite numbers (head teachers, attendance officers, EWOs) to meet and to prepare reports and statistics for exchange and comparison. In our view this time was well spent, and we appreciated the LEA's support in their publication of four issues of *School Attendance Matters* during the project (Kent County Council, 1993, 1994a, 1994b, 1994c). This occasional broadsheet provided an opportunity to celebrate and share successful strategies during the project.

The statutory framework

The statutory framework within which schools and LEAs work on improving school attendance is addressed in Chapter 1 of this volume, but a significant influence following the Kent Attendance Project was the appearance in May 1994 of the Department for Education's *School Attendance: Policy and Practice on Categorisation of Absence* (DFE, 1994), which offered detailed advice on the reasonable exercise of discretion in authorising absence, where that is permitted in law. Although this advice did not have the force of law, the accompanying letter to head teachers included the caveat: 'Schools should note that their practices in relation to the recording of absence of pupils of compulsory school age will be given particular attention as part of the school inspection process.' The revised *Guidance on the Inspection of Schools* (OFSTED, 1995c) stated that judgements should be based on the extent to which pupils' attendance exceeds 90 per cent. This figure had already become part of the mythology associated with OFSTED inspections and therefore provided the project schools with a minimum target for improvement.

There was one year group, however, in which it was an unattainable target: Year 11. DFE (1994) defined work experience and study leave (both features of the Year 11 programme in most secondary schools) as 'authorised absence' (DFE, 1995: 51–3, 65).[1] Two weeks of work experience, which has become a valued part of the Key Stage 4 curriculum, together with study leave 'in the period immediately prior to public examinations and during the period of examinations themselves' (DFE, 1995: 64) – usually the whole of May and beyond – amount to a minimum of four weeks out of the total of 31 weeks used for annual performance tables (September to May inclusive). This means that it was impossible for a Year 11 pupil to achieve more than 87 per cent attendance even if every available school session were fully attended. Yet OFSTED (1994) guidelines for the inspection of schools, and for the identification of those with serious weaknesses, use 90 per cent as the line below which attendance, either for the whole school or for any year group, should not fall without reasonable explanation! Assuming that Year 11 was exonerated for the above reasons, a level of 87 per cent attendance in that year still had a knock-on effect on the overall percentage for the school. Even with the best possible attendance in Year 11, the rest of the school had to maintain an attendance level of at least 91 per cent. Allowing for a typical level of 7 per cent authorised absence for other reasons such as illness and interviews in Year 11, the target for the rest of the school would have had to increase to 92 per cent actual attendance.

The Secretary of State's announcement in September 1997 (DFEE, 1997a) that from the summer of 1998 all Year 11 pupils will be expected to attend full-time until the end of June is likely to exacerbate the problem of the knock-on effect, despite the White Paper's expressed hope that this change 'will equip a significant minority of young people better for lifelong learning' and claim that 'each year as many as 17,000 young people, *many of them capable of securing good GCSE results* leave school with no qualifications at all' (my emphasis). It has been my experience at more than one large secondary school that nearly all pupils qualified to leave at Easter have in fact stayed on to take their examinations if they had a realistic chance of 'securing good GCSE results'. From the summer of 1998, many schools and EWOs will find themselves hard-pressed to enforce the continued attendance of the small number of pupils for whom the current examination system offers little chance of tangible achievement.

Starting points

During the years leading up to the start of the project, our overall attendance had tended to fall below 90 per cent, with the characteristic decline in Years 10 and 11 (then known as Years 4 and 5). During the project it was our objective to find out why this was happening, and then to take steps to maintain levels of attendance throughout the time our pupils were on our roll. Table 7.1 shows that we succeeded to a degree; we were particularly pleased to see that the Year 9 cohort from 1989/90 avoided the falling off that had characterised their predecessors' attendance pattern when they went into the last two years.

Table 7.2 traces each year cohort from 1989/90 through to 1992/3; it gives an encouraging picture for the original Year 7 but also shows that their fellow-pupils in Year 8 had a consistently lower overall attendance throughout their school career.

This year group included a number of travellers' children whose lifestyle meant prolonged periods of absence during which they were out of the reach of school staff and the EWO, but DFE guidance (DFE, 1991) appeared to require us to count their absence as unauthorised, which we did until advised by the EWS that we could reasonably categorise up to 20 weeks as authorised. The DFE (1994) later ratified this approach. When travellers' children were known to be back in the catchment area, they were encouraged to return to school by the school's Traveller Liaison Officer. She was a

Table 7.1 Swanley School attendance figures, 1989–93 (%)

Year group	1989/90	1990/1	1991/2	1992/3
Year 7	91.60	93.29	92.97	91.50
Year 8	88.63	91.96	92.25	90.00
Year 9	89.19	90.12	90.83	88.80
Year 10	85.57	91.65	89.82	90.00
Year 11	81.21	84.26	90.76	88.50
Total	87.24	90.26	91.28	89.80

learning support assistant who had developed a sympathetic understanding of traveller lifestyle and cultural traditions, consequently gaining the trust and support of most of our traveller families. She encouraged the school to recognise and celebrate the traveller culture, for example with a splendid mural on a school wall and a magazine, *Cushti*, in which the pupils and their families described their traditional lifestyle. Nevertheless, there were several traveller pupils who remained outside the system and whose very occasional attendance had a depressing effect on the overall figures.

The other four secondary schools involved in our part of the Kent project – a boys' and a girls' secondary school in each of two other towns in north Kent (Schools B1, B2, G1 and G2) – had similar initial attendance levels to that of Swanley (Table 7.3)

Comparable schools were identified in the vicinity of three of the project schools as controls. They received no additional resources in terms of EWO support but were given computerised registration facilities. It is interesting that they also improved their attendance during the project period – indicating that the national focus on attendance and the interest being shown by Kent LEA were having the intended effect.

Pursuing attendance issues

When the Kent project began, there was no uniform procedure for pursuing attendance issues, so during the first year a common EWS referral form was

Table 7.2 Swanley School year cohorts traced, 1989–93 (%)

Cohort	1989/90	1990/1	1991/2	1992/3
Year 7/89	91.60	91.96	90.83	90.00
Year 8/89	88.63	90.12	89.82	88.50
Year 9/89	89.19	91.65	90.76	
Year 10/89	85.57	84.26		
Year 11/89	81.21			

Table 7.3 Attendance figures for project and control schools (%)

School	1989/90	1990/1	1991/2	1992/3	1993/4
Swanley	87.49	90.45	91.28	90.34	89.80
S control	87.98	89.55	na	na	na
B1	83.40	85.40	88.40	na	na
G1	82.82	86.94	89.58	na	na
B2	88.00	86.00	89.00	na	na
B2 control	88.66	89.67	90.00	na	na
G2	86.50	88.00	91.00	na	na
G2 control	90.67	89.83	90.50	na	na

adopted and a common system of recording reasons for absence in school registers was developed. Both these initiatives were then introduced across the LEA. Staff at Swanley School recognised many of the factors outlined in the HMI paper *Attendance at School* (DES, 1989b) as contributing to our own pupils' non-attendance. Nevertheless, we felt that there were some pupils whose habitual absence was not attributable to their financial circumstances, or to their experience of school, nor to deep-rooted psychological problems leading to school refusal. We devised our own checklist (Figure 7.1), to be used in a non-threatening interview between any pupil returning after a dubious absence and a trusted member of staff.

During the three-year period of the project, we used this checklist with approximately 40 pupils. Although it did not provide a reliable research base, it did give us some understanding of the individual pupils' concerns and their reasons for non-attendance. It enabled us to provide them with focused counselling sessions with the EWO or pastoral tutors, and helped us to select suitable candidates for the 'circle time' described later in this chapter.

The checklist also alerted us to the existence of a group of de-schooled young people who had either been excluded or had become permanent truants. The older members of this group were past school leaving age and were surviving on the black economy. They had several bases – either their own flats or the homes of permissive parents – and they encouraged younger siblings, their sexual partners and other friends to take days off school and join them. This was a very persuasive alternative to attending school for impressionable teenagers, especially if the current boy- or girlfriend was already part of the group. Countering the 'School's not Cool' philosophy called for skilful counselling rather than repeated statements of our disapproval. For these youngsters, permanent exclusion was seen as a rite of passage, so any uncharacteristically provocative behaviour when they did attend school became recognised as a warning sign that a boy or girl was bidding for full-time membership of the de-schooled group. The counsellors gave a lot of time to these individuals, alerted their group tutors and subject

ESG ATTENDANCE PROJECT: CHECKLIST FOR RESEARCH

NOTE: In questioning pupils about their reasons for truanting, direct questions such as 'Why?' or 'When' are likely to produce short responses, which can then 'trigger' further encouraging questions to focus on more detailed reasons. The following checklist is designed to suggest further questions, and to provide a convenient means of unobtrusively recording the answers in a methodical way.

1. Please complete the following details:

PUPIL'S ADMISSION NUMBER: .... GENDER: M F   YEAR 7 8 9 10 11

PATTERN OF TRUANCY: One-off   Occasional   Regular   Continual

2. Please note reasons for truancy by ticking any that appear in the following checklist, and/or writing other reasons in the appropriate spaces.

Q.	'TRIGGER' RESPONSE	FURTHER Q/ ENCOURAGEMENT	DETAILED REASONS	
WHY?	'BORING'	'Tell me about it.' 'Is there …?'	Too much talk	—
			Too much writing	—
			Don't understand	—
			Can't do	—
			Other	
WHY?	'USELESS'		No good for career	—
			No good for real life	—
			Not doing the exam	—
			Other	
WHY?	'FRIENDS'		Row with friend	—
			Friend was going out	—
			Friend was off school	—
			Friend has left school	—
			Friend doing something (e.g. fishing, concert)	— —
			Other	
WHY?	'TEACHER/S'		Picks on me	—
			Can't understand him/her	—
			Just goes on	—
			Can't work in lesson	—
			Cover teacher	—
			Other	
WHY?	'BULLIED'		Dirty looks	—
			Threats	—
			Name-calling	—
			Interference with work	—
			Interference with property	—
			Physical hurt	—
			Other	
WHY?	'FAMILY'		Needed at home	—
			Rows with neighbours	—
			Other	
WHY?	'SOMETHING BETTER'		Rather be in bed	—
			Work	—
			Hobby	—
			Messing about	—
			Other	

Q.	'TRIGGER' RESPONSE	FURTHER Q/ ENCOURAGEMENT	DETAILED REASONS	
WHEN?	'START OF THE DAY'	Could lead to any of these ...	Particular lesson	__
			Easiest time	__
WHY?	'AFTER DINNER'		Something better to do	__
			Get tired by Friday	__
WHY?	'END OF WEEK'		Nice weather	__
			Other	__
HOW?	'STAY AT HOME'		Pretending to be ill	__
			Really feeling ill	__
			Parents go out early	__
			Parents don't care	__
			Parents don't want me to go to school	__
			Other	__
	'BUNK OFF'		Everyone does it	__
			Easy to get out	__
			Teachers don't check	__
			Cover teachers	__
			Other	__

Please add any other reasons which do not fit into the above:
....
....
....

Figure 7.1 The checklist

teachers to the 'need to greet' them when they made an appearance in lessons, and to take every opportunity to praise and encourage them. Some were given in-school work experience with the caretaker, the grounds staff or the school office and responded really well to being given responsibility and learning some practical skills. Although we did not succeed with all members of this group, we found that we were able to counter the attraction of truancy for a significant number of vulnerable pupils.

Changing the curriculum

During the time of the project we had begun to accumulate evidence through the questionnaire that a significant number of our non-attenders were staying away for reasons that were not related to the school learning experience. Nevertheless, there have been several imposed changes in the curriculum during recent years which have increased the dangers of frustration and failure for some pupils. During the project period we had a very popular post-14 CSE course in Community and Vocational Education. This gave the pupils a non-academic opportunity to develop their inter-personal and social skills in a community placement with supportive mentoring from a teacher. Following the advent of the GCSE, the course continued to receive national accreditation until 1996, since when it has been certificated only by the school. At the same time the compulsory modern foreign language at Key Stage 4 has squeezed the time available for substantial out-of-school experience and provided another academic hurdle for the less able to negotiate.

There have been positive changes, though. For example, we have introduced Business and Information Studies into the Key Stage 4 curriculum and we are planning to develop the Foundation GNVQs as they come onstream. With additional funding from the Basic Skills Agency, since 1996 we have provided an intensive programme for Year 7 pupils whose literacy and numeracy skills on entry signalled that they were unlikely to cope with the curriculum.

Furthermore, a grant from the Prince's Trust in 1996 enabled us to set up an out-of-school club – 'Zone 90' – from 8 a.m. before school and until 5 p.m. after school. Pupils are encouraged to come into a comfortably furnished annexe to the school library, where they can make a simple snack and then do their homework or play indoor games. Volunteer teachers offer help with homework and fill 'guest spots' in the after-school sessions, introducing pupils to new activities such as origami or mime.

These initiatives are all designed to discourage failure and to encourage positive feelings about the school. Initial evaluations are encouraging, and it is hoped that the pupils will continue to find good reasons for coming to school regularly as they grow into young adulthood. All the other schools reviewed the relevance and value in their curriculum from the viewpoint of the potential non-attender. There was general agreement that the most important element in the programme of learning was the frequent opportunity to succeed.

Additional EWO time

The ESG funding for the Kent project was largely spent on increasing the availability of Education Welfare Officers in the five schools. Three additional officers were appointed, which released three experienced EWOs to give their full-time support to the project schools: one to Swanley, one to each of the other pairs of project schools. Each was provided with an on-site office and telephone – fortunately both pairs of schools in the other two towns were on adjacent sites. Their briefs included liaison with feeder primary schools and collecting comparative data from the control schools. In addition a member from the Juvenile Offender Liaison Team (JOLT) in north Kent was seconded half-time to investigate possible links between non-attendance and juvenile crime across the area and to offer counselling sessions to pupils referred by the other project schools.

The appointment of a full-time EWO had a marked and lasting effect on attendance at Swanley School. Once established in his office in September 1991, he began by scrutinising all the registers, writing to all the families where pupils' attendance was poor, pointing out the facts and asking for their support in ensuring regular attendance in the future. Where this correspondence had no effect, he made home visits on the first day of absence which produced a mixed reaction from parents but had a salutary effect on many pupils. He regularly checked the school gates at changes of lessons to discourage post-registration truancy and became a familiar sight at the local market, a favoured haunt for non-attenders, on Wednesdays. Every morning he began with a briefing from the pastoral staff and would then set off straight away to visit youngsters who were suspected of unauthorised absence, in many cases bringing them into school himself. Spot checks, where morning registers were compared with teaching group registers later in the school day, showed that we had very little post-registration truancy, thus enabling us to focus as a school on those pupils who were at risk through habitual, and often parentally condoned, absence.

This initial activity might be seen as mere policing, but the EWO's longer-term contribution was in raising the profile of good attendance throughout the school, which he achieved through regular meetings with the pastoral staff. These colleagues in turn encouraged all the teaching staff to make their contribution, and the quality and accuracy of registering and monitoring attendance improved across the school.

Regular meetings also enabled prompt and sustained feedback about referred pupils and improved communication between school and home. For every parent who saw the EWO as an enemy, either hiding behind the curtains or giving him a mouthful of abuse, there were several who saw him as an ally in persuading a reluctant attender to go to school. More families showed a willingness to come into school to discuss their problems with the staff and to receive regular reports on their children's progress.

As part of his brief, our EWO established a sound relationship with the head teachers and staff of our feeder primary schools, and the early identification of children at risk of becoming poor attenders enabled us to target them in a positive way when they transferred to Swanley School. Such was the value of his support during the project that I had little difficulty in persuading the governors to buy in an extra day per week of his time from 1994 onwards – and at the time of writing he still has his office at Swanley School.

All the schools in the project found that the full-time services of their EWO had an immediate effect on their attendance, especially in Years 9 and 10. The officers themselves enjoyed having a broader role as counsellors and leaders in extra-curricular experiences, some of which are described later in this chapter. Another important contribution was the regular gathering of accurate statistics that were used by the schools in various ways to raise the profile of attendance with staff, pupils, parents and governors. For example, the EWO in one of the pairs of project schools established a baseline attendance figure of 84 per cent. She calculated weekly attendance for each form, and graphs were displayed in every classroom. Classes with 90 per cent or higher attendance were congratulated by the head teacher in assembly and given a certificate. Certificates for 100 per cent attendance were presented to individual pupils on a termly basis. Reluctant attenders were identified and attempts made to integrate them on a gradual basis with a reduced timetable, sometimes staying with one teacher. The EWO personally collected pupils for the first few days until they were ready to come on their own. Known truants were visited and picked up on their first day of absence. The EWO also ran a drop-in centre and counselling sessions at the girls' school. By the end of the project, attendance in both schools had increased overall by 7 per cent.

In all cases, the EWO had a brief that included liaison with the secondary school's main feeder primary schools, which enabled them to identify potentially poor attenders before they made the transfer. This was helpful in identifying youngsters who would particularly benefit from the 'circle time' and out-of-school provision described later in this chapter.

In-school incentives

One of the main thrusts of the project was to raise the profile of attendance throughout the school. This was achieved through assemblies, letters and publications to parents and personal certificates for good attendance. At first we introduced termly individual certificates for individuals who achieved 100 per cent attendance. It soon became clear that in most cases we were rewarding those pupils whose attendance was exceptional but habitual; we were not targeting those pupils whose non-attendance was a cause for concern. We therefore lowered the ceiling and gave certificates for good attendance to those who achieved 95 per cent. It was a logical step from there to move to certificates for *improved* attendance over a shorter period of time, and it was by this means that we really reached the individuals at risk by giving them their own targets.

Another incentive that involved a degree of peer pressure was the introduction of George, an amiable white teddy bear, who was given as a mascot each week to the tutor group with the highest overall attendance. The appeal of George was not restricted to the younger pupils; on one occasion an upper sixth-former was dragged from his bed by fellow students anxious to retain the ursine trophy for a second week. George completed six years' service in the summer of 1998, and he is still in good shape and much sought after. Like all systems, the mascot approach is not perfect. There will always be groups whose regular absentees prevent them from winning the recognition they otherwise deserve. As a means of keeping attendance in view, however, George and his fellow-mascots in other schools do an excellent job. The project schools all found that the development of incentives was more effective than the application of sanctions.

Targeting individuals and groups

While project schools were developing ways of raising the whole profile of good attendance in schools, it soon emerged that there were individual pupils and groups of young people who were particularly unlikely to attend regularly unless they were targeted for particular attention and encouragement.

During the second year of the project at Swanley School, a group of 12 pupils in their first two years were identified as potentially non-attenders. Their parents' permission was sought and given for them to form a group that met weekly on neutral territory (the local youth club) with a non-teaching youth worker and the area JOLT officer. The meetings were organised on the principle of 'circle time', during which they were encouraged to share their thoughts and worries about school in a non-threatening atmosphere. They knew that what they had to say would be listened to, taken seriously and possible personal strategies could be explored. The attendance pattern for eight of the 12 improved significantly as a result of this regular support. Several other pupils preferred to seek individual counselling with the school's attendance officer, a member of the pastoral staff, and they all made progress. Although the discussions at 'circle time' and in counselling sessions remained confidential, it was important that all the teaching and support staff were made aware that these youngsters were making an effort to attend more regularly. Staff agreed on a strategy to support the initiative, which included a low-key but friendly welcome when pupils returned after an absence and a bridging plan for helping them to catch up with work that had been missed.

At another school the EWO and a youth and community worker followed a groupwork programme with nine boys along similar lines. After clarifying objectives and agreeing basic rules at their first session, they moved on to exercises to help increase self-confidence and self-knowledge. Sessions four and five dealt with the interplay of feelings between the boys, their peers, parents and teachers, focusing on bullying and coping with difficult situations. All on the course had experienced physical or emotional bullying. Session six was spent on self-defence and the final session reviewed progress. At the end of each session, held in the local youth club from 11 a.m. to 1 p.m., 20 minutes was devoted to games. From 12.20 p.m. (the start of the school's lunch break) food could be eaten at any time. During the term following the course, there were no referrals for non-attendance on any of the nine boys.

A third Kent school established a Welcome Week, aimed at easing the transition of vulnerable pupils from primary to secondary school, through the adoption of a proactive rather than a reactive response to the potential problem of transferring. Ten children were identified as failing already or being at risk of failing to attend their new secondary school because of poor social skills or low self-esteem. With parental support, they attended a programme of activities during the week before the end of the summer holidays. The programme included a trip to London and outdoor activities including canoeing and orienteering. The group remained in contact with each other and the EWO after transfer to secondary school, and the rapport established with the parents continued during their time at the school.

Computerised registration

The use of computerised register systems such as the SIMS Attendance Module is now commonplace (see Walton and Stokes in this volume for a more detailed discussion of computerised registration). At the time of the project the system was being piloted and, initially, there was some resistance from teaching and support staff, who found its operation more time-consuming than traditional practice. For those staff involved in the Kent project, however, the print-outs made it easy to publish up-to-date information and maintain the high profile. The winners of George the Bear were always announced first thing on Monday mornings, making a positive start to the week. Personal attendance records gave graphic illustration of patterns of non-attendance, and in due course it became possible to demonstrate the relationship between attendance to achievement. Generally, all the project schools found that computerised registration helped in raising attendance. A much more complex system of electronically recording attendance and pupil location through the use of swipe cards was installed at only one school.

Conclusions

Improvement in attendance rates increase when attendance is given an increased profile by all members of the school and allied staff. It is also important to reward improvement in attendance, focusing particularly on pupils at risk, who often require group or individual counselling. The ultimate challenge to the project will be to maintain the momentum after initial enthusiasm – and funding – is spent.

Note

1 When referring to the 'Kent Attendance Project' in this chapter I mean the group of five schools in north-west and west Kent that worked together from 1990 to 1993. During the same period there were also two schools in east Kent

that took part in a similar GEST-funded project in conjunction with the EWS and the Youth and Community Service. I have included examples of good practice developed by those schools in the section of this chapter entitled 'Targeting Individuals and Groups'.

2 The Changes to Pupil Registration Requirements: The Education (Pupil Registration) (Amendment) Regulations 1997 (SI 1997 No. 2624) redesignated work experience placements (together with field trips, educational visits, sporting activities and link courses in FE), but not study leave, as an 'approved educational activity' with effect from 1 January 1998.

8

PROACTIVE PRIMARY APPROACHES TO NON-ATTENDANCE

Beverley Lewis

Introduction

Although concern about exclusions from primary school has provided a focus on the educational difficulties of younger pupils (see, e.g., Hayden, 1996; Parsons, 1996), there has been little corresponding interest in attendance problems for this age group. Most of the research and GEST (Grants for Education Support and Training) initiatives have concentrated on secondary school pupils. Where primary school pupils have been mentioned, this has been largely concerned with easing the transition from primary to secondary school for the benefit of the latter (see, e.g., Felsenstein, 1987). However, the overall satisfactory attendance rate (approximately 90 per cent) of primary school pupils masks some worrying attendance trends at this level. Stokes and Walton (in this volume) found that attendance at primary school peaks in the middle years, with Year 6 and reception classes having the lowest attenders. Stokes and Walton's additional finding that schools with nursery units show even lower attendance in the reception year further highlights the problematic nature of transitions for young pupils. The GEST initiative described in this chapter arose from similar concerns about primary school attendance levels.

Complacency about overall satisfactory levels of primary school attendance also underestimates the importance of establishing regular attendance at an early age, as recognised by the Department for Education and Employment (1997a). Frones (1995) refers to the primary school years as a crucial period of childhood; a phase where 'competence for depth' develops. By 'depth', he means the development of concentration, commitment and the intimacy of friendship – the ability to work with a task over a protracted period, the ability to concentrate and probe matters in depth, the ability to think long-term; all essential qualities in modem society and dependent on a commitment to regular attendance. Disruption to primary education and the social isolation that accompanies it may be difficult to compensate for later when the basic skills of reading, writing and social interaction have not been well established (Hayden, 1996).

The importance of the primary school effect on basic educational skill acquisition has been clearly demonstrated (Mortimore *et al.*, 1988; Goldstein and Sammons, 1995). Although *attainment* is heavily influenced by home background, *progress* is more likely to be influenced by school, with primary school effects being greater and longer lasting than those of secondary school. The development of social skills is equally important:

> It is well established that problems in peer relationships are frequently present in a wide range of psychiatric disorders. Indeed, of all individual items of behaviour, it shows one of the strongest and most consistent associations with disorder.
>
> (Rutter and Rutter, 1993: 151)

Despite this, schools tend to use the Education Welfare Service mostly at secondary level when attendance problems have become entrenched, leading to unproductive home visits and time-consuming court action that rarely improves attendance (see, e.g., Hoyle, 1998; and Blacktop *et al.* and MacIldowie in this volume). The Education Welfare Officer (EWO) is faced with home–school liaison that is often characterised by confrontation, whereas earlier contact would have had a better potential for the establishment of positive relationships. There exists some information on initiatives to ease the transfer from primary to secondary school via leaflets and inter-school visits (see, e.g., Blyth and Milner, 1997), and the use of peer mentoring to encourage a sense of responsibility and consideration in Year 7 pupils as well as ensure a successful transition (see Bardsley and Haworth in this volume). However, the effects of transition from nursery and reception classes on school attendance and the development of basic skills have been largely ignored. The Department for Education and Employment's draft guidance on school attendance recommends that both LEAs and, specifically, their Education Welfare Services should focus 'more directly' at the primary level, to:

- encourage in children the habits of regular and punctual attendance, reliability and responsibility;
- firmly establish at an early age to parents and children both the importance of education and that unauthorised absence will be challenged; and
- reduce the risk of attendance problems at secondary school transfer.

(DFEE, 1997a: para. 79)

This chapter aims to demonstrate how these issues can be tackled in a simple but comprehensive and effective programme, tailored to the needs of individual schools. Central to this is the fostering of early links with a wide range of families to explore assumptions and prejudices about primary school education, and to establish effective relationships involving children, parents, schools and support services, including education welfare. What follows are descriptions of proactive approaches used in the Lancashire GEST Project to raise awareness of the importance of continuous education.

Lancashire County Council initially secured GEST funding in 1991 under the 'Reducing Truancy/Improving School Attendance' initiative launched by the Department for Education. Continued funding has been obtained in subsequent years to enable the continuation and expansion of this project. The objective of the project has been to develop school-based initiatives that encourage all members of the school community and support services to participate in 'whole-school' approaches to attendance (see, e.g., Learmonth, 1995). The emphasis of the work undertaken has been on 'school-led' activities. This rests on the assumption not only that responsibility for promoting good attendance lies, initially, within the school itself, but also that, if schools, in partnership with support agencies, give sufficient priority to attendance, they will identify strategies that are relevant and meaningful for their own situation and which are more likely to effect long-lasting change. By 1995/6 45 schools in Lancashire were involved in the project: four infant schools, 27 primary schools and 14 secondary schools.

Pre-school family initiatives

Reception departments in the project primary schools have a policy of making home visits to the families of their new pupils to introduce learning packs, equipment and information to parents of children about to start school. This policy is founded on the importance of forming sound links with parents in partnership with schools. Resources deployed at this stage reduce some of the concerns families may have and encourage the family's interest in their children's work and progress, enabling them to establish and maintain good attendance. The EWO taking part in these visits discusses concerns about getting children to school on time, especially when there are other children in the family who may be attending different schools.

The most basic source of information about a school that the family receives is the school brochure. This is aimed at helping families to understand the school and their involvement with it and includes clear statements about the school's expectations regarding punctuality and attendance. Brochures can only be a beginning, with further reinforcement needed of a more personal nature. Some families are wary of professionals, with good reason. They may have experience of being patronised, or parents' past experiences from their own school life have led them to be wary. However, most families are supportive of school when their children first start, and although they may lack the confidence or ability to be active supporters of their child's learning, the experience from the project is that they will try if efforts are made to involve them.

Schools invite families to meetings, but the parents who most lack confidence are generally those least likely to respond to such invitations. This situation will be compounded throughout the child's school life if it is not addressed at the beginning. While the EWO can usefully liaise with the family and invite them to be partners in the new school, it is often reception teachers – who have regular contact with most families through the daily contact of a parent dropping reception children off at school in the morning – who develop relationships with families. These reception teachers become skilled in involving families in the school day and with their own child's learning out of school. As children get older and move up the school, this regular contact is at risk of being diminished unless each transition is monitored and contact nurtured.

Time-keeping awareness initiatives

Reception teachers often suggest that attendance problems may begin with poor time-keeping. Families with young children often have many demands on their time and, although they bring their child to school, they sometimes come late. Very often some families do not see the importance of their young children being at school on time, regarding the first 10 or 15 minutes of the school day as not that significant. Even the regular 10 minutes' lateness can have disastrous effects, however, as children then begin to learn that punctuality is not especially important. Reception teachers who are tolerant of late-corners in the belief that it is important that children come at least for part of the day, who feel that to put pressure on parents, or apply sanctions, could lead to more entrenched non-attendance, may inadvertently compound the problem. While it is undeniably difficult to impose penalties on pupils who are too young to bring themselves to school, those pupils who constantly come late to nursery and reception classes, and continue to do so, find that penalties are imposed when they reach secondary school, if not before.

Parents who fail to ensure their child arrives on time frequently do not understand the importance of timeliness, nor of the difficulties they are building up for their child. For the primary school pupil the first half-hour of the school day is the most important. It is often the settling down time when pupils are introduced to the day's activities. Rules and expectations are explained and then there is the social aspect of school that is often the aspect pupils are most likely to remember. The embarrassment of arriving late and either missing assembly or having to sit at the front or the back away from friends can be very distressing and inhibits learning for the rest of the day. Late attenders become isolated from the beginning and are made to feel different.

Reception teachers address this in a variety of ways. Displays that show parents what happens in the first 30 minutes of the school day can be very effective, especially when linked to National Curriculum attainments and the structure of the school day. Also helpful can be photographs of children listening to the teacher explaining what will happen on that day and the activities that will take place. Parent groups who enjoy coming into school to see what is happening have enjoyed videoing activities undertaken by the children. Other parents are always interested in seeing photographs of their own children. Emphasis can be placed on the disruption to children's learning if they arrive persistently late.

Initiatives aimed at involving parents with children's learning of organisational skills, including attendance and time-keeping

Schools often have extensive Personal and Social Education programmes that are aimed at developing an element of self-monitoring for children to assume a degree of personal responsibility. Primary schools are concerned with the development of independence and the personal and social skills needed to equip them to cope effectively with school and beyond. One description of a reception class initiative is described below.

The reception teacher and EWO designed a programme where simple skills were identified, for example 'I can put away my toys', 'I can dress myself'. Once identified, these skills were listed in blocks that built up to a whole shape. The reception teacher then held a workshop to which parents were invited to become involved with the monitoring of the skills and assist the pupils in colouring in the blocks. Only 30 per cent of parents attended the first workshop, so the reception teacher approached individual parents directly immediately before and after school, enabling another 30 per cent of parents to become involved. The EWO paid home visits to the remaining parents, encouraging another 10 per cent of parents to become involved at school and working with the remainder of parents in their homes. The EWO worked with the pupils in school in pairs, specifically focusing on time-keeping and attendance, setting weekly targets. All the families attended a final ceremony celebrating pupils' success and their future involvement with the school was established, making a time-consuming initiative well worthwhile.

Another initiative involved pupils at Key Stage 1 working through state-ments divided into seven areas in the class situation: listening; communication; responsibility for others; responsibility for the environment; sharing; co-operation; and respect (a statement within 'respect' would be 'I am always on time for school'). Parents' involvement was encouraged by sending them individual sheets to show the skills being developed in class and providing suggestions about how they could help. The EWO followed up the letter to offer support. After completing the target statements within each category, the pupils gained a sticker which was placed on the inside of the skills booklet, with stickers in the seven areas comprising the pupils' 'passport' to Key Stage 2. Again, success was celebrated with families.

Records of Achievement have proved to be a most effective way of enhancing confidence and self-esteem in pupils and in fostering better pupil–teacher relationships. The process of being able to identify goals and celebrate their success has enormous potential for learning. Achievement that is celebrated across the phases provides an anchor point that enables pupils to reflect on and consolidate what they have learned before facing another transition. Additionally, a final document is built up in the primary school that can be used in the transition to secondary school. Displays in the receiving secondary school or samples of children's own favourite or 'best' work facilitate links between the primary and secondary school.

One attempt to involve the family more directly in Year 6 was to timetable EWOs to make home visits during school time with individual pupils, sharing the Record of Achievement to enable discussion and real involvement of the family in the compiling of the record. Given this precious resource of time and the realisation that the school regarded this highly, families were able to add to the Record, setting their own goals which they felt their child could achieve. Families were involved in their children's learning, especially those life skills including time-keeping, taking responsibility and making choices. Families were able to talk about concerns regarding transition and discuss the continuation of learning, building on the achievements of their child.

This provided an important link, consolidating home–school relationships, with families and children being positive about the experience. When there was a difficulty, families had confidence in contacting their EWO. For those families where there wasn't a specific problem, the experience was still valued and it gave pupils an invaluable opportunity to discuss their achievements with an adult and their family.

Rewards and recognition of achievement for punctuality and attendance

Observations of classes showed that teachers gave punishments far in excess of rewards. If we are to reward achievement and believe it is an important reinforcement to learning, it has to be built in to the system. The award of a badge in recognition of punctuality and good attendance, and designing and making badges, has proved to be a highly successful and popular activity in both primary and secondary phases. Badges are a desirable item amongst pupils and are worn with pride. Year 6 pupils can be involved in the development of rewards for reception children and have responded positively to consideration of appropriate rewards and then the development of them. A design project was used as a competition where designs were submitted to a panel of judges. Those pupils with the winning designs made the badges. Alternatively, those children with 100 per cent attendance formed the badge-making team.

Every school needs a policy that rewards attendance and good time-keeping, especially when, as an industrial society, we rate these achievements highly in the workplace. Equally, schools need to have the pupil for a period of time to be able to demonstrate to the youngster what school can offer. If school does not value attendance, then pupils quickly feel that this is not important and that learning can be 'caught up'. This really challenges what we think learning is about.

Initiatives for families to observe and participate in the school day

Children who are absent often miss out on those special 'one-off' occasions that many children enjoy. Also learning often demands interaction with others and needs a teacher rather than a worksheet. Families do not always understand the importance of this aspect of the school day, thinking that work missed can be easily caught up. One school felt that families that took their child away on holiday in school term time misunderstood what the school was about. In this instance the school was in the tourist area where there was an ethos of taking holidays in term time out of season because school holidays are the time when many are employed by the tourist industry. The school tackled this problem by holding a family day that showed a number of activities that didn't involve working from a book or, indeed, writing anything down. The activities included a drama lesson, an art lesson, a maths investigation lesson, a physical education lesson and an English lesson. All these lessons involved children interacting and learning from each other's work in an active way. Parents were invited to be involved and emphasis was placed on the importance of pupils interacting and the fact that the learning could not be replaced by setting work to be done on holiday. At the end of the day an awards ceremony for attendance took place. EWOs were involved in encouraging parents to attend the day and partici-pate in the learning process. Those families who attended recorded within their evaluation their enhanced understanding of what teaching and learning were about.

Initiatives to involve pupils in recording their own attendance and punctuality and monitoring their own performance

The importance of accurate recording of progress in any specific area is acknowledged in many different fields. I have always had a problem with my weight, and with any diet club have been encouraged to record exactly what I have been eating. You can always cheat of course, but that doesn't detract from the process of recording, because you know you are cheating. Likewise for attendance and punctuality, pupils don't always realise just how much time they are having off or how often they are coming late. Recording this can come as a shock. Recording can happen in a variety of different ways – by colouring shapes, collecting stickers, and wall charts, such as 'Humpty Dumpty's Wall', where a brick is coloured in each day each child arrives on time. This then becomes a visual display of time lost and restriction on progress by the whole class because of constantly restarting lessons. Very young pupils need short-term goals of a week and achievement of goals must be recognised and celebrated.

One school that had been involved in a badge design project sent letters home to explain about the project and the self-monitoring that was going to take place over the next three weeks. A further questionnaire sent to parents and followed up by the EWO revealed that less than half admitted or remembered receiving the letter, although most of the families knew of the project because their child had talked about the badge designing and their own self-monitoring and were talking to their families about getting to school on time. Letters home are not the only or even the most effective way of communication.

Initiatives to raise the attendance profile within the whole community

Local firms are often very enthusiastic about becoming involved with initiatives to promote good attendance and time-keeping. This is a major concern for them and there is now a developed network of Compact initiatives throughout the country. In the primary school these initiatives can be even more productive because of the often closer links with families, especially when aimed at the transition to secondary school. Transfer of information across the phases very often consists of academic details, with personal and social skills being devalued by the fact that the secondary school neither asks for, nor receives, information in these areas. It is also the case that the receiving secondary school finds it difficult to use all the information that is sometimes sent from different primary feeder schools. One way that a group of schools accommodated this was by a number of primary schools, together with associated secondary schools, developing a project in which children in Year 6 were involved in the targeting of personal and social skills and success was acknowledged by the secondary school and associated industries.

At the beginning of Year 6, the secondary school teacher responsible for transition visited the primary school and spoke to the children about the importance of personal and social skills, particularly those to do with self-organisation, working co-operatively, attendance and punctuality, both in the primary school and in the secondary school. At the same time as this visit, a representative from a local firm and/or a local football team visited the school and reinforced the importance of these skills in the workplace. Following these visits, the children were involved at regular intervals in setting targets for themselves and reviewing progress. A representative from the local firm visited the school to talk to individuals about their progress and offer support and one-to-one mentoring, assisted by the EWO. Pupils were encouraged to set their own targets, with three successes identified and included in a statement prepared at the end of the year. Pupils were awarded certificates at the end of the year, displaying a joint logo of the two schools and the local firm. The primary head teacher, the secondary head teacher, the representative of the local firm, the EWO, parents and pupils, attended the awards ceremony.

The scheme achieved a number of objectives. All pupils received a certificate identifying individually negotiated successes. These certificates transferred to the secondary school and became a part of the secondary Record of Achievement. Both the world of secondary school and the world of work were represented, acknowledging the importance of developing personal and social skills for adult life.

Other initiatives included visits to local firms or the local football team, where managers explained how a concern depends on all its employees being there. Failure of a canteen worker to turn in can, by a chain of events, lead to the team losing the match on Saturday. Equally football teams can and have forfeited games because of late arrival. Biscuit firms described the havoc that is created by a missing worker on the production line. Food chains described the skills programme that their employees go through to enable them to progress in the firm. Sometimes local firms can bring young people from their workforce back into school to make the message more relevant to young pupils, especially when those young people went to that primary school. Often small local firms have far more credibility with young children and their families than larger national industries.

Supporting pupils 'at risk' before transfer to another class, group or school

Any transfer involves anticipation of new experiences and expectations, but it is the responsibility of schools and teachers to ensure that the move fulfils that excitement and expectations of new beginnings and at the same time builds on skills and knowledge already acquired. Schools can concentrate on the more positive aspects of the move to raise pupils' confidence and self-esteem. One way of achieving this was by helping pupils to identify their own strengths. Ideas are brainstormed and then categorised. For example, 'I can tidy up behind myself' is listed under 'responsibility'. Pupils are then given the task of producing simple sentences relating to their own skills, aiming for at least five statements. These statements of skills are kept by the pupil and added to whenever pupils feel that they have developed or demonstrated a skill that might be useful at secondary school.

Other initiatives included working with a group of disaffected pupils and building more positive attitudes that they will hopefully take on to the secondary school by providing a number of positive adult role models willing and able to share an interest in them. Role models included youth workers, EWOs and teachers from the receiving school. Through this approach it was hoped to increase the trust and confidence the pupils have in adults and help them adjust more readily to new experiences and situations. The pupils became used to different people being in the classroom working with them in small groups on a common task. They became more accustomed to different approaches demonstrated by the different adults within the security of the classroom. While progress was variable, the subsequent transition between the primary and secondary phase was successful.

For many pupils the summer holiday is a long time. It is a time when worries about future schools can magnify and get out of all proportion. Links with the primary school are lost and new links with the secondary school have not yet been forged. The good relationships established with the EWOs through the primary school initiatives can be utilised at this time to provide the reassurance and support that some families need, and prompt action can prevent transition problems becoming entrenched.

Conclusions

The initiatives described have been developed and implemented by different schools within the GEST Improving Attendance Project. The cost of using EWOs in the ways suggested is high but cost-effective when compared with the time they may spend in fruitless home visits to families where patterns of irregular or non-attendance are entrenched and educational achievements not realised. The cost to the community of young people who leave school with few or no qualifications as a direct consequence of non-attendance is also very expensive. The cost to the nation of disaffected, unmotivated youngsters with few aspirations is one we should not be prepared to bear. The outcome of this work since 1991 shows that when schools take seriously improved attendance and punctuality, and are supported in doing so, significant improvements can be made in attendance and time-keeping. Schools need to be exciting and challenging institutions, but children have to acquire the habit of attending to be able to judge whether the school has something to offer. That habit is best encouraged from the first moment the child begins education in a spirit of positive home–school partnership.

9

RAISING EXPECTATIONS AT DON VALLEY HIGH SCHOOL

Bob Johnson

Introduction

This chapter is about the struggle of Don Valley High School to improve the quality of education it provides for its pupils and the outcomes they have achieved. The work undertaken is described as a 'struggle' because it is never-ending and its progress is never smooth and progressive; rather, it is very erratic and difficult to predict. Sometimes there are setbacks, and the challenge is to remain optimistic and positive. This chapter will be like a diary of all the measures that the staff of the school have carried out to improve attendance and achievement. There are many initiatives to talk about; some will be particular to Don Valley and others will be more general and, therefore, reproducible in other contexts. Perhaps one of the most rewarding facets of involvement in this work is the sense that staff are really making a difference to the future of young people who do not start life with advantages that many other pupils have. Having staff who feel that they can make this difference and who are tenacious about the job is vital to success.

In my experience, planning for improvement is not a sequential-type process. School improvement is about culture change, and changing cultures in a school requires progress on a number of different initiatives at any one time. Clearly, to change culture it is vital that staff are involved in the audit (the shopping list) and the setting of priorities at the outset and that there is adequate time allocated for full involvement.

The beginning

Don Valley High School is a maintained 11–18 mixed comprehensive school situated on the northern outskirts of Doncaster in South Yorkshire, serving Bentley and Scawthorpe, a catchment area where there is considerable social deprivation; indeed the 1991 census data show Bentley to be one of the most socially deprived areas in Doncaster. Over 30 per cent of children are entitled to free school meals. The school population has grown considerably since starting the initiatives described in this chapter. In 1990, the school population was 820 pupils. In 1998 there are 1320 pupils on the roll, and the pupil population is projected to grow to 1500 in the next few years. The reasons for the growth in pupil numbers are various and will be discussed in greater detail later, although one major reason for the increase in pupil numbers over the eight years was the fact that the school reorganised in 1993 from an age 12 entry to an age 11 entry school. The school had been losing around 30 pupils per year prior to 1990 to two nearby comprehensive schools because of parental preference. In 1990 many parents, governors and staff considered that the school had a poor reputation in the local community. There was a great feeling of concern in the school about reducing pupil loss from the catchment area and many staff were working very hard to try to improve the reputation of the school.

Soon after my appointment as head teacher at the school in September 1990, it became very clear that the staff, as a group, had very little confidence in the abilities of pupils. They were defensive and defeatist. Staff made comments at meetings such as 'This is too difficult for our pupils', or 'The CATS [Cognitive Abilities Tests] scores are low and that is why our students do not do well at examination'. A culture change was needed so that all staff could believe that pupils could perform better. Based on the work of Rosenthal and Jacobsen (1968), staff needed to reaffirm the adage of 'what you expect from children is what you get from children'. The culture change needed was to raise expectations among both staff and pupils about what could be achieved, and the only way to do this was with the full co-operation and collaboration of all the staff, since the message from Rosenthal and Jacobsen's work applied to staff equally as well as to pupils. Staff talked through the issue at a management team meeting and agreed that more time was required to discuss and develop strategy. Therefore, an away weekend was organised. Fortunately the local education authority organised and funded a weekend each year when management teams from different secondary schools would meet with a consultant to work on any development issues they had identified.

The management team were very clear about their agenda and quickly set about contacting the nominated consultant to arrange a meeting to discuss raising expectations in the school. The meeting proved extremely important and the consultant played an influential role in the way work progressed.

At the first meeting, the consultant suggested that he should interview as many staff as possible to obtain some idea about how they saw the issues facing the school so that he could act as the voice of the staff when the issue was tackled during the weekend meeting and ensure that discussions remained grounded in the reality of Don Valley High School. He met with a cross-section of staff (about 12) and produced a report, with the permission of the staff concerned, containing anonymised direct quotes, which were listed under various headings. These quotes provide an accurate picture of the feeling in the staffroom at the time (December 1991):

The school needs to be more positive. That's where the problems start.

A key issue is the extent of underachievement...and acknowledging that pupils do underachieve.

A key issue is staff expectations. There is a view that you don't get clever kids here – they go to another school. That seems to be a prevalent view that is distressing. Moreover, it is a view shared by the middle schools. It is changing, though.

We have to have clear expectations of ourselves. If we accept lower standards, that reinforces their low expectations.

Their expectations may be low because of the messages from parents ('It's not good to do well at school') and from other pupils they are called 'boff'. This makes them happier with D grades.

How we teach children is an important issue....An awful lot of emphasis is put on 'discipline' rather than 'behavioural management'. This is a throwback to a negative discipline model. It means kids get passive and don't have to think for themselves. They don't need to work until we make them. They begin to take the line: 'Come on – make me work. Make me behave.' I think that underpins a lot of underachievement. They are not responsible for their own achievement. Therefore, for me teaching and learning is important and the environment less so.

'Standards are fairly low on, for example, dress, presentation of work, hanging up coats, etc. There is a lack of consistency. There is nothing in the staff document, except about dress, so we all do our own thing. We need to be clear about the basics – having books, pens, etc. There should be something from above.

A lot is about changing staff attitudes and behaviour – the fear among staff is that another set of rules will be imposed.

It is important, though, that we don't just rearrange the deckchairs.

It's got to start from the top. Consistency is the key word. The Senior Management Team has to have expectations for everyone else to have them. It has to be prepared to work on expectations. There has to be an enforcement role and working together, negotiating.

We need to keep pushing, saying, 'Yes, we know there are prob-lems, but keep pushing.' It's easy to slip into excuse-making. It's easy to blame 'the area' – that's quite an acute problem.

It will be obvious to anyone reading this synopsis of staff quotes what the agenda for the future school development plan should be, and this enabled the management team to feel confident about the way forward.

Background to developments in the school

The 'Raising Expectations' initiatives started at the end of 1991. Prior to this, the school had been involved in a considerable measure of change. One development on its own cannot create the change in culture required to bring about progress. It is, therefore, important to mention the develop-ments the school had been working on prior to the end of 1991, because the changes will have contributed to the culture change so necessary for any major school improvement. Within months of my appointment as head teacher the management structure and curriculum of the school were subject to an internal audit. In addition, a community group was started and two other groups, the Don Valley Bridge Group (a group of senior citizens) and a playschool group, started later in the academic year. The community group started to organise social events and the Don Valley Bridge Group became very successful by meeting twice a week to swim in the school swimming pool and arrange various activities like visits, bingo and keep fit. The playschool attracted around ten parents and children and they used the school pool. All groups are currently still active in the school.

The audit of the curriculum and the management of the school produced great structural change without, perhaps, too much cultural change. It was decided that more flexibility was needed in the timetable to deliver the sort of curriculum that would meet the needs of the pupils. The only way such flexibility could be increased was to change the number of periods in a week. After much debate it was agreed that the timetable should be based on a six-period day and a 30-period week. In addition, changes to the timing of the school day to start and finish earlier were agreed because staff believed that learning is more effective in the morning and, therefore, why not use more of it? The audit of the management structure of the school produced consid-erable debate and resulted in the production of a whole-school pay policy, which was finally agreed by staff, governors and professional associations and unions in March 1992.

By the end of 1991, the school was already developing, not so much in a cultural sense but more in a structural sense, tackling some of the important problems that had easy solutions. It is far easier to change something like the timing of the day in a school than it is to get complete staff ownership for, say, a behaviour policy that includes staff and pupil behaviour. One sort of change is about mechanical matters and the other is about hearts and minds.

One of the great strengths of Don Valley High School has always been the staff. In 1990 there were a large number of staff who had spent more than 15 years in the school and yet were very ready to embrace change. There was great concern about the fact that the school was not seen as popular in the community, and some staff felt the threat of losing 20 to 30 pupils from feeder schools every year and the likely effect it would have on staff numbers. Threat does focus the mind.

'Raising Expectations Mark I'

The management team and the consultant met for their weekend meeting in December 1991. It took about 12 hours of discussion to define the strategy that staff thought would be successful in raising achievement and expectations in the school. Two strands were identified: Strand One was to do with celebrating and rewarding achievement in school; and Strand Two was to do with achievable standards which had staff support. The discussion initially was much focused on celebrating achievement, staff talking at great length about rewarding pupils' work and learning. It was the consultant who reminded the team that there were some more difficult issues to deal with and these were centred on standards involving pupil discipline and conduct and linked to the quality of the environment and our role in these issues. The team would probably not have addressed these difficult and potentially divisive issues had it not been for the consultant's intervention and contribution. It is very tempting to retreat to the comfort zone.

Discussions about Strand One were very clear by the end of the weekend, culminating in the following suggestions for staff action:

- more display of pupils' work in classes and around school;
- set up a staff group to make recommendations about presentation of awards, merits, and certificates for each year group annually and to make clear the criteria by which rewards are given to pupils;
- create a culture where verbal praise and a positive view of pupils' work is common – a staff group to be asked to make recommendations;
- the need for a whole-school homework policy;
- the need for a whole school marking policy;
- the need for performance indicators so that we know when we have raised expectations and achievement.

Strand Two was less clear by the end of the weekend. Staff knew they had to deal with things like punctuality, pupil movement around school, tidy classes, litter, behaviour at lesson changes, and the condition and use of toilets in the school (this latter issue was quite unsavoury!). The suggestion to all staff was that another staff group be established, the 'Positive Culture' group, in the hope that this group could find solutions that would gain consensus. Management team members joined all staff groups formed.

The staff received the suggestions well and the staff meeting in January 1992 was to be the start of the real work to raise expectations in the school. Display of pupils' work around school increased enormously from that date. Money was allocated for display materials and INSET (InService Education and Training) time was arranged to help staff to display work more effectively. The school now allocates INSET time annually to the display of pupils' work, such is the importance attached to this activity. The 'Presentation of Awards' group reported in June 1992 and proposed the institution of two types of award, 'ongoing' awards and 'annual' awards. Ongoing awards are for merits and attendance. If a teacher deems a piece of work worthy of merit, he or she stamps it with a merit stamp; for every 20 merits the pupil accumulates, he or she will receive a certificate in assembly during the year. Attendance certificates are awarded for 100 per cent and 95 per cent attendance during a term. Much later in 1996 the merits policy was amended to limit it to pupils in lower school (Years 7–9) and commendations were awarded to pupils in upper school (Years 10–11). A commendation is a nomination from a department concerning the good performance of the pupil during the term related to the pupil's own prior performance.

Annual awards were to be made in five categories and would be awarded at an annual presentation evening in December for all year groups in the school. Because of the numbers of pupils involved, three separate evenings were organised: for Years 8 and 9; Years 10 and 11; and the sixth form, where GCSE and A level certificates and sixth form awards are presented. The presentation to each pupil is for the previous year's work and, therefore, Year 7 will receive their awards in Year 8. The five categories of awards (a certificate and a £5 book token) are: merits and commendations, attendance (100 per cent only), outstanding commitment to extra-curricular activity, personal achievement in the curriculum, and community awards. Staff are very careful to ensure that pupils of all abilities are nominated and are equally careful to ensure that not only is academic achievement celebrated – as the school is a comprehensive, all abilities and achievements must be recognised. The presentation evenings have proved to be very worthwhile and prestigious events in the school calendar. Approximately 60 to 70 pupils from each year group of around 200 pupils are invited with their parents each year and a guest speaker is also invited. This started in December 1992 and the tradition has been sustained, despite the large costs and work involved in the organisation of the evenings. Many of the staff feel that the evenings make a very important contribution to the success of the school's 'Raising Expectations' initiatives.

The homework policy group reported in late 1992, and one of the most important points the group recommended was that each pupil should be provided with a printed prestigious student planner externally produced and customised for Don Valley. The group argued that if homework is to be important in the minds of the child and parents, this must be reflected in the way it is recorded. The student planner also records merits and notes from parents to form teachers as well as being a personal diary for the pupil. Despite the annual £3,000 bill, it has been a very worthwhile investment. The group was clear to point out homework monitoring responsibilities and homework is monitored twice a year. The marking policy group reported towards the end of 1994, although the impact of this particular initiative has been small, not because of the ideas contained in the policy, which are very good, but more because insufficient time was spent on INSET to ensure its success. Our successful second OFSTED inspection in October 1997 pointed out the need for a whole school Literacy Policy and a staff group is currently working on this and its assessment in the school.

Performance indicators were identified very early on in February 1992 because staff needed to know whether the work they were initiating was having a positive effect. The performance criteria agreed included: measurement of the success of the student planner system; improved examination results; improved attendance; pupil numbers in Year 7; post-16 numbers; positive pupil opinions; parental opinion/praise. It was agreed that performance would be monitored every September starting in 1993. Some of the criteria are difficult to measure; staff have never been exhaustive in their analysis of, say, parental opinion, but the question is asked collectively, and a view obtained. Criteria like examination results, attendance and pupil numbers are easily monitored, of course, and data will be provided later in this chapter to show how the initiative improved performance.

Strand Two was much slower to develop, because the issues under consideration, that is, standards, are much more complex. The positive culture group met during 1992 and into early 1993 and the very first thing it decided to do was to survey staff opinion concerning pupil movement around school and arrangements for lunch- and break-time. Staff were asked for general comments and any proposals/solution they might have. The group worked very hard, made various recommendations in the form of policy documents, and articulated judgement; they produced a code of conduct policy and a movement about school policy that was accepted readily by staff in June 1993. Solutions to address the other issues were suggested and funds were allocated to provide more litter bins and to decorate and tile pupil toilets. By September 1993, the year the school was to be reorganised, all staff were clear about what pupils were expected to do when they move around school, which stairs they should use to get to a particular room, how they should behave, and so on. On the first day of term staff went through the policy with form groups and there was a large degree of ownership by staff and pupils so that the school's first day as a 1,000-plus 11–18 comprehensive school went with reasonable smoothness.

Did 'Raising Expectations Mark I' work?

It is very difficult in any action research situation to identify that which is causal. As noted earlier, the work identified as 'Raising Expectations Mark I' was not the only development going on in the school. Far from it, during the period 1992/3 staff worked on the National Curriculum, school pay policy, staff development policy, collective worship, and many other things. To say, therefore, that the school improvement was caused only by the work identified as 'Raising Expectations' is uncertain. However, 'Raising Expectations Mark I' contributed greatly to success in improving performance. The data contained in Table 9.1 support our improved performance from 1991 to 1994, the year of the school's first inspection by OFSTED.

Table 9.1   Don Valley High School performance data 1990–4

	GCSE 5 A–C (%)	GCSE no pass (%)	GCSE av. pts score	A level av. pts score	6th as % Year 11	Lost Year 7 pupils	Attendance (%)
1990	9.8	30.0	–	9.2	16.0	31	84.0
1991	13.5	29.0	–	9.6	17.1	25	84.0
1992	15.0	13.2	18.7	9.4	40.3	19	82.0
1993	22.4	9.4	21.9	7.5	45.4	14	86.0
1994	22.7	14.8	23.3	9.6	55.0	15	85.4

The first OFSTED inspection occurred on 28 January 1994 and the report was very complimentary about the school, after, of course, it had pointed out that it was performing below national average in public examinations. The inspectors felt that the Mark I initiatives were having a positive and observable effect. They said:

Seek to extend the raising of expectations through an emphasis on increased rigour in learning.

The school provides care and support through a well-structured pastoral system. The categories of the successful merit and presentation policy enable the school to promote positively its range of values as well as raising pupil self-esteem.

The clearly defined code of conduct gives guidance to pupils and staff about expected pupil behaviour and specific sanctions to minor offences. Parents and pupils are also informed of the school expectations through their own prospectus. Both parties are asked to sign an agreement giving support to the observance of these guidelines. The merit system for good work and effort is motivating and valued in Key Stage 3. The school's positive attitude towards behaviour is conducive to raising expectations and contributes to the quality of work. Parents reported that behaviour in the school is good and there is immediate action if problems arise.

The school's aims and the new objectives were agreed in 1993. The evidence is that these are understood by staff and widely supported. The major issue of raising pupil expectations and equality of opportunity are both seen in the working of the school.

The fact that OFSTED had recognised the impact of the work was extremely pleasing. Not only had they valued it, but also they were telling staff in 'key issues for action' to continue and concentrate on rigour. Another key issue was attendance. The overall attendance figure prior to inspection was 85.4 per cent and the school was told that it must look at strategies to improve attendance to 90 per cent or more. This provided the agenda for our school development plan to this date and became 'Raising Expectations Mark II: Rigour'.

'Raising Expectations Mark II: Rigour'

In October 1994 the school's management team organised another weekend to deliberate over strategies that would improve attendance and make learning more rigorous. This time the consultant was not able to participate because he had other commitments, and, in retrospect, it was probably a mistake because it would have been very interesting to see if he could detect any evidence of a shift in staff expectations. However, a larger management team of nine meant a broader cross-section of staff's views was represented.

It was a productive weekend that produced a 'shopping list' of strategies that were written up in a paper for staff and governors to consider. Like the first try at 'Raising Expectations', Mark II has two strands, 'Attendance' and 'Rigour in Learning'.

Attendance

The school serves a community where parentally condoned absence from school is not uncommon, and this makes the job of motivating pupils to come to school a very difficult one. Like many schools in Britain, there are parents for whom education, sadly, is not important. Their experience when they were at school themselves was not good and they pass on their value system to their children. Working with families like this depended on setting up procedures in school that were persistent, in the hope that 'persistence wears down resistance'. However, the school remained aware that the reasons for non-attendance at school are very different for each individual child and his or her family, and sometimes they are school-related. Schools cannot point the finger of blame at families only for non-attendance at school. The following strategies were devised:

- to develop an attendance policy that outlined what is done, when and by whom;
- to develop a class register system that is available when staff are absent;
- to increase support from the Education Welfare Service;
- to involve governors in the problem of non-attendance;
- to appoint a clerical assistant with responsibility for attendance;
- to reward good attendance;
- to redesign the pupil leave of absence form;
- to send attendance letters to parents.

The attendance policy was to summarise all the procedures in school to do with pupil absence, starting from if 'John' is away what happens? There was strong agreement about the need for first-day contact with parents, but this was not reasonable to ask of a busy teaching staff. Therefore, a case was put to governors to appoint an attendance clerical assistant whose job would be to telephone home when a pupil was absent. The head of year would have been informed by the form teacher about concerns over the absence of the pupil and would ask the clerical assistant to contact home on the first day of absence for pupils with known attendance problems or where there was suspicion; others would be contacted on the second or third day of unexplained absence. After contacting home the attendance clerk would write a reply and return this to the year team and/or Education Welfare Officer (EWO).

OFSTED made the point that in a few classes a register was not called at the beginning of the lesson. This became a staff awareness problem, but it did raise the issue of what happens when the member of staff is absent and there is no class register. There was a clear need to develop a class register system that operated when a member of staff was absent, and a staff group worked on this problem. After a few meetings the staff group suggested that we have emergency registers in all teaching areas containing the class lists of each class that is taught in that area. It is the class teacher's responsibility to ensure that the lists are correct.

The work of the EWO is vital to any attendance initiative and the school is very fortunate in having a very committed EWO who has worked very closely with the school. The management team felt that it needed to get the whole-hearted support of the Education Welfare Service and met with the Principal EWO and school EWO to discuss procedures.

Governors have a very significant role to play in pupil welfare. The school's governor committee already dealt with pupil welfare problems so why not extend the role of the committee to deal with attendance problems?

There was immediate support for the idea that a Governors' Attendance Committee be established. The committee is convened to meet with parents who are known to condone the absence of their child from school. First and second governors' warning letters are sent after 200 sessions and 200 plus 100 sessions respectively. The attendance of pupils nominated will normally be well below 80 per cent. The governors' procedures run in parallel with EWO procedures. If parents do not attend the governors' meeting, the school pursues them tenaciously. To date the Governors' Attendance Committee has proved very effective; the majority of cases heard by governors have resulted in improved attendance which has been sustained over a long period, although some persistent absenteeism is very difficult to change.

If attendance is important, it must be rewarded. Attendance certificates are presented for 95 per cent and 100 per cent attendance termly, and pupils who maintain 100 per cent attendance throughout the year are invited to the annual presentation evening to receive their awards. In addition, it was agreed that year teams would publish percentage attendance figures weekly for each form and the form that has achieved the best attendance in one term will be presented with a cake at the end of term!

The existing pupil leave of absence form made it too easy for parents and pupils to take holidays during term time. It did not point out the vital education that would be missed and that there should be an expectation that work missed would be learned when the pupil returned. For some parents this is a once in a school career occurrence, so the school targeted those parents who took it as an automatic right that their child should have two additional weeks off each year. Often pupils for whom leave during term time was requested regularly were poor attenders and the parents of poor attenders needed reminding that attendance at school is vitally important. Letters are sent to parents after 100, 200 and 300 sessions if attendance is less than 80 per cent. Warning letters are sent at the same mile-posts if attendance deteriorates to 85 per cent.

Rigour in learning

Discussions concerning increased rigour in learning in the school ranged extensively. Clearly, there are an enormous number of strategies to tackle this issue, and the task was to classify it and pick out the most productive and effective strategies to work upon. The following areas were identified for consideration as a whole staff group:

- academic monitoring throughout the whole school;
- department liaison arrangements;
- formal examinations for Years 7 and 8 (those for Years 9–13 were already formal);

- involvement of all schools in the pyramid of raising expectations;
- Year 11 mentoring;
- more rigour in marking and homework (including use of student planners).

Academic monitoring was defined in two ways: one was needed to monitor the progress of a whole year group or sex group to ensure that the school was being effective (adding value); and the other was needed to monitor the progress of individual pupils to identify those who were underachieving and to guide remedial action. Since the beginning of 1995, systems in school have been steadily developed to help establish whether the school is adding value. This involves testing pupils in Year 7 using CATS (Cognitive Abilities Tests) by the NFER (National Foundation for Educational Research) and MIDYIS (Middle Years Information Service from Durham University). In Year 9 there are, of course, SATS (Standard Attainment Tests); in Years 10 and 11 YELLIS (Year Eleven Information Service from Durham University) is used and in the sixth form ALIS (A Level Information Service from Durham University). All of these tests are standardised and within particular levels of confidence will predict outcomes in public examinations for individuals and cohorts. The monitoring of pupils for individual progress is far from complete. There exists an effective system in the sixth form, but the developing system in the main school needs to be tenaciously pursued. There is an enormous amount of academic information available on each individual pupil and a computer network throughout the school may be needed so that all academic information on that pupil may be accessed and kept up to date. The problem is very much one of information handling and the school expects to have the system in place for 1998/9.

In 1995, department liaison arrangements with the management team were formalised. It was agreed with staff that all members of the management team would have a pastoral/development role with respect to a particular department. The senior manager attends department meetings, supports the head of department, observes lessons and reports back to the department on a particular focus (this happens twice a year), and is very aware of the current problems facing the department. Lesson observation is purely developmental and arrangements to decide which lessons are to be observed are made with the head of department so that staff are aware. Many staff in the school would say that the liaison system has many advantages; the major two being the greater awareness in the management team of department activity and the help given to departments to help them become more effective.

In 1996, formal examinations for Year 7 and Year 8 pupils in the Summer Term were introduced because lower school pupils were showing a low level of factual recall and, furthermore, the OFSTED inspectors commented on this. Developing a whole-school study skills policy, completed in 1997/8, has supported this move. This policy is taught in departments and in the context of the subject.

The school has eight feeder primary schools and regular meetings take place of the head teachers of all the schools in the pyramid. In 1995, it was agreed to look at raising expectations as a whole pyramid and the pyramid head teachers were supportive of the idea. The General Inspector for schools in the pyramid was also supportive and managed to fund the support of Manchester University to assist this development. This work is currently ongoing and focuses on cohort academic monitoring; a pyramid group of English co-ordinators meets regularly to compare standards of written work and to discuss effective methodology. Recently the pyramid of schools and another neighbouring pyramid of schools has been successful, through an LEA bid, in getting funding through the Government Single Regeneration Budget, and this will help support work on various initiatives involving working with parents, literacy, raising achievement and the Pathways project, which focuses on the work-related curriculum.

In 1996, the Year 11 mentoring system was introduced and the system was refined for 1997. Pupils are arranged into groups of around eight and the year team and management team support those pupils from January through to the examinations in the following June. Staff meet parents and go through the same agenda with pupils so that they are well prepared for June. Many staff feel that this initiative has had a very positive effect on the outcomes achieved by the pupils.

Rigour is to do with monitoring and revisiting things. A large comprehensive school has a number of changing priorities and the school's view is that it cannot just accept that once the policy is in place then everything in it will happen. In June 1994 the homework policy was revisited and made much more rigorous. It includes a monitoring programme and clear responsibility for involvement in the monitoring of homework. Student planners are inspected by year teams and there is a report to staff council (the policy-making body in school). Heads of departments are intimately involved in the monitoring. The way pupils are using their student planners is also monitored, and, like litter, this will be one to revisit as time goes on.

Did 'Raising Expectations Mark II' work?

It has already been stated that it is very difficult to find out what is causal in education, and clearly the work on 'Raising Expectations Mark II' has not really had enough time to show itself. There is much left to do. However, analysis of performance indicators is very pleasing, and this is detailed in Table 9.2.

Comparison of Tables 9.1 and 9.2 shows that there has been a steady reduction in the number of pupils lost to neighbouring schools during the

Table 9.2   Don Valley High School performance data 1994–7

	GCSE 5 A–C (%)	GCSE no pass (%)	GCSE av. pts score	A level av. pts score	6th as % Year 11	Lost Year 7 pupils	Attendance (%)
1994	22.7	14.8	23.3	9.6	55.0	15	85.4
1995	19.4	10.9	23.8	9.3	36.8	10	86.0
1996	25.0	20.0	25.5	13.2	39.2	0	89.0
1997	27.0	7.0	28.6	12.7	55.0	0	88.6

eight-year period. While pleasing, it is not possible to say precisely what has caused this change. In addition to the 'Raising Expectations' initiatives, there have been many other changes in the school during that period. Many staff feel that these changes have been equally effective as the 'Raising Expectations' initiatives in enhancing the school's performance. For example, the impact of the human relationships and the staff and governor changes that have occurred during the eight-year period (clearly a vital factor in school improvement) is difficult to estimate. Perhaps one of the most influential changes has been in the primary liaison arrangements, whereby Don Valley High School staff teach in primary schools during the week and primary school pupils visit Don Valley in Years 5 and 6 for specialist days in addition to the usual parents' evening and staff primary school visits. However, the fact that parents now say many positive things about the school and there are now, for the first time, admissions appeals reinforces the positive effect the 'Raising Expectations' initiatives have had in the school.

Over the eight-year period, pupils' GCSE results have improved considerably. They needed to. The base of 18.7 average points score per pupil moved to 28.6 points in five years. The 'A' Level average points score per student has also risen around three points in that time. Many staff consider that the work completed under the banner of 'Raising Expectations' has contributed greatly to this improvement. Progress to improve attendance has been slow and hard-fought. Although overall attendance throughout the school has moved closer to 90 per cent over the period, there is still more work needed in this area despite the large number of changes made. In October 1997 the school had its second OFSTED inspection. The OFSTED report stated:

> The school makes considerable efforts to secure good attendance by pupils. It has carefully reviewed its procedures for securing and monitoring attendance and has improved and extended them significantly since the last inspection. They include a system of rewards for good attendance and an efficient telephoning of the homes of pupils who are disposed to absence. The school's efforts are having mixed success. In the third week of the autumn term of the current academic year attendance was a satisfactory 90–91 per cent in Years

7–9, but fell to 88 per cent in Year 10 and to a poor 83 per cent in Year 11.

The report added:

> Standards of attainment and progress have, however, risen steadily but surely since the last inspection.

Conclusion

The challenge now facing Don Valley is the challenge facing the nation. How is progress to be made to address the major issue of the 'long tail' of underachievement; the 30 or 40 youngsters (mostly boys) in each year group who go through school each year and obtain few or no GCSE passes, attend very poorly and try to 'play the adult' far too early in life? Part of the solution must be to do with increased accountability and more rigorous academic monitoring. Ralph Taberrer, then Deputy Director of the NFER, speaking at a conference in Doncaster in July 1996, suggested that schools must take on the role of 'air traffic controller' with children who are failing. Schools must identify very early on those children who are likely to 'drop out of the sky' and target their resources accordingly.

The children can be identified as early as Key Stage 1, sometimes in Years 1 or 2, and the government White Paper *Excellence in Schools* (DFEE, 1997b) will, hopefully, help primary schools to target their work at that stage. For those in Don Valley, the school must develop more intense intervention strategies to ensure they do not fail.

Pupils who are at the 'tail' of attainment in Don Valley exhibit associated and persistent attendance problems. That is not to say that every pupil who exhibits low attainment does not attend well, but many do have an attendance well below 90 per cent. This stubborn problem will persist as long as the legislation is not focused on those parents who connive with and condone non-attendance at school. Meanwhile, the school will remain tenacious and vigilant toward non-attendance. Some pupils, through their prolonged absence from school, have lost the skills to access the curriculum and the will to view their reinduction into school imaginatively.

The challenges facing schools like Don Valley that serve needy areas are therefore immense. There is no other option open than to continue repeatedly to take an optimistic and tenacious attitude towards them. To take the other option of excusing failure because of social problems will not raise expectations and has an end of certain downfall. It is hoped that this chapter has shown that, with the commitment of staff, pupils, parents and governors, the first option can work.

10

DOING BETTER

Improving the educational experiences of looked-after children and young people

Eric Blyth, Dorothy Jessop and Judith Milner

Lessons from research

Under provisions of the Children Act 1989, local authorities in England have a responsibility to 'look after' both young people placed in their care by the civil or criminal courts and young people whose own parents or carers are unable to care for them. Educational difficulties, such as exclusion from school and poor attendance, frequently contribute to social work intervention, including the possibility of being accommodated by the local authority (e.g. Sinclair *et al.*, 1993; Parsons *et al.*, 1994). Where the state performs a parental role, it might be expected that, with the weight of the state behind them, any erstwhile educational disadvantages accompanying such young people into public care might be tackled by the co-ordinated efforts of social services and education authorities acting as 'corporate parent'. However, any such assumption receives scant support from available evidence. Looked-after young people experience poor-quality education where this is provided by social services agencies as an alternative to mainstream schooling (Fletcher-Campbell and Hall, 1990; DES, 1992; SSI and OFSTED, 1995). In addition, they also experience considerable difficulties in mainstream education, for example exhibiting comparatively high levels of disturbed behaviour in school, engaging in relatively high levels of absenteeism, being more likely to be excluded from school, and performing poorly on measures of academic attainment, the latter frequently resulting in limited employment prospects (see, e.g., Fletcher-Campbell and Hall, 1990; Heath *et al.*, 1989, 1994; Biehal *et al.*, 1992; Cheung and Heath, 1994; Colton and Heath, 1994; Stein, 1994; SSI and OFSTED, 1995; Utting *et al.*, 1997; Social Exclusion Unit, 1998).

Identifying the precise impact on educational experience and outcomes of the care experience itself, as opposed to that of the circumstances preceding a young person's admission to care, has been more elusive. This is because looked-after young people do not necessarily have comparable experiences; they may enter and leave care at different stages of their lives and experience care and different types of placement for varying lengths of time, often interspersed with periods of living with their family.

However, the research does identify particular features of care experiences that may contribute to such outcomes. Although many young people have already experienced severe disadvantage prior to entry into care, existing educational difficulties are frequently compounded by the fragmentation and weakening of family and neighbourhood ties following placement (Stein, 1994). Analysis of data from a major longitudinal developmental survey indicates that the effects of 'care' on educational achievement and employment outcomes are influenced by the age of entry to care and the length of time spent in care, those entering care at a young age and those spending longer in care experiencing greater achievement and employment disadvantage (Cheung and Heath, 1994).

In general, young people in residential care appear to fare less well than those in foster care, although many will have experienced both forms of care, sometimes interspersed with periods with their families (Fletcher, 1993). The specific ways in which residential care may disadvantage young people educationally include residential care workers' own limited educational experiences, which may result in their low educational aspirations for young people in their care; and lack of privacy for study and high turnover of both staff and residents, causing difficulties for young people establishing and sustaining long-term relationships with staff members who might take an active interest in their education (Jackson, 1988–9). Young people who enter public care are predominantly from the most disadvantaged sectors in society, and social workers and teachers alike too readily excuse poor behaviour, achievement or attendance as the inevitable outcomes of a disadvantaged background and about which little can be done (Fletcher, 1993; Heath et al., 1994; Stein, 1994). More insidiously, researchers such as Stein and Carey (1983) and young people's advocates such as Fletcher (1993) provide evidence of young people's exposure to stigma and discrimination by teachers and other students.

Placement change and consequent disruption to education are common experiences for looked-after young people. The longer a young person is looked after, the more likely he or she is to experience changes in both placement and school, many experiencing multiple placement changes. Placement moves, including a return home, rarely take adequate account of the young person's education, in many instances resulting in delay in obtaining a school place and lack of information being provided for a receiving school (Millham et al., 1980; Stein and Carey, 1983; Stein, 1994, 1986; Bullock et al., 1994). Neither do such moves take sufficient account of the young person's own views:

Many [looked-after] children feel that they are not meaningfully involved in the decisions being taken about them, including those relating to moves of home or school.

(DFE and DOH, 1994: 9)

Formal explanations for the relatively low priority given to education for looked-after young people by social workers include: a view that education is only one factor among many and that placement availability takes precedence over other considerations, however desirable; priority being given to young people's emotional rather than their educational needs; social workers' lack of awareness of how education and schooling might contribute to the young person's development and long-term future; and social workers' views that it may be unfair to give looked-after young people educational advantages their parents are unable to provide, or that poor parents of similar young people are unable to provide (e.g. DFE and DOH, 1994; Jackson, 1994). These factors manifest themselves in a variety of ways in practice. For example, social workers' expectations of schools may be limited to judgements about their ability to cope with 'difficult' young people and being sympathetic and 'child-friendly', rather than on their academic record. A government report (SSI and OFSTED, 1995) notes that social workers generally have little accurate knowledge about the academic achievement of looked-after young people for whom they are responsible and that social services departments appear reluctant to challenge educational decisions in the way that a young person's own parents are likely to do, such as appealing against exclusion, because of the risk of harming relations with schools.

Prioritising education for looked-after young people

The evidence from research, formal inspections and reports has prompted concrete recommendations for policy frameworks and improved professional practice at both national and local levels (e.g. Dartington Social Services Research Unit, 1995; SSI and OFSTED, 1995; Fletcher-Campbell, 1997; Leeds City Council, 1997; Murray and Godfrey, 1997). The corner-stone of such initiatives is an explicit acceptance of the need to prioritise the education of looked-after young people:

Care authorities should act to remedy the educational disadvantage of children in their care, and do all that a good parent would do to ensure that children's needs are met.

(DOH, 1991b: 10)

Specifically, prioritising education for looked-after young people requires: promoting young people's rights to education; replacing a culture of non-achievement with a culture of achievement; encouraging inter-agency and inter-professional awareness and co-operation; and developing corporate management and co-operation.

Promoting young people's rights to education

In the longer term one of the most significant contributions teachers, social workers and carers can make to the lives of looked-after young people is to ensure their acquisition of marketable skills, in particular literacy and numeracy. Fletcher-Campbell and Hall (1990) argue that the promotion of equal educational opportunities for looked-after young people should focus on the *outcomes of*, rather than merely *access to*, education. The rights to educational equality and opportunity of looked-after young people must be advanced by having the weight of the local authority behind them. This means that local authorities should exercise more forcefully the role of 'concerned parent', engaging with schools on behalf of the young people in their care.

Taking corporate parenting seriously means: accessing published school performance data to seek the best school for a looked-after young person and negotiating admission where a change of school is required; ensuring the young person goes to school; setting appropriate educational targets and keeping them under review; supporting schools to maintain young people in school to prevent the risk of exclusion; using appeals procedures if the young person is excluded from school, notwithstanding the tensions this may cause if he or she is excluded (as a corollary, a greater readiness to activate appeals procedures may encourage head teachers to seek alternatives to exclusion); securing high-quality alternatives when a young person is unavoidably out of school, and working towards getting out-of-school young people (back) into school as soon as possible; ensuring access to appropriate careers and further education advice; making links with prospective employers to optimise employment prospects and help reduce the likelihood of looked-after young people ending up in poorly paid, 'dead-end' jobs – or having no job at all; and improving the management of transitions, especially taking account of any implications a child's care plan will have for their educational career. It means explicitly questioning whether any necessary change in placement also requires a change of school.

Encouraging a culture of achievement

Prioritising education means challenging the 'non-achieving welfare culture' (Stein, 1994: 358) and replacing this by a culture of attendance and achievement, setting explicit achievable educational targets for attendance, behaviour, academic progress and involvement in the social and extra-curricular life of school. Given their prior experiences of education, many looked-after young people may be neither particularly enthusiastic about education nor the most amenable of students. They are likely to need additional support, not only from teachers, social workers and carers, but also from specialist education support staff such as educational psychologists, to make up for educational deficits (McParlin, 1996).

The population of looked-after young people is likely to contain a disproportionate number of students with special educational needs, especially those with statements indicating emotional and behavioural difficulties. All too often so-called 'special education' has in effect been 'second-rate' education, and the rights of these young people to decent-quality education needs to be ensured (Barnes, 1994).

Improving knowledge and awareness across agency boundaries

Many of the practice recommendations from research and inspections identify the need for inter-professional and inter-agency training. However, given the pressurised nature of professional training, few initial qualifying programmes provide opportunities for teachers to learn about the roles, responsibilities and agenda of social services or for social workers to appreciate the value of education, to learn about the operation of the educational system, or how they can ensure that looked-after young people receive a fair deal from it. Beyond qualifying training, much necessary training is already provided by local authorities for staff, carers and school governors, although its benefits across agency boundaries could be further developed.

Developing corporate management and co-operation

Perhaps one of the greatest failures of local authorities has been their signal inability to secure effective inter-departmental co-operation. This is primarily because resources tend to be allocated to particular services (e.g. social services or education) rather than directed towards particular needs. Recent requirements to produce Children's Service Plans provide opportunities to ensure a much greater level of co-operation at all levels, and in some parts of England, at least, the opportunity has been taken to develop integrated local authority services for young people (Cohen and Hagen, 1997). However, government imperatives encouraging collaborative inter-agency and inter-professional endeavour have had to compete with legislative and policy developments promoting fragmentation and competition within and between public services, making such co-operation more, rather than less, difficult. A teacher employed by Manchester Social Services Department urges teachers and social workers to recognise the potential mismatch between education and social services' time-scales, work patterns and bureaucracies which militate against the right kind of intervention being delivered at the right time, and to work around these (Walker, 1994).

The different – and potentially conflicting – policy agendas of education (schools being more likely to think in terms of 'early warning') and social services (favouring 'minimal intervention') also need to be acknowledged and addressed. Professionals owe it to the young people for whom they are responsible not to be overwhelmed by these problems or by excessive pessimism about the impracticality of meaningful co-operation. When resources are limited, there is even more reason to ensure that they are appropriately deployed. A considerable amount of professional workers' time is currently spent, unproductively, on 'debris management' (Parsons *et al.*, 1994). For example, residential care staff may need to be employed for additional hours to care for young people without a school place – whether as the result of exclusion or for other reasons – and frequently doing little more than 'containing' the young person (Fletcher-C................ le the time and effort of t...ent in dealing with the ....on and alienation, which n..................

If local authori...nt and utilisation rather t...ink in terms of *investing* ι.....................................*pending* them reactively, li...............................ιιectively. The positive us..ιιs educational needs are recognised..........................work with the young person and his or her family ....ιιore effective. Proposed measures to facilitate inter-agency ιιιson include an identified individual having oversight of educational matters in each residential establishment (Jackson, 1988–9); a senior manager in social services taking responsibility for the education of looked-after young people (DOH, 1991b; Levy and Kahan, 1991); and making a senior member of teaching staff responsible for looked-after young people (DFE and DOH, 1994).

It is fundamental that all those working with looked-after young people are clear about their own roles and those of others, and that young people know that the different professionals and carers in their lives are working together. This means sharing relevant and important information, while paying due regard to confidentiality, so that schools don't find a young person on their doorstep about whom they know nothing, or young people are not inadequately prepared for a new school. There are now clear expectations that both education and care plans will be produced for looked-after young people and that all those contributing to the care and education of the young person should be actively involved in developing and regularly monitoring these plans (SSI and OFSTED, 1995).

Since the working lives of social workers and care workers are less ruled by timetables than those of teachers, they generally have better opportunities to initiate positive and effective networks including both professionals and parents. Forging effective partnerships with the young person's parents may not be easy, especially where the young person is living away from home, where conflict and discord between the young person and his or her parent(s) have played a part in the young person becoming looked after, and where the parent(s) appear(s) to have little interest in or contribution to make to their child's education. However, one of the consistent messages from research studies is that success in residential care (including educational success) is strongly correlated with the maintenance of family and parental contact (e.g. Weiner and Weiner, 1990).

Implications for practice

Evidence about the impact of education and schooling in the lives of young people, especially those who are experiencing disadvantage and disruption in other areas of their lives, including those in public care, indicates that school can provide one — sometimes the sole — element of stability, continuity and positive relationships (see, e.g., Rutter, 1991; Bullock *et al.*, 1994). Similarly, the evidence above indicates that social work, care and education professionals are frequently failing to ensure that young people in public care obtain optimum benefit from their educational opportunities.

The concerns discussed in this chapter raise certain general implications. Education social workers need to be aware of the range of educational difficulties which looked-after children may be facing and should also ensure that they know the identity of looked-after young people in the schools for which they have a responsibility. They should be competent in inter-agency and multi-disciplinary practice, an essential aspect of which is the accurate knowledge of the identity and role of key participants in the inter-agency/multi-disciplinary network. This will also require them to encourage those responsible for the welfare of the young person to work collaboratively to promote the young person's interests. National and local policies to promote the educational interests of looked-after young people promote effective inter-agency/multi-disciplinary effort. Where they do not already exist, education social workers are clearly well placed to encourage their development.

The Northorpe Hall Trust scheme

Northorpe Hall Trust is an independent charity in Kirklees aiming at improving the quality of life for children, young people and their carers. Its activities range from the provision of practical services, such as a young carers' group, to organising multi-agency training for professionals in health, education and welfare. As such, it was ideally placed to provide a forum in which an integrated approach to improving the educational experiences of looked-after children could be developed, setting up a multi-agency steering group in 1996 alongside the existing project which promoted the health needs of looked-after children and young people. In order to develop corporate management and co-operation to enable the local authority to fulfil its role as 'concerned parent', the promotion of education project consisted of three complementary parts: a training programme for professionals and carers; an action group; and a literacy support group, focusing on improving reading skills.

The training programme

The aim of this programme was to improve the confidence and effectiveness of participants in safeguarding and promoting the education of looked-after children and young people and improve multi-agency co-operation. Initially all the residential homes in the authority were visited to assess what sort of support, guidance and knowledge course participants required, and this was followed up with a series of day seminars which outlined current legislation and guidance. In addition, a ten-week evening course provided more intensive training, covering topics such as:

- the responsibilities of the local authority
- what schools and LEAs should do to safeguard and promote the education of looked-after children
- the law on special educational needs
- attendance and admissions
- exclusion from school
- education otherwise than at school
- options in Year 11 – work experience, transition planning, etc.

Participants could opt for a single session, but, for those attending all 10 sessions, the course was also designed to meet the requirements of post-qualifying study, the assessment including evidence of how learning integrated into practice. In all, the course attracted 183 participants, including social workers from residential, field and education settings; teachers and education support workers; school governors; and foster carers. The course not only increased participants' knowledge and improved inter-agency awareness, but also provided a core group of concerned individuals for stage two of the project – the action group.

The action group

Initially, this group consisted of an educational adviser, the principal education social worker and the residential services manager. This group agreed resource allocation to promote the educational experiences of looked-after children and identified the education of young people admitted to the reception unit as its first priority so the unit manager, mentor and a residential social worker (who had completed the course) were enlisted for the development of the first action plan.

The reception unit was chosen for the first part of the project because of the difficulties being experienced by residential staff in getting residents to school at all and the influence this had on subsequent placements in the authority. Young people newly admitted to the unit found refusing to go to school the easiest form of protest against their more general turmoil and a way of effecting some sort of control over their lives. A culture had developed of non-school attendance, with young people quickly losing good habits of attendance as they sought solidarity in the resident group. Staff were struggling with this general resistance, which was compounded by problems around young people being admitted in an emergency without school uniform so that schools were sending pupils back to the unit on the grounds that they were improperly dressed; some young people having very long journeys to their schools which resulted in them having too many opportunities to find something more interesting to do before they got there; young people feeling embarrassed in the school peer group at no longer having a 'normal home'; and a widespread practice of unofficial exclusions. The lack of knowledge about the appropriate named teacher to contact in each school meant that individual difficulties were not easily sorted out. Unit staff were also concerned that young people who were exhibiting a 'won't go' attitude to school attendance might well develop a 'can't go' attitude as their period of non-school attendance increased and was compounded by the subsequent move to a medium-stay unit (see Bardsley *et al.* in this volume). Additionally, non-school attendance effectively ruled out foster placements for the young people as well as put them at increased danger from the pimps and drug pushers who target new admissions to the unit.

With much of the preparatory work having been already done in phase one of the project, it was relatively easy to actualise the action plan – the multi-agency support and resource allocation already being in existence. The current non-attenders were provided with flexible packages by their schools to aid reintroduction to school and taxis were provided to remove the travel problems. The flexible packages looked not only at curricular modifications to help the young people catch up with academic work whilst maintaining a GCSE level profile that would give them appropriate qualifications, but also took account of their emotional and social needs. For example, one very angry young man was provided with a room to go to when he was about to 'blow up' and teaching staff were informed not to challenge his sudden departures from the classroom; one young woman was allowed to stay in school at break-time until she felt able to mix with other pupils.

Some older pupils were offered packages that gave them part-time study in college and opportunities to study in the home via computer packages in basic English and maths. These packages were introduced via the pupil referral unit and the support of PRU staff in training residential staff in the use of the packages was invaluable. At the same time the mentor concentrated on the educational needs of the residential staff – as noted earlier, residential staff themselves often suffer from educational disadvantage and they can hardly be expected to be confident about assisted reading, homework groups and general negotiations with schools if their confidence in such matters is not attended to.

Education also became an urgent issue for new admissions to prevent any falling off in school attendance habits. The pre-planning meeting that had previously been held within the first five days of admission was brought forward with a meeting held within 24 hours. The identified, named teacher and field social worker were invited to this meeting, which was chaired by the young person's link worker in the unit, thus ensuring an emphasis on educational needs. These meetings quickly sorted out the irritating difficulties to do with school uniform and transport and laid down the foundations of educational needs in the longer-term care plan. The care plan was monitored by means of a weekly action plan agreed between the young person and his or her link worker. The results of the scheme were dramatic – within six weeks not only were all the residents in school on a regular basis, but staff were more confident and optimistic.

The action group then invited medium-stay residential units to take part in the project. Interestingly the units that responded all had a member of staff who had undertaken the introductory course. The action proposed contained all the elements of the first stage of the scheme but had a slightly different focus to meet the individual needs of the units. Two main needs were identified: young people with long-term non-attendance patterns who had developed into a 'can't go' category; and young people whose schools were some distance from the new placement, thus removing the young person from easy contact with friends.

The first group of young people tended to respond well initially to flexible school packages but found returning to school much harder than they had anticipated; their early efforts soon diminished, with a knock-on effect on school and social work staff, who felt 'let down' by the young person, losing enthusiasm for the project. It was found that the packages needed to be particularly flexible in terms of time-scales, teachers tending originally to expect a carefully phased return to full-time schooling. Where the young person felt consulted about the plan and in charge of how it developed, much more success was achieved. Additionally, a full-time dedicated education social worker to the scheme proved vital in helping residential and teaching staff design and support an appropriate package of reintroduction to school. This led in some cases to the young person's link worker attending school with the young person in the early stages; a seemingly expensive resource but one that worked for the young person – and increased the residential workers' knowledge of the school and education process.

The second group of young people needed a slightly different approach. The units were already skilled in introducing the new admission to the other residents with a carefully planned programme of meal-time visits and overnight stays, but needed to pay more attention to the difficulties the change of address would have on the young person's social life. In some instances this will require a carefully planned change of school, even where the young person is already established in a school, but mostly it will involve plans to help the young person maintain existing social relationships. The development of this stage of the project has yet to be established, but what is clear is the need to consult with the young person carefully and honestly to prevent both parties from feeling that their efforts are not being reciprocated. One year on, the project has been sufficiently successful to hold a 'Celebration of Achievements' Day at which forty young people looked after by the local authority received certificates in recognition of significant improvement at school or college. The young people were nominated by a wide range of professionals – foster carers, social workers, support workers and counsellors – all of whom enjoyed a day where they could focus on achievement rather than failure, showing that developing a culture of achievement clearly benefits adults as well as young people.

The literacy support scheme

Some of the successful practical measures which have been introduced elsewhere to promote a culture of educational achievement focus on literacy schemes (e.g. Jackson, 1998–9; Menmuir, 1994; Brodie, 1997; Fletcher-Campbell, 1997), so it was felt vital to the success of the project generally to support it with a book-buying and reading scheme. The Northorpe Hall project applied the Who Cares? Trust 'Book of My Own' scheme (Bald *et al.*, 1995). This aims to:

- encourage young people's interest and pleasure in books and reading;
- give looked-after children the opportunity to choose and own books;
- encourage adults and children to enjoy reading together as partners; and
- help children gain the reading skills needed for success in education.

The scheme provides the young person with an allocation of £25 which can be spent on books over a three-month period, and where the young person has no suitable reading partner, it provides one who will both help with the purchase of books and listen to reading. The response to the scheme has been enthusiastic and varied, ranging from young people in residential units who are paired with their link workers to foster carers. There is even one young person on the scheme who has returned home. This young person and her family have special educational needs so Northorpe Hall Trust has provided a reading partner for her. There are opportunities to extend the scheme on a peer pairing basis as the looked-after young people's group meets at Northorpe Hall. The National Literacy Scheme subsequently supplied books for the young people participating in the 'Celebration of Achievement' event.

Conclusion

Change is rarely effected by informing a group of teachers or social workers that they are failing children. They have mostly tried hard to access education for looked-after young people at some time in their careers and met with more disappointment than success. The Northorpe Hall Trust scheme shows that what works best is a building up of existing expertise and a regeneration of enthusiasm via the co-ordinated efforts of concerned management. Having a neutral base such as Northorpe Hall Trust also helps to break down inter-agency barriers.

Promoting educational achievement for looked-after young people does not require vast amounts of money or large numbers of working parties. The key to initial success lies in providing a forum in which individuals are listened to and their existing skills recognised and utilised. This includes both professionals, who need to be consulted about their training needs, and the young people, who are the best experts on the difficulties in their own lives. Successful schemes grow from the identification of expertise, not imposed solutions.

11

STUDENT SUPPORT GROUPS

Mike Haworth and Kay Bardsley

The work described in this chapter has developed from a number of projects with which we have been involved. This work has been carried out with students presenting challenges in terms of their school attendance and/or their behaviour. The focus of this chapter is on groupwork aimed at helping students to improve their attendance; it is based largely on work undertaken by the Leeds Attendance and Behaviour Project, although examples from the Preventing Exclusions Project are also used.

The Leeds Attendance and Behaviour Project grew out of a three-year GEST- funded initiative aimed at raising attendance in five inner city high schools. This project focused on helping schools to develop a whole-school approach to improving attendance. Work was undertaken at whole- school, classroom and individual level. Groupwork formed an important part of the intervention undertaken with individual students.

Support groups were set up for chronic non-attenders, who might otherwise have been progressing onto committee and court (The Leeds Education Welfare Service [EWS] operates a system whereby the decision to refer a case to court is taken by a panel which includes some members of the Education Committee and senior EWS staff. The panel meets with the parents/carers and the child.) Other groups were also available to students whose attendance was deteriorating or whose punctuality was poor. This work has been continued by a series of one-year GEST-funded projects, which have tackled attendance and behaviour. It has included groupwork with:

- students at risk of being excluded from school
- primary school students about to undergo the transition to high school
- parents/carers of children with challenging behaviour (run in parallel with groups for the children themselves)
- students who are the victims or perpetrators of bullying

Groupwork (student support groups, social competencies groups, social skills groups, etc.) can often be seen to offer a miracle 'cure' to the challenges presented by children with attendance or behavioural difficulties. This is a temptation that needs to be avoided. Not only can groupwork with 'disaffected' students be extremely challenging, it very rarely offers the wished for miracle (although we know of a number of instances where such groupwork has provided the turning point for individual students). More importantly it can prove a red herring preventing schools from addressing other key issues relating to the needs of disaffected students. Student support groups must be seen within the context of the whole school system and indeed beyond. Work with disaffected students must take place at a range of levels from the individual to the whole school. To do otherwise is to risk problematising the students and avoid examining other issues within schools, such as bullying or racism (see, e.g., Blyth and Milner, 1996).

Poor school attendance is usually a symptom of other problems. These may be:

- rooted in home circumstances and can be social or emotional in nature
- individual difficulties, special needs or behaviour
- school-based problems such as difficulties accessing parts of the curriculum; in forming social relationships with teachers and peers or because of unmet learning difficulties
- wider issues such as racism both at school and outside.
  The manifestation of this myriad of problems in poor school attendance means that a groupwork approach to the issue must be carefully thought through.

Group members may bring a combination of these problems with them to the group. So whilst the common factor amongst members will be poor school attendance, they may present such diverse problems as caring for other family members, involvement in solvent abuse, experiencing racial harassment, working illegally to supplement the family income, being bullied at school, and so on.

Common to all these students is the need to return to school and access their education. The emphasis of an attendance group must be to help individuals tackle the issues affecting them. Because these are so diverse, the approach taken by the project has been to introduce members to problem-solving strategies which can be applied in a variety of different contexts. At the same time we have endeavoured to improve self-esteem through involvement in the group and offer support by bringing students together and engendering a feeling of positive peer group pressure.

The vehicle for teaching these problem-solving strategies has been a programme based on life and social skills issues; equipping the young people with the necessary life and social skills to return to school and access their education.

Considerations for running a group

There is, then, no single ideal way of running a group. It has to be tailored to the needs of the particular individuals who are to be in the group that is being run as well as the needs of the school at that particular time. There are, however, a number of common considerations to be made.

Why do you want to run a group?

At the outset, anyone considering running a group needs to be clear what they hope to achieve. What are the challenges that are being presented? Are there enough suitable individuals to make up a group? Is a group the best way to meet these challenges or would an individual approach be more appropriate? Are there adequate resources available to run a group?

Groupwork or individual support?

To a certain extent this is a non-question. We have always tried to incorporate some individual work with groupwork. This enables focused follow-up work, clearer monitoring and more comprehensive target setting and planning. There are, of course, resource implications here. One of the attractions of groupwork is its apparent cost-effectiveness. As a minimum we have found an initial individual session invaluable. This enables you to:

- introduce yourself to the student
- assess the issues affecting the student's attendance/behaviour
- identify problem areas that the student wants to work on
- explain what will happen in the group and check that the student understands this
- discuss any anxieties
- check that the student wants to be part of the group

Figure 11.1 shows a questionnaire that we have used (often in part only) during individual and group sessions to help identify some of the issues, at both group and individual level, that need to be addressed. We have also used variants of this format for evaluation purposes.

If further individual sessions are possible, a programme for these sessions should be drawn up otherwise there is a danger that they become unfocused 'chats' or 'pep talks'. These sessions can be useful in setting targets and working on plans that will achieve these targets. They should also be used to review progress and reinforce the work from the group. The approach we have used is generally known as a problem-solving approach (Searle and Streng, 1996):

	YES	NO
1 It is easy for me to listen to someone who is talking to me.		
2 I ask for help in a friendly way.		
3 I have the materials I need for classes (i.e. books, pencils and paper).		
4 I understand what to do when directions are given and I follow these directions.		
5 I finish my schoolwork.		
6 I try to help an adult when I think he/she could use the help.		
7 I decide what I don't understand about my schoolwork.		
8 I decide on something I want to work for and keep working until I get it.		
9 When someone says they like something about me, I accept what they say.		
10 I tell others I'm sorry after I do something wrong.		
11 I know how I feel about different things that happen.		
12 I let others know what I am feeling and do it in a good way.		
13 I try to tell how other people are feeling.		
14 When I am angry, I deal with it in ways that will not hurt other people.		
15 I try to understand other people's angry feelings.		
16 I keep my temper when I am upset.		
17 I know that when I have to ask to do something I want to do, I should ask in a friendly way.		
18 When somebody teases me, I stay in control.		
19 I try to stay away from things that may get me into trouble.		
20 I think of ways, other than fighting, to take care of problems.		
21 I think of ways to deal with a problem and think of what might happen if I use them.		
22 When I do something I shouldn't have done, I accept what happens.		
23 I decide what I have been accused of and why, and then think of a good way to handle it.		
24 I know when a problem happened because of something I did.		
25 I tell others without getting mad or yelling when they have caused a problem for me.		
26 When I don't do well at something on a test, or doing my chores, I decide ways I could do better next time.		
27 When I am told 'no', I can keep from becoming upset.		
28 I say 'no' to things that might get me into trouble or that I don't want to do, and I say it in a friendly way.		
29 When a group of students want me to do something that might get me in trouble or that is wrong, I say 'no'.		
30 I keep from taking things that are not mine.		
31 I tell the truth about what I have done, even if I might get into trouble.		

Figure 11.1 Pupil questionnaire

- identifying the problem
- setting goals or targets
- developing plans to achieve the targets (these need to be quite detailed and examine the consequences of each step of the plan)
- putting the plan into action
- reviewing progress
- reviewing the targets or modifying the plans.

Venue

Apart from the usual considerations about cost, adequate space, accessibility, facilities, and so on, there are a number of other issues which need to be addressed for school attendance groups. Should the group be held on school premises? The non-school attender may transfer negative associations with school to the group. Holding the group at school may also exclude those students who have not attended on the day of the group. The venue for the group is important. It must have an atmosphere conducive to enabling group members to feel secure and relaxed. The following features should be considered when choosing a venue:

- creating the right atmosphere
- room to meet together as a large group or in smaller groups
- adequate seating
- space to display materials on the wall
- room to store equipment, materials and work
- toilet facilities for both sexes
- facilities for making drinks.

It is essential that the same room is used for each session (one of us had a disastrous experience being moved around a school every week) and that the space is private and free from interruptions.

Who will run the group?

We have tried running groups solo. This can be very hard work and, based on our experience, we would advise against this if at all possible. Not only is planning easier in a team, but it gives the students more chance of forming a relationship with a group leader. You may find that you develop particular strengths and your other team members will also have strengths that help create a strong 'blend'.

We would also advocate an apprenticeship model so that less experienced workers team up with more experienced workers. This is a good way of developing skills in groupwork.

In a mixed group you would want a balance of male and female workers.

There are also issues about race and gender to consider when deciding who might run groups. The projects that we have worked with have run or supported groups which have been single-sex and for groups of students from minority ethnic groups (or both). It is appropriate that the group leaders reflect the composition of the group if important issues around race and gender are to be covered in an open way that group members feel comfortable with.

There are definite advantages to having school staff involved in running groups. The skills of running groups become part of the range of expertise of the school staff. Relationships formed during groups may be helpful outside of the group setting and using school staff can mean greater flexibility and sometimes availability. There can, however, be disadvantages. The students may be anxious about the presence of school staff and may not be 'open' or receptive. Groups can be seen as low priority if there is staff absence leading to cancellation, giving the message that the group is not important.

If school staff do run or help run groups, consideration will need to be given to whether there are staff available with adequate groupwork skills or who are willing to learn. You will need to ask if there is training available, and know where to look. It might be tempting to use staff whose timetable is more flexible (e.g. senior management) but whose general role in school conflicts with their role in the group. Year heads who are responsible for some aspects of 'discipline' might find it difficult to establish trust and openness with a group.

The school Education Welfare Officer (EWO) may be an ideal figure to run or be involved in the group: EWOs are detached from the school and yet familiar with its staff, structures and procedures; they are not part of the school hierarchy and yet they understand the organisation so they can help and advise students. Most of the students invited to an attendance group will be known to the EWO and the EWO may have visited the family home. EWOs are in a good position to be able to follow up absentees from the group and to form vital links with carers.

Supervision

Do you want to be supervised, and if so, who might do it? Having someone not directly involved in the group offering impartial views can be very helpful, particularly if the group is demanding and you feel that little progress is being made or that you are stuck. Meetings with the group supervisor should be scheduled to take place at the planning and operation stages, with a review after the group has finished.

Who should be in the group?

Attendance groups can be run around specific issues such as punctuality, internal truancy, behaviour and attendance problems, chronic poor attendance or intermittent absence. The criteria used for selection will depend upon the problem that has been identified. Consideration should be given to the balance of gender, ethnicity and age that is represented amongst the membership. Too broad a range of ages may make the group unworkable as the different developmental stages of members may militate against effective group functioning. Discussion-based work may be difficult, as might activities where a certain degree of literacy and comprehension competence is required. However, a group comprising individuals separated by a year or two may be beneficial in enabling the older members to develop pride in the support they are able to give to younger ones and the younger ones to model their behaviour on their older peers.

As noted above, we have successfully run groups targeted solely at, for example, girls or students of Asian origin. There may be occasions when it is necessary to address issues that are pertinent to one such group and the nature of the discussion may require a commonality of experience that would exclude other groups. For example, a punctuality group for girls in a school where punctuality was a particular issue amongst girls; similarly an exclusion group that targeted black students who wished to discuss issues of racism and their responses to racist attacks.

It is very tempting to put all students presenting the most challenging behaviour or attendance problems into social competency groups. It is very easy to end up creating the 'group from hell', where the students are reluctant to participate, or, at the other extreme, where too many students exhibit the type of poor behaviour or attendance that led to their referral in the first place! A group focused on the poorest attenders may flounder. The low attendance rate within the group may give credence to poor attendance amongst the members. A mix of better and poorer attenders enables the better attenders to support the poorer ones by suggesting strategies and ideas for improving their attendance. It also provides the poorer attenders with positive role models and healthy competition. It is necessary to consider what sort of mix you want to create.

Given that there is a fair amount of discussion involved, a group full of introverted students who are reluctant to join in oral work would not work well. Similarly, too many dominant individuals can make groupwork hard going. To a certain extent who is in your group will not be a question that you can answer in isolation from questions about what you want to focus on in your group. For example, if you want the group to focus on conflict resolution, then the group composition will to a certain extent 'fall out' of this decision.

The widespread introduction of computerised registration has facilitated the easy identification of students occupying a given target category. It is easy to generate a list of students with less than 85 per cent attendance or with more than five 'lates' in the previous four weeks. However, having generated the list, teachers and EWOs must work together to identify those students who would benefit from a groupwork approach in tackling their problems. Some students may need help but not benefit from belonging to a group, and one-to-one individual attention may be more useful to them.

Decisions about who will be in the group and whether or not you need criteria for selection will also have to be made. Should heads of year decide? Should it only be for children for whom a lot of reports have been made? Some sort of referral system avoids the students being placed in a group because there was a difficulty with them that morning! Experience has shown that a detailed referral form can help in selecting the right students for the group. The referral form should enable teachers and other agencies involved with the family to make comment on the child. It is also useful to ask parents for their views on the child and his or her difficulties.

One of the problems we have found is trying to provide groupwork for students who are already involved with a variety of other agencies. Sometimes the work can tend to cross-cut rather than complement what we are trying to achieve; for example, working on a behaviour group with students who are referred to the Pupil Referral Unit. As noted above, it is useful to meet potential recruits before the group begins. Workers can then begin to build a relationship with these children, explain to them what the group is about and see whether they are likely to commit themselves to participating and attending. Workers can then try to select a balance of students and a combination that appear as if they would gel. Such a system needs to be clear to staff, even though the criteria or target group might change.

The number of children in the group is crucial. It will depend to a certain extent on the experience of the group leaders, the students themselves and what you are trying to achieve. As a general rule, groups over 12 can become unwieldy.

Parents

A child's involvement in an attendance group will usually involve obtaining parental consent. This may be a legal necessity where the group does not include a teacher, insurance cover may involve collecting consent forms before the group begins. It is also a matter of good practice to try to enlist the support of parents for their child's involvement in the group. The intervention of EWOs will involve meeting the whole family to agree strategies that can be tried to improve pupil attendance. Membership of an attendance group may form part of that work.

Clearly the support and encouragement of parents may be crucial to the success of the group in improving school attendance. The majority of parents will be interested to know what their children are doing; moreover, they may be able to provide valuable insights into the reasons why their children are missing school and useful assistance in supporting their return to school. There may be instances, particularly with younger children or where youngsters are performing a caring role within the family, where there is some parental collusion in the child being away from school. Home visits prior to the group may help to unveil some of these issues and alert the parent to your concern.

Figure 11.2 shows a section of a questionnaire used to structure parent interviews and as part of the evaluation. (This particular example is from the Preventing Exclusions Project.)

Rules and contracts

Consideration of the 'rules' or 'codes of conduct' is very important. They must be clear from the outset, as must be the consequences of breaking them and equally important, the consequences of keeping them. The same considerations apply as they would when students are negotiating other sets of rules, for example class rules. It is particularly important, however, that issues of confidentiality are clear and that the group is a pleasant and safe environment for everyone. A common issue that arises is around the comments students will make about staff. The important thing is to be clear. Rules work best when they have been negotiated and agreed by group members themselves. Group leaders will still need a clear idea of what issues the rules need to cover, however. It is worth considering whether to draw up individual contracts for group members to sign. These should specify the expectations on both sides and the consequences of meeting these expectations or not.

Non-attendance at attendance groups!

Attendance groups are often sporadically attended. Students with problems that militate against them going to school may find it difficult to maintain a commitment to attending a regular group meeting. There is a dilemma for the attendance group worker. To remove children from their school lessons in order to attend a group about school attendance can be criticised as legitimising non-attendance. However, it can be hard to motivate students who are daunted by the need to turn up at school every day to come to a group which is run after school.

Our experience suggests that it is beneficial to offer transport to and from the group. There are also issues about what to do when group members do not turn up. Even if you have planned well and organised transport, with a group of poor attenders it is possible that there will be sessions when attendance is low. There is no easy answer to this. Experience has taught us the

1.How do you think _____ is doing at school?

2. Are you aware of any problems with _____ at school?

YES		NO		Please tick

What are they?

_____

_____

3. If yes, how worried are you about it? PLEASE TICK

Very worried		Worried		Slightly worried		Not worried	

4. Have you any concerns with _____ at home?

YES		NO		Please tick

5. If yes, what sort of concerns?

6. How would you rate the communication from school? PLEASE TICK

EXCELLENT		5		4		3		2		1		Poor	

7. If poor, how could it be improved?

_____

_____

8. Have you been asked to be involved in any school matters involving

_____ ?

YES		NO		Please tick

9. If so, what sort of involvement

_____

_____

Figure 11.2 Parent/carer questionnaire

wisdom of having some standby or alternative activity. Discussion-based activities and role play are impossible with insufficient numbers. If numbers are very low and running the session later is possible, using the time for individual work should be considered. In this way the core of the work is not missed. If this is not possible, some thought must be given to how students who have missed a session can 'catch up' and how they might be brought back into the group.

As a minimum follow-up, absentees should be contacted by either letter or telephone before the next meeting. Ideally they should be visited at home or seen in school so that contact is not lost and they do not begin to drift.

Programme content

There are many possible curricula and to a certain extent questions about content are inseparable from questions about teaching approaches. Some of the most important questions are about whether a specific content is adopted, such as conflict resolution or anger management, or whether a more general approach is taken, such as problem-solving, into which different issues may be slotted. Typically we have run groups that provide a mixture of the two, which has allowed us to cover areas appropriate for members of any particular group but also to teach them problem-solving skills which they can apply to a wide range of challenges that they will face. There are now a number of good resource books to 'tap into' (see, e.g., McConnon, 1990, 1992a, 1992b; Brown and Fabry, 1993; Fitzpatrick *et al.*, 1994; Douglas, 1995; Freeman and Fabry, 1995; Dwivedi, 1996).

If you are running the group in tandem with individual sessions for group members, you need to consider how the two (groupwork and individual work) will marry. The individual work may come out of the groupwork and the group may be used to support individual targets, or individual work may follow on from the groupwork (i.e. after the programme has finished).

Timing

The number of sessions in a programme, the length of each session and the frequency of sessions may well be determined by the timetable, although the groups we have run have generally run for about ten weeks. Where flexibility is possible it is important that sessions do not drag. Conversely the session must be long enough to generate productive discussions and to complete the activities. Timing also depends upon the age of the group members; older children usually have a longer attention span than younger ones. As a general rule an hour and a half seems to be the optimal length for a session. Our experience has been largely based on once-weekly sessions, although an intensive groupwork programme may benefit from a second session in the week. There are implications here of course for staff time and the extra planning and organisation involved.

The number of sessions in a programme should be decided at the beginning and stuck to: extending the life of the group because it is going well will not necessarily benefit the youngsters involved. In fact, it could delay their development by extending their dependency on the group and the workers. Indeed, the group ending should be planned at the beginning. Consideration should be given to the support structures that will be available to the members and any further contact that the workers might have with them. For example, there may be a member of staff in school whom students can see if they have any problems.

Content

The content of the programme will vary depending on the problems that the students in the group present. One model, which has been used, is as follows:

- introduction – getting to know each other
- 'keyhole' exercises and assessments
- reasons and excuses for absence
- positive reasons to attend school
- personal, social and legal consequences of absence
- practicalities: morning routines
- dealing with authority figures
- peer group relationships
- family relationships
- the future: jobs and leisure
- end session and goodbye.

The more serious the attendance problem that the group members present, the more individual support is offered to help students.

What methods/approaches will you use?

There are many methods that you might consider using in groupwork sessions. We have found that incorporating pace and variety keeps students engaged and motivated to attend sessions. It is preferable to develop a session structure that is used throughout the programme, although this must be flexible enough to incorporate other approaches when the occasion demands. One such structure is outlined below:

- welcome
- 'get it off your chest' – five minutes discussing any pressing issues

- feedback on homework
- activity – tabletop tasks completed individually or in groups
- discussion
- role play
- games
- setting homework.

The aim is to use a variety of groupwork methods and give students the opportunity to discuss issues and practise skills or strategies that they may have learned. Although group leaders must be prepared to 'go with the flow' of the session to a certain extent, the objectives for each session need to be clear to avoid it meandering into irrelevant areas. Some children will be very good at taking sessions to regions they've never been before!

Some of the approaches we have used are listed below.

Video work

This can include making videos. You will need to feel confident about the technology (technical gremlins are an anathema to groupwork), be clear about why you are using it (i.e. not just as a gimmick), and allow plenty of time. It can take up a lot of time and result in very 'stop-and-start' sessions, but it can be useful to provide visual feedback to students on their performance. Pre-recorded videos can help to illustrate a point or provide a starting point for discussion.

Cartooning

Group members depict an event that prevents them from going to school; for example, meeting friends on the way to school or problems getting up in the morning. Each frame in the cartoon illustrates a part of the sequence of events that result in non-school attendance. With the aid of group leaders they can identify when things start to go wrong and draw an alternative version.

Group discussion

To a certain extent this is an obvious approach, although it requires a good deal of skill and planning on behalf of the group leaders. It is vital to ensure that the discussion feels safe to the students and that it doesn't leave them feeling exposed or that they have covered too much in a session.

Circle time

There are a plethora of resources on 'circle time' (e.g. Bliss and Tetley, 1993; Bliss *et al.*, 1996), and we have found the techniques useful even with younger groups of children. The group sit in a circle and each member of the group is given the opportunity to speak, perhaps finishing statements such as 'I didn't go to school this week because...'. All group members have the right to pass if they cannot think of anything to say. It can also be a useful way of ending the group: 'The thing I liked best about the group today was...'; 'One thing I will do differently next week is ...'.

Role play

Role play can be used for students to act out situations and practise alternative responses. It enables them to practise dealing with situations in a safe environment and can prove invaluable in helping them develop interpersonal skills. It has been used to particular effect enacting conflict situations in school between teachers and students. Students can learn that by reacting differently to a teacher the conflict can be dissipated.

Questionnaires

While these may provide a challenge for the less able students, they can provide useful information in helping the student and the member of staff to analyse the reasons why a pupil is missing school or misbehaving. Closed questions are easier to complete than open ones and questionnaires can be simplified for younger or less literate children by using tick box smiley faces rather than complex rating scales. Questionnaires should be completed in small groups where a groupworker can go through each of the questions and help students to complete their responses. They are, of course, also a useful tool for group evaluation.

Audiotapes

Group members may wish to record examples of their work or discussion onto audiotape and it may be a useful tool for evaluation and reflection. We have also used audiotape to play music and look at relaxation techniques.

Drawing

Group members can be encouraged to express their ideas through drawing or painting. Again, this visual record can be a useful way for the less literate or younger child to express his or her feelings, or to depict events.

Games

Games are an important way to develop trust and confidence amongst the group members. A variety of books which are packed with ideas are available (McConnon, 1990, 1992a, 1992b; Brown and Fabry, 1993; Fitzpatrick *et al.*, 1994; Douglas, 1995; Freeman and Fabry, 1995; Dwivedi, 1996). Many of these have sections on trust building, concentration, confidence building, and so on. They are important in developing a sense of group cohesion and identity. They also provide useful icebreakers at the beginning and end of the sessions.

Attendance charts

An attendance chart (Table 11.1) forms a substantial and important part of each of the sessions. This takes the form of a wall chart on which group members plot their level of school attendance.

Table 11.1 An attendance chart

Name of group member	Attendance achieved over previous week	Points awarded	Target attendance for next week	Running total of points achieved
Ian	6/10	6	8	20
Simon	4/8	5	6	15
Jason	0/10	0	1	8
Charlotte	10/10	15	10	30
Aziz	3/8	5	4	20
Winston	5/10	6	8	14
Susan	9/10	10	10	25

The attendance chart can accommodate the fact that group members may have been unable to attend for a full week due to a school closure or training day. The points awarded to members reflect the amount of effort they have put into attending school. A point will usually be given for each day the student attended school and the group may decide to give extra points where they feel a member has made exceptional effort to get to school by overcoming difficult problems, or where he or she has improved his/ her attendance dramatically from the previous week. The target attendance for the following week is negotiated, taking into account how well the pupil has attended. Strategies to help individuals get back to school may also be discussed as part of the process of negotiating the points.

Some of the feedback we have had from group members about the attendance chart includes:

The other group members made me feel that I should attend.

It made me realise that other members of the group had problems with their attendance as well.

It made you proud if you attended well.

Why homework?

There is evidence to suggest that even when people change their behaviour within the context of a social competency group, change in different contexts is much more difficult to achieve. Setting tasks based on the groupwork sessions can help to transfer newly learned strategies to new situations. Typically students might be asked to monitor the way they dealt with a particular type of situation, how they felt, note what the consequences of their behaviour was, or try out a new approach in a number of low-risk situations. Of course, 'homework' (or rather not completing it) should not become a reason for students not to come to the group. It should be presented as part of the groupwork that it is important for students to attempt, not as something they will be punished for not doing! We have had many useful discussions with groups as a result of homework exercises. One of the most important teaching (and learning) points has been that not everything works first time. It has enabled some students to reflect on what works (or doesn't) and to establish some perseverance and build on their experience.

Planning time

It is essential to build in time for debriefing and planning after each session. It may sometimes be tempting to forget these sessions and enjoy a well-earned rest. If you can defer your gratification, however, time spent discussing what went well, what didn't, noting individuals who worked well, and so on, will bring considerable benefits to your planning and increase the probability of a successful next session.

Where planning and evaluation time have been programmed in, the sessions are more productive. Without this the planning falls on one individual and the other workers become glorified support workers who are unable to effectively participate in leading the session as they are unsure what has been planned and why the topics/activities have been included.

Outcomes (evaluating the success [or otherwise] of your group)

For some teachers, evaluation is the last thing on their minds. When you are involved yourself in running a group it is very difficult to evaluate objectively. We have found that unless a system is in place, evaluation of a whole programme can easily consist of whether the last session went well. Unless evaluation is considered at an early stage, you will hear yourself saying, 'I wish we had collected that information before we started.' Some of the things you might want to consider are:

- Has the students' attendance improved?
- Has the students' behaviour changed?
- Do the students perceive it as having changed?
- Do teachers or parents perceive it as having changed?
- Have you taught what you intended to/have the students learned what you wanted them to?
- Are any changes long-lasting?
- Do students value the changes?
- Did students enjoy the groupwork sessions? Which aspects did they enjoy the most?
- What did they feel about the venue/ timing of the group?

The 'how' of evaluation can be more problematic. We have developed questionnaires to answer most of these questions. Attempts to use the Behaviour Database © (a computerised system developed by Leeds City Council 1998) to monitor group members' behaviour and measure any change have had limited success. Computerised attendance programmes offer a straightforward approach to one aspect of evaluation, but some of the benefits to the students might not be immediately apparent. The benefits might be long term or they might be other than a straightforward improvement in attendance. Self-monitoring by students themselves probably offers the most scope. Many students are unable to self-monitor (they may well, for example, not recognise their rising anxiety and what increases it and so not be able to do anything to reduce it), but by equipping students with strategies to monitor their own behaviour we can evaluate and provide support at the same time.

Apart from asking students, we have also asked the opinions of teachers and parents. It is necessary to be clear what information you want, that is, what will be valuable for the individual students and what will help you improve your approach with future groups. There is a limit to what you can expect others to do to support your evaluation. Teachers, for example, may not appreciate the burden of more paperwork. It is often difficult to pick up the more subtle changes in behaviour through questionnaires. In particular it is perhaps impractical to expect a teacher who has struggled with the challenging behaviour of a student in the past to notice that the same student now grunts at him more politely! All of these methods using questionnaires are 'rough and ready' but the qualitative (and sometimes anecdotal information) can be very useful in planning the next step with a student.

Below are some of the comments members of one, fairly typical, group have made:

Q.1: Please write down one or two things that you have enjoyed about being part of the group.
Answers:
'I work now ...I want to work'
'Talking'
'Laughter'
'Seeing the brothers'
'Being able to come in and say stuff about the teachers'
'Talking to someone in confidence'

Q.2: In what ways has the group helped you at school?
Answers:
'Know what my rights are'
'Learn from my mistakes'
'Be more calm'
'Know how to control my temper'
'How to speak to teachers'
'Think before we act'

Q.3: In what ways has the group helped you at home?
Answers:
'How to control my temper'
'No change really'
'No, I've been grounded for four weeks'
'I don't know – the same'
'Mum not getting so much hassle from school'

Q.4: At school, has your attitude to teachers changed?
Answers:
'Learn to laugh at them instead of getting angry'
'Yes, a bit'
'Yes it's good now'
'I can see their point of view'
'In conflicts, yes, but not normally'
'Realise that if we can't get on with teachers, still got to get on with work'

Q.5: Has your attitude towards your peers changed?
Answers:
'Sort of'
'It's good talking in the group'

'I don't beat up so many people now'
'It wasn't bad in the first place'

Q.6: Do you find it easier to accept instruction now?
Answers:
'If they're normal instructions, yes'
'I don't answer back'
'I don't get so angry now'
'No – still gets me mad – they go too far'

Q.7: Do you find it easier to deal with difficult situations?
Answers:
'Confrontations – yes'
'Learn how to handle your arguments'

Q.8: Any other comments?
Answers:
'Interesting and helpful'
'Fun'
'Exciting'
'Would like to do it again'
'The teachers should have a group'
'I needed it'
'I haven't told anyone things before'

Ratings for why students attended the group included 'I enjoyed it' and 'I wanted to see my friends'.

A feeling that echoed through the group evaluation was 'being made to feel important', providing a sense of self-worth and the feelings that someone cared and that others were in the same situation.

Belonging to a group was sometimes reported to have little impact on the way group members feel about the school; some attitudes were still negative: 'Nobody likes school.' Similarly, attitudes to teachers/parents and EWOs were unchanged. What was remarked upon was how attitudes to themselves had changed: 'I've learned to control my temper' and 'I have got more confident about myself'. Several felt that it had helped them to improve their attendance 'a little bit'. The overall response to the group was that they had 'enjoyed it'. Moreover, there was greater confidence about attending school – 'Because I would know what to expect and how to react' – and an increase in organisational skills – 'It made me think about setting the alarm at the right time.'

Reporting back information to parents and teachers

For groups to work well there needs to be good support from school and good communication with all parties. Sometimes poor communication from group leaders to school staff and others can lead to a lack of follow-up work with group members. Further, it can leave staff wondering what the group was for and reticent about lending their support in the future.

Qualitative information can sometimes pick up on the benefits of group-work that quantitative information may miss. This was illustrated by one of the students involved in an attendance group. Katie was a very able girl who attended sporadically through Year 9 and had block absence throughout Year 10. Katie attended an attendance support group that ran after school for ten weeks, despite not attending school during the period of the group. However, after the group, as she began Year 11 she returned to full-time attendance:

> I never did a full week in the 10 weeks – it just clicked – I started going back to school, I wanted to prove I could do it, to everyone who said I couldn't do it.

She attributed her return to the effect of the group, saying that it had helped her to build her confidence and to realise that others were in a similar situation:

> I had more confidence because I went back to school....I had a bad attitude but it helped going to the group.

She also commented on the support that attending the group had conferred:

> The longer I left it the more catching up I had to do – I didn't want to go, everyone took it out of me for not going. The group showed that someone was bothered – it helped you.

Because the impact of the group was long term rather than immediate with this student, analysis of her attendance as the group was in progress would not have been very impressive. However, the long-term impact was of great benefit.

Continuity

The more often that students attend the group, the more likely their attendance was to improve. The continuity of the group was also found to be important. It is important to ensure that the group wasn't disrupted by other events such as exams, Christmas or school outings. Workers should also plan to minimise disruption caused by staff sickness. Having a 'reserve' worker is useful where possible, thus avoiding the need to cancel sessions.

Finally

Have you been deterred by the long list of considerations that this chapter contains? There is no doubt that running groups for students disaffected from school is not a soft option. It is also true that evaluating these groups is not straightforward, that you can spend more time 'evaluating' than 'doing'. We are convinced, however, that there is a good deal of potential in this area. The evaluation and feedback from students is almost invariably positive, it is generally positive from parents and, not infrequently, positive from teachers (not involved in running the groups). Some of the comments from students indicate that being part of a student support group was a unique experience for them, and one that altered the course of their problematic school careers. This has made the hard work worthwhile for us.

REFERENCES

Association of Metropolitan Authorities (AMA) (1995) *Reviewing Special Educational Needs: Report of the AMA Working Party on Special Educational Needs*, London: AMA.

Audit Commission (1996) *Planning and Supply of School Places and Parent Satisfaction*, London: HMSO.

Bald, J., Bean, J. and Meegan, J. (1995) *A Book of My Own*, London: Who Cares? Trust.

Ball, S. (1993) 'Education Markets, Choice and Social Class: The Market as a Class Strategy in the UK and the USA', *British Journal of Sociology of Education*, 14, 1: 3–19.

Barnes, C. (1994) *Disabled People in Britain and Discrimination: A Case for Anti-Discrimination Legislation*, London: Hurst and Co.

Berg, I., Consterdine, M., Hullin, R., McGuire, R. and Tyrer, S. (1978) 'The Effect of Two Randomly Allocated Court Procedures on Truancy', *British Journal of Criminology*, 18, 3: 232–44.

Berg, I., Hullin, R., McGuire, R. and Tyrer, S. (1977) 'Truancy and the Courts: Research Note', *Journal of Child Psychology and Psychiatry*, 18: 359–65.

Biehal, N., Clayden, J., Stein, M. and Wade, J. (1992) *Prepared for Living? A Survey of Young People Leaving the Care of Three Local Authorities*, London: National Children's Bureau.

Bliss, T., Robinson, G. and Maines, B. (1996) *Developing Circle Time*, Bristol: Lucky Duck Publications.

Bliss, T. and Tetley, J. (1993) *Circle Time*, Bristol: Lucky Duck Publications.

Blyth, E. and Cooper, H. (in press) 'Schools and Child Protection', in Violence Against Children Study Group, *Children, Child Abuse and Child Protection: Placing Children Centrally*, Chichester: John Wiley and Sons.

Blyth, E. and Milner, J. (1987) 'The Juvenile Court and Non-Attendance at School', *Justice of the Peace*, 151, 51, 19 December: 854–7.

—— (1996) 'Black Boys Excluded from School: Race or Masculinity Issues?', in E. Blyth and J. Milner (eds) *Exclusion from School: Interprofessional Issues for Policy and Practice*, London: Routledge.

—— (1997) *Social Work with Children: The Educational Perspective*, Harlow: Addison Wesley Longman.

REFERENCES

Bourdieu, P. and Passeron, J. C. (1990) *Reproduction in Education, Society and Culture*, London: Sage.

Bowen, D. E. (1985) 'Education – Whose Care? A Consideration of the Educational Effect of Making Care Orders in Respect of Non-Attenders at School', unpublished MSc dissertation, Cranfield Institute of Technology.

Bowles, S. and Gintis, H. (1976) *Schooling in Capitalist America: educational reform and the contradictions of economic life*, New York: Basic Books.

Boyd, B. (1993) 'Letting a Hundred Flowers Blossom', unpublished PhD thesis, University of Glasgow.

—— (1995) 'Research and Staff Development', *Interchange*, 33, Edinburgh: SOEID.

Brazier, M. (1988) *Street on Torts* (8th edn), London: Butterworth.

Broadfoot, P. and Osborn, M. (1987) 'Teacher's Conceptions of their Professional Responsibility: Some International Comparisons', *Comparative Education*, 23, 3: 287–302.

Brodie, I. (1997) 'Education on the Agenda: An Educationally Effective Children's Home', *Children's Residential Care Unit Newsletter*, 4: 15.

Brown, J. and Fabry, L. (1993) *Overcoming Bullying*, Milton Keynes: The Chalkface Project.

Bullock, R., Little, M. and Millham, S. (1994) 'Children's Return from State Care to School', *Oxford Review of Education*, 20, 3: 307–16.

Campbell and Cosans v. *United Kingdom* (1982) Series A, vol. 48.

Carlen, P., Gleeson, D. and Wardhaugh, J. (1992) *Truancy: The Politics of Compulsory Schooling*, Buckingham: Open University Press.

Casey, B. and Smith, D. (1995) *Truancy and Youth Transitions: England and Wales Youth Cohort Study*, Cohort Report No. 34, London: Policy Studies Institute.

Central Advisory Council for Education (CACE) (1967) *Children and their Primary Schools* (The Plowden Report), London: HMSO.

Charter, D. (1995) 'Church School Parents May Lose Opt-Out Voice', *The Times*, 28 October: 8.

Cheung, S. Y. and Heath, A. (1994) 'After Care: The Education and Occupation of Adults Who Have Been in Care', *Oxford Review of Education*, 20, 3: 361–74.

Cohen, B. and Hagen, U. (eds) (1997) *Children's Services: Shaping up for the Millennium*, Edinburgh: The Stationery Office.

Colton, M. and Heath, A. (1994) 'Attainment and Behaviour of Children in Care and at Home', *Oxford Review of Education*, 20, 3: 317–27.

Coombes, F. and Beer, D. (1984) *The Long Walk from the Dark*, Birmingham: National Association of Social Workers in Education.

Cooper, G. and Brown, C. (1997) 'Blair Puts Parents in Firing Line Over School Attendance', *The Independent*, 9 December: 7.

Corrigan, D. (1996) 'Creating Collaborative Systems: Implications for Partnership', in J. McCall and R. M. MacKay (eds) *Teacher Education in Partnership and Cooperation*, papers from the 21st Annual Conference of ATEE, Glasgow: University of Strathclyde.

Cullingford, C. (1991) *The Inner World of the School*, London: Cassell.

—— (1993) 'Children's Attitudes to Bullying', *Education 3–13*, 23, 2: 11–17.

—— (1995) *Parents, Education and the State*, Aldershot: Ashgate.

—— (1996), in D. Whitcutt (ed.) *Towards Employability: Addressing the Gap between Young People's Qualities and Employers' Recruitment Needs*, London: Industry in Education.

Cullingford, C. and Morrison, J. (1995) 'Bullying as a Formative Influence: The Relationship between the Experience of School and Criminality', *British Educational Research Journal*, 21, 5: 547–60.

—— (1996) 'Who Excludes Whom? The Personal Experience of Exclusion', in E. Blyth and J. Milner (eds) *Exclusion from School: Interprofessional Issues for Policy and Practice*, London: Routledge.

—— (1997) 'Peer Group Pressure within and outside School', *British Educational Research Journal*, 23, 1: 61–80.

Dartington Social Services Research Unit (1995) *Looking After Children: Assessment and Action Records*, London: HMSO.

Department for Education (DFE) (1991) *The Education (Pupils' Attendance Records) Regulations, Circular 11/91*, London: DFE.

—— (1992a) *Choice and Diversity: A New Framework for Schools*, Cm 2021, London: HMSO.

—— (1992b) *Education into the Next Century: The Government's Proposals for Education Explained*, London: DFE.

—— (1994) *School Attendance: Policy and Practice on Categorisation of Absence*, London: DFE.

—— (1995) 'Statistics on School Performance Published', *DFE News, 43/95*, 28 February, London: DFE.

Department for Education and Department of Health (1994) *The Education of Children Looked After by Local Authorities*, Circular No. 13/94. DH LAC (94) 11, London: DFE and DOH.

Department for Education and Employment (DFEE) (1995a) *National Pupil Absence Tables 1995*, London: DFEE.

—— (1995b) *Protecting Children from Abuse: The Role of the Education Service*, Circular 10/95, London: DFEE.

—— (1996) *National Pupil Absence Tables 1996*, London: DFEE.

—— (1997a) *Draft Guidance on School Attendance and the Role of the Education Welfare Service*, London: DFEE.

—— (1997b) *Excellence in Schools*, London: The Stationery Office.

—— (1998) *Section 550A of the Education Act 1996: The Use of Force to Control or Restrain Pupils, Circular 10/98*, London: DFEE.

Department of Education and Science (1975) *A Language for Life* (The Bullock Report), London: HMSO.

—— (1989a) *Discipline in Schools: Report of the Committee of Inquiry Chaired by Lord Elton*, London: HMSO.

—— (1989b) 'Attendance at School', *Education Observed, 13*, London: DES.

—— (1991) *The Education (Pupils' Attendance Records) Regulations, 1991*, Circular No. 11/91, London: DES.

—— (1992) *Education in Social Services Establishments: A Report by HMI*, 4/92/NS. London: DES.

Department of Health (DOH) (1991a) *The Children Act 1989: Guidance and Regulations vol. 7*, London: HMSO.

—— (1991b) *Children in the Public Care*, London: HMSO.

Douglas, T. (1995) *Basic Groupwork*, Cambridge: Cambridge University Press.

Durham University (undated-a) *ALIS (A Level Information Service)*, Durham: School of Education, Durham University.

—— (undated-b) *MIDIS (Middle Years Information Service)*, Durham: School of Education, Durham University.

—— (undated-c) *YELLIS (Year Eleven Information Service)*, Durham: School of Education: Durham University.

Dwivedi, K. (1996) *Groupwork with Children and Adolescents: A Handbook*, London and Bristol, PA: Jessica Kingsley Publications.

Elliot, V. and Pierce, A. (1998) 'Parents Facing Jail in Campaign against Truancy', *The Times*, 11 May: 4.

Essex CC v. *B* (1993) 1 FLR: 866–82.

Farrington, D. (1996) 'Later Life Outcomes of Truants in the Cambridge Study', in I. Berg and J. Nursten (eds) *Unwillingly to School* (4th edn), London: Gaskell.

Farrington, D. and West, D. J. (1990) 'The Cambridge Study in Delinquent Development: A Long-Term Follow Up of 411 London Males', in H. J. Kerner and G. Kaiser (eds) *Criminality: Personality, Behaviour and Life History*, Berlin: Springer Verlag.

Felsenstein, D. (1987) 'Strategies for Improving School Attendance', in K. Reid (ed.) *Combating School Absenteeism*, London: Hodder and Stoughton.

Fitzpatrick, P., Clarke, K. and Higgins, P. (1994) *Self Esteem*, Milton Keynes: The Chalkface Project.

Fletcher, B. (1993) *Not Just a Name: The Views of Young People in Foster and Residential Care*, London: National Consumer Council and Who Cares? Trust.

Fletcher-Campbell, F. (1997) *The Education of Children Who are Looked After*, Slough: National Foundation for Educational Research.

Fletcher-Campbell, F. and Hall, C. (1990) *Changing Schools? Changing People? The Education of Children in Care*, Slough: National Foundation for Educational Research.

Freeman, P. and Fabry, L. (1995) *Overcoming Truancy*, Milton Keynes: The Chalkface Project.

Frones, I. (1995) *Among Peers: On the Meaning of Peers in the Process of Socialization*, Oslo: Scandinavian University Press.

Ghate, D. and Daniels, A. (1997) *Talking About My Generation: A Survey of 8–15 Year Olds Growing up in the 1990s*, London: NSPCC.

Gilligan, R. (1998) 'The Importance of Schools and Teachers in Child Welfare', *Child and Family Social Work*, 3: 13–25.

Gleeson, D. (1992) 'School Attendance and Truancy: A Socio-Historical Account', *The Sociological Review*, 40: 437–90.

Golden, J. and Hopkins, N. (1997) 'Mother's Homework: Court Rules Girl, 15, Can Leave School to Care for Son', *Daily Mail*, 21 March: 5.

Goldstein, H. and Sammons, P. (1995) *The Influence of Secondary and Junior Schools on Sixteen Year Olds' Examination Performance: A Cross-Classified Multilevel Analysis*, London: Institute of Education.

Gow, L. and McPherson, A. (1980) *Tell Them From Me*, Aberdeen: Aberdeen University Press.

Graham, J. and Bowling, B. (1995) *Young People and Crime*, Home Office Research Study 145, London: Home Office.

Gray, J. and Jesson, D. (1990) *Truancy in Secondary Schools amongst Fifth Year Pupils*, Sheffield: University of Sheffield.

Grenville, M. (1988) 'Compulsory School Attendance and the Child's Wishes', *Journal of Social Welfare Law*, 1: 4–20.

Hamilton, S. and O'Reilly, J. (1997) 'Tory School Opt-Out Drive Hits Buffers', *The Sunday Times*, 16 March: 12.

Hansard (1997) 1 July: 112–14, London: House of Commons.

Harris, N. with Pearce, P. and Johnstone, S. (1992) *The Legal Context of Teaching*, Harlow: Longman.

Hayden, C. (1996) 'Primary School Exclusions: The Need for Integrated Solutions', in E. Blyth and J. Milner (eds) *Exclusion from School: Interprofessional Issues for Policy and Practice*, London: Routledge.

Heath, A., Colton, M. and Aldgate, J. (1989) 'The Educational Progress of Children In and Out of Care', *British Journal of Social Work*, 19, 6: 447–60.

—— (1994) 'Failure to Escape: A Longitudinal Study of Foster-Children's Educational Attainment', *British Journal of Social Work*, 24, 3: 241–59.

Heath, S. B. (1983) *Ways with Words: Language, Life and Work in Communities and Classrooms*, Cambridge: Cambridge University Press.

Hibbett, A. and Fogelman, K. (1990) 'Future Lives of Truants in Family Formation and Health-Related Benefits', *British Journal of Educational Psychology*, 60: 171–9.

Hibbett, A., Fogelman, K. and Manor, O. (1990) 'Occupation and Outcomes of Truancy', *British Journal of Educational Psychology*, 60: 23–36.

HMI Audit Unit (1994a) *The Homework File*, Glasgow: QIE, University of Strathclyde.

—— (1994b) *Scottish Schools: Costs 1993/94 to 1995/96*, Edinburgh: SOEID.

—— (1995) *The Truancy File*, Glasgow: QIE, University of Strathclyde.

—— (1996) *Examination Results in Scottish Schools 1994–1996*, Edinburgh: SOEID.

—— (1997a) *Attendance and Absence in Scottish Schools 1995/96*, Edinburgh: SOEID.

—— (1997b) *Close to the Mark*, Glasgow: QIE University of Strathclyde.

—— (1998) *Leaver Destinations from Scottish Secondary Schools 1994/95 to 1996/97*, Edinburgh: SOEID.

HMSO (1994) *The UK's First Report to the UN Committee on the Rights of the Child*, London: HMSO.

Holmes, G. (1989) *Truancy and Social Welfare*, Manchester: Boys' and Girls' Welfare Society/Manchester Free Press.

Hoyle, D. (1998) 'Constructions of Pupil Absence in the Education Service', *Child and Family Social Work*, 3: 99–111.

Humes, W. M. (1986) *The Leadership Class in Scottish Education*, Edinburgh: John Donald.

Jackson, S. (1988–9) 'Residential Care and Education', *Children and Society*, 4: 335–50.

—— (1994) 'Educating Children in Residential and Foster Care', *Oxford Review of Education*, 20, 3: 267–79.

Jeffs, T. (1995) 'Children's Educational Rights in the New ERA?' in B. Franklin (ed.) *The Handbook of Children's Rights: Comparative Policy and Practice*, London: Routledge.

Joseph Rowntree Foundation (1997) *Communities that Care (UK): A New Kind of Prevention Programme*, London: CTC (UK).

Kent Education (1993) *School Attendance Matters Issue No. 1*, Maidstone: Kent County Council.

—— (1994a) *School Attendance Matters Issue No. 2*, Maidstone: Kent County Council.

—— (1994b) *School Attendance Matters Issue No. 3*, Maidstone: Kent County Council.

—— (1994c) *School Attendance Matters Issue No. 4*, Maidstone: Kent County Council.

Lansdown, G. (1995) 'The Children's Rights Development Unit', in B. Franklin (ed.) *The Handbook of Children's Rights: Comparative Policy and Practice*, London: Routledge.

—— (1996) 'Implementation of the UN Convention on the Rights of the Child in the UK', in M. John (ed.) *Children in our Charge: The Child's Right to Resources*, London: Jessica Kingsley Publishers.

Lavalette, M., Hobbs, S., Lindsay, S. and McKechnie, J. (1995) 'Child Employment in Britain: Policy, Myth and Reality', *Youth and Policy*, 47: 1–15.

Learmonth, J. (1995) *More Willingly to School? An Independent Evaluation of the Truancy and Disaffected Pupils GEST Programme*, London: DFEE.

Leeds City Council (1993a) *Awards and Incentives*, Leeds: Leeds Attendance and Behaviour Project, Department of Education.

—— (1993b) *Home/School Links*, Leeds: Leeds Attendance and Behaviour Project, Department of Education.

—— (1993c) *Good Practice Document on Illegal Employment*, Leeds: Leeds Attendance and Behaviour Project, Department of Education.

—— (1994) 'Sample Attendance Policy', in *Analysing Attendance at Schools: A Summary of the Research and Development Work undertaken by the Leeds Attendance and Behaviour Project 1993–1994*, Leeds: Leeds Attendance and Behaviour Project, Department of Education.

—— (1998) *The Behaviour Database©: A Behaviour Monitoring System* (version 4.1), Leeds: Leeds Attendance and Behaviour Project, Department of Education.

Levy, A. and Kahan, B. (1991) *The Pindown Experience and the Protection of Children: The Report on the Staffordshire Child Care Enquiry*, Stafford: Staffordshire County Council.

MacBeath, J. (1992) *Education In and Out of School: The Issues and the Practice in Inner-Cities and Outer Estates*, Edinburgh: SOEID.

McConnon, S. (1990) *Your Choice – Conflict: A Personal Skills Course for Young People*, Hong Kong: Nelson.

—— (1992a) *Your Choice – Assertiveness: A Personal Skills Course for Young People*, Hong Kong: Nelson.

—— (1992b) *Your Choice – Self-Esteem: A Personal Skills Course for Young People*, Hong Kong: Nelson.

McParlin, P. (1996) 'Children "Looked After" (in Care): Implications for Educational Psychologists', *Educational Psychology in Practice*, 12, 2: 112–17.

McPherson, A. and Raab, C. (1988) *Governing Education: A Sociology of Policy Since 1945*, Edinburgh: Edinburgh University Press.

Magistrates' Association (1994) *Notes of a Meeting Held on 28 October 1994 between the Magistrates' Association and Representatives of Agencies Involved with Prosecution of Parents under the Education Acts*, London: Magistrates' Association.

Malcolm, H., Thorpe, G. and Lowden, K. (1996) *Understanding Truancy: Links between Attendance, Truancy and Performance*, Edinburgh: Scottish Council for Research on Education.

Menmuir, R. (1994) 'Involving Residential Social Workers and Foster Carers in Reading with Young People in their Care: The PRAISE Reading Projects', *Oxford Review of Education*, 20, 3: 329–38.

Millham, S., Bullock, R. and Hosie, K. (1980) *Learning to Care: The Training of Staff for Residential Social Work with Young People*, Aldershot: Gower.

Montgomery, J. (1996) 'Truants' Parents Feel the Force of Law', *The Times Educational Supplement*, 10 May: 5.

Mortimore, P., Sammons, P., Stoll, L., Lewis, D. and Ecob, R. (1988) *School Matters? The Junior Years*, London: Open Books.

Munn, P., Cullen, M.A., Johnstone, M. and Lloyd, G. (1997) 'Exclusions and In-school Alternatives', *Interchange*, 47, Edinburgh: SOEID.

Murray, V. and Godfrey, E. (1997) *The Education of Looked After Children and Equal Chances Projects*, Bradford Metropolitan District Council.

National Association of Schoolmasters and Union of Women Teachers (1995) *Child Abuse Allegations against NASUWT Members*, Birmingham: NASUWT.

National Association of Social Workers in Education (NASWE) (1996) *NASWE Data Book*, NASWE.

National Union of Teachers (NUT) (1992) *Survey on Pupils' Exclusions: Information from LEAs*, May, London: NUT.

NCH: Action for Children (1994) *The Workhouse Diet and the Cost of Feeding a Child Today*, press release, 1 February, London: NCH: Action for Children.

Newell, P. (1991) *The UN Convention and Children's Rights in the UK*, London: National Children's Bureau.

OECD (1995) *Income Distribution in OECD Countries*, Paris: OECD.

OFSTED (1994) *Handbook for the Inspection of Schools* (consolidated edn), London: HMSO.

—— (1995a) *Access, Achievement and Attendance in Secondary Schools*, a report from the Office of Her Majesty's Chief Inspector of Schools (Ref 16/95/NS), London: OFSTED.

—— (1995b) *The Challenge for Education Welfare*, a report from the Office of Her Majesty's Chief Inspector of Schools (Ref 17/95/NS), London: OFSTED.

—— (1995c) *Guidance on the Inspection of Schools*, London: HMSO.

O'Keeffe, D. (1994) *Truancy in English Secondary Schools*, London: HMSO.

O'Reilly, J. (1997) 'Return of the Wagman in Crackdown on 1m Truants', *The Sunday Times*, 15 June: 13.

Parsons, C. (1996) 'The Cost of Primary School Exclusions', in E. Blyth and J. Milner (eds) *Exclusion from School: Interprofessional issues for policy and practice*, London: Routledge.

REFERENCES

Parsons, C., Benns, L., Hailes, J. and Howlett, K. (1994) *Excluding Primary School Children*, London: Family Policy Studies Centre.

Patten, J. (1992) reported in *Education*, 179, 19, 8 May: 370.

Petre, J. (1994) 'Tougher Fines for Parents of Truants Urged', *The Sunday Telegraph*, 3 July: 8.

Pond, C. and Searle, A. (1991) *The Hidden Army: Children at Work in the 1990s*, Low Pay Unit Pamphlet 55, London: Low Pay Unit.

Power, S., Fitz, J. and Halpin, D. (1994) 'Parents, Pupils and Grant Maintained Schools', *British Educational Research Journal*, 20, 2: 209–26.

Power, S., Halpin, D. and Fitz, J. (1996) 'The Grant Maintained Schools Policy: The English Experience of Educational Self-Governance', in C. Pole and R. Chawla-Duggan (eds) *Reshaping Education in the 1990s: Perspectives on Secondary Schooling*, London: Falmer Press.

Pugh, G. (1997) 'Early Childhood Education Finds its Voice: But is Anyone Listening?' in C. Cullingford (ed.) *The Politics of Primary Education*, Buckingham: Open University Press.

Pye, J. (1992) *Invisible Children*, Oxford: Oxford University Press.

Quinn, V. (1997) *Critical Thinking in Young Minds*, London: David Fulton.

Ranson, S. (1984) 'Towards a Tertiary Tripartism: New Codes of Social Control and the 17+', in P. Broadfoot (ed.) *Selection, Certification and Control*, Lewes: Falmer Press.

—— (1990) 'From 1944 to 1988: Education, Citizenship and Democracy', in M. Flude and M. Hammer (eds.) *The Education Reform Act 1988: Its Origins and Implications*, Lewes: Falmer Press.

Re: DJMS (A Minor) (1977) 3 All ER, 582.

Re: 0 (A Minor) (Care Order: Education Procedure) (1992) 2 FLR FD: 8–13.

Robertson, I. (1996) 'Legal Problems', in I. Berg and J. Nursten (eds.) *Unwillingly to School* (4th edn), London: Gaskell.

Rosenthal, R. and Jacobsen, L. (1968) *Pygmalion in the Classroom*, New York: Rinehart and Winston.

Rubenstein, D. (1969) *School Attendance in London 1870–1904*, Hull: Hull University Press.

Rutter, M. (1991a) 'Pathways from Childhood to Adult Life: The Role of Schooling', *Pastoral Care in Education*, 9, 3: 3–10.

—— (1991b) 'Services for Children with Emotional Disorders', *Young Minds Newsletter*, 9, October: 1–5.

Rutter, M. and Rutter, M. (1993) *Developing Minds: Challenge and Continuity across the Life Span*, Harmondsworth: Penguin.

Rutter, M., Maughan, B., Mortimore, P. and Ouston, J. (1979) *Fifteen Thousand Hours: Secondary Schools and their Effects on Children*, London: Open Books.

Sage, G. (1993) *Child Abuse and the Children Act: A Critical Analysis of the Teacher's Rôle*, London: Association of Teachers and Lecturers Publications.

Samson, A. and Hart, G. (1995) 'A Whole School Approach to the Management of Pupil Behaviour', in P. Farrell (ed.) *Children with Emotional and Behavioural Difficulties: Strategies for Assessment and Intervention*, London: Falmer Press.

Scanlan, D. (1998) *The Crime and Disorder Act 1998: A Guide for Practitioners*, London: Callow Publishing.

Scott-Clark, C. and Burke, J. (1996) 'Who, Me?', *The Sunday Times*, 19 May: 10.

Scott-Clark, C. and Syal, R. (1996) 'Running Wild', *The Sunday Times*, 28 April: 12.

Scottish Consultative Council on the Curriculum (SCCC) (1986) *More Than Feelings of Concern*, Dundee: SCCC.

—— (1996a) *Teaching for Effective Learning: The Heart of the Matter*, Dundee: SCCC.

—— (1996b) *Teaching for Effective Learning: Climate for Learning*, Dundee: SCCC.

Scottish Council for Research on Education (SCRE) (1992) 'Truancy and Attendance in Scottish Secondary Schools', *Spotlights*, 38, Edinburgh: SCRE.

Scottish Council on Crime (1975) *Memorandum on Crime and the Prevention of Crime*, Edinburgh: HMSO.

Scottish Education Department (1965) *Primary Education in Scotland* (The Primary Memorandum), Edinburgh: HMSO.

—— (1977a) *The Structure of the Curriculum in the Third and Fourth Years of the Scottish Secondary School* (The Munn Report), Edinburgh: HMSO.

—— (1977b) *Assessment for All: Report of the Committee to Review Assessment in the Third and Fourth Years of Secondary Education in Scotland* (The Dunning Report), Edinburgh: HMSO.

—— (1977c) *Truancy and Indiscipline in Scotland* (The Pack Report), Edinburgh: HMSO.

Scottish Office Education Department (SOED) (1990) *Management Training for Head Teachers*, Edinburgh: HMI.

—— (1991) *Action on Truancy in Scotland*, consultation paper, Edinburgh: SOED.

—— (1995) *Parents' Charter: Information for Parents – Authorised and Unauthorised Absence*, Circular 1/95, Edinburgh: SOED.

Scottish Office Education and Industry Department (SOEID) (1995) *Higher Still – Opportunity for All*, Edinburgh: SOEID.

Searle, Y. and Streng, I. (1996) *Lifegames: The Social Skills Game*, London: Jessica Kingsley Publishing.

Sim v. Rotherham Metropolitan BC and other actions (1966) 3 All ER: 387–416.

Sinclair, R., Garnett, L., Beecham, J. and Berridge, D. (1993) *Social Work and Assessment with Adolescents*, London: National Children's Bureau.

Social Exclusion Unit (1998) *Truancy and School Exclusion*, report by the Social Exclusion Unit, London: Cabinet Office.

Social Services Inspectorate (SSI) and Office for Standards in Education (OFSTED) (1995) *The Education of Children Who are Looked After by Local Authorities*, London: DOH and OFSTED.

Solihull Metropolitan Borough Council (1992) *Legal Enforcement – School Attendance*, Report by Director of Education, 8 January, Solihull: Solihull Metropolitan Borough Council.

Stein, M. (1986) *Living Out of Care*, Ilford: Barnardos.

—— (1994) 'Leaving Care, Education and Career Trajectories', *Oxford Review of Education*, 20, 3: 349–60.

Stein, M. and Carey, K. (1983) *Leaving Care*, Oxford: Blackwell.

Stirling, M. (1996) 'Government Policy and Disadvantaged Children', in E. Blyth and J. Milner (eds) *Exclusion from School: Interprofessional Issues for Policy and Practice*, London: Routledge.

Stoll, P. A. and O'Keeffe, D. J. (1989) *Officially Present: An Investigation into Post-Registration Truancy in Nine Maintained Secondary Schools*, London: Institute of Economic Affairs.

Strathclyde Regional Council (1988) *Young People in Trouble*, Glasgow: SRC.

Sutherland, A. E. (1995) *Persistent School Absenteeism in Northern Ireland in 1992*, Belfast: NICER Research Unit, School of Education, The Queen's University of Belfast.

UN Committee on the Rights of the Child (1995) *Consideration of Reports Submitted by States Parties Under Article 44 of the Convention – Concluding Observations of the Committee on the Rights of the Child: United Kingdom of Great Britain and Northern Ireland*, Geneva: United Nations.

Utting, W., Baines, C., Stuart, M., Rowlands, J. and Vialva, R. (1997) *People Like Us: The Report of the Review of the Safeguards for Children Living Away from Home*, London: The Stationery Office.

Van Oppen v. *Clerk to the Bedford Charity Trustees* (1989) 3 All ER 389 (CA); 1 All ER 273.

Walker, T. (1994) 'Educating Children in the Public Care: A Strategic Approach', *Oxford Review of Education*, 20, 3: 329–47.

Webb, R. (1994) *After the Deluge: Changing Roles and Responsibilities in the Primary School. Final Report of Research Commissioned by the Association of Teachers and Lecturers*, London: Association of Teachers and Lecturers.

Weiner, A. and Weiner, E. (1990) *Expanding the Options in Child Placement: Israel's Dependent Children in Care from Infancy to Adulthood*, New York: University Press of America.

West, D. J. and Farrington, D. P. (1997) *The Delinquent Way of Life*, London: Heinemann.

White, C. (1996) 'New Order', *Community Care*, 2–8 May: 16–17.

White, R. with Brockington, D. (1983) *Tales Out of School*, London: Routledge.

Whitehead, M. (1996) 'Plea for Tougher Law on Truancy', *The Times Educational Supplement*, 31 May: 2.

Whitney, B. (1994) *The Truth about Truancy*, London: Kogan Page.

Williams v. *Eady* (1893) 10, TLR 41, CA.

Williamson, I. and Cullingford, C. (1997) 'The Uses and Misuses of "Alienation" in the Social Sciences and Education', *British Journal of Educational Studies*, 45, 3, pp. 263–75.

INDEX